PRIVATE PRISONS AND PUBLIC ACCOUNTABILITY

Richard W. Harding

Open University Press
Buckingham

Open University Press
Celtic Court
22 Ballmoor
Buckingham
MK18 1XW

First Published 1997

A catalogue record of this book is available from the British Library

ISBN   0 335 19849 X (pb)   0 335 19850 3 (hb)

Typeset by Type Study, Scarborough
Printed in Great Britain by Biddles Ltd, Guildford and King's Lynn

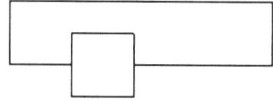

Contents

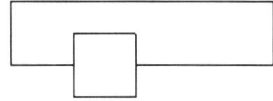

Acknowledgements

This book was written whilst I was on sabbatical leave at the University of Wales Cardiff. I wish to express my thanks to the School of Social and Administrative Studies at that university and to the head, Dr Sara Delamont, for the wonderful support I received during that time. I also wish to thank my home university, the University of Western Australia, for the opportunity to take sabbatical leave to complete this project.

My research into private prisons extended over a period of more than four years. During that time I visited many prisons in the USA, the UK and Australia. In the course of doing so, I conversed with prison administrators, programme and other specialist staff, custodial officers and inmates. These people are too numerous to identify by name, but without their ready assistance my understanding of the issues would be circumscribed. In prison research there is no substitute for the experience of the people whose daily lives revolve around the operation of the institutions.

Head-office personnel in all countries – including New Zealand – also gave generously of their time. None of the doors I tried to go through was closed against me. Nor was I denied documentation when I sought it. Indeed, several of these senior people helped, unsolicited, by sending me important material of which I might otherwise have remained ignorant. In much the same way, private prison personnel – both in the prisons themselves and at corporate head offices – were unstintingly co-operative. Quite evidently, in a context where rapid change was occurring all around them yet a cohesive analytical overview was so far lacking, people on both sides of the fence saw my research as possibly being of some assistance to themselves. In this regard I hope that they will not feel themselves disappointed.

It would be invidious to identify by name the persons falling into the above categories. There are so many of them that one would risk inadvertently omitting some, thereby seeming to downgrade their particular contribution. They all know who they are, and to all of them I express my sincere thanks.

However, three persons must be singled out for specific mention. They are Professor Mike Maguire, Mr David Biles and Professor Charles Thomas.

Professor Maguire was my colleague at Cardiff whilst this book was being written. He assiduously read all my early drafts, and his perceptive comments invariably served to push me to a deeper level of analysis. His extensive knowledge of penal practice and policy in the UK particularly anchored my analysis of the place of privatization in that country. David Biles, consultant criminologist and former deputy director of the Australian Institute of Criminology, played a comparable role with regard to the Australian scene, as well as giving me invaluable feedback on the early drafts. Professor Charles Thomas, director of the Private Corrections Project at the University of Florida, gave me inestimable help during a research trip to the USA and subsequently by commenting on the manuscript. His help pre-dated this period, however; for he is the author of the regular *Private Adult Correctional Facility Census*. This is the single most important and informative source of factual data available in the USA about private prisons in that most significant market. To all three, then, I express my particular gratitude.

The text of this book was essentially completed in June 1996. The information upon which it is based, therefore, does not purport to go beyond that date. Nevertheless, some later matters of particular importance were able to be included, and where this was done they will be found in the endnotes of the relevant chapter.

Finally, this book is dedicated with love to my daughter Louise.

Richard W. Harding

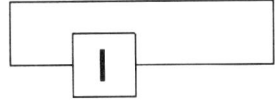

The growth of private prisons

What is meant by 'private prison'? In this controversial area of penology and public administration even the terminology provides a battleground. Prison administrators tiptoe gently through the area talking about 'contract management' – a phrase calculated to reassure critics, as well as themselves, that these prisons are still *their* prisons and thus subject to the prevailing standards of public accountability. By contrast, observers who are ideologically opposed to this development emphasize the notion of 'privatization' – a concept already partially discredited in the western world because of its association with inflated profiteering and abandonment of the public interest. Some critics then go so far as to embrace derived terms such as 'privateers', redolent of piracy and pillage, to describe the private sector operators (Baldry 1994a).

Ambiguity in the contemporary use of the word 'privatization' has been cogently identified by Donahue (1989: 215). The first use

> involves removing certain responsibilities, activities or assets from the collective realm. This is the chief meaning of privatization in countries retreating from post-war, post-colonial experiments with socialism, as they separate factories, mines, airlines and railroads from public control . . . The second meaning . . . [is] retaining collective financing but delegating delivery to the private sector.

It is evident that some of the critics of prison privatization attack the idea as if it were being implemented in the first sense, by way of total divestiture, rather than the second sense, by way of delegated service delivery. In this regard they are perhaps marooned in the experience of the eighteenth and nineteenth centuries, where the notion was indeed associated with the disposal of prisoner labour to entrepreneurs and the opportunity to charge prisoners or their families for subsistence costs (Feeley 1991; Moyle 1993).

However, this simply is not the modern connotation of private prisons.

Rather, at the end of the twentieth century, privatization typically refers to a process whereby the state continues to fund the full agreed costs of incarceration but the private sector is paid to provide the management services, both 'hotel' (including custodial) and programmatic. Variants of this include arrangements whereby the private sector also provides the physical plant itself and, more unusually, joint ventures where custodial responsibility may rest with one sector and other hotel and/or programmatic responsibilities with the other sector. Whichever of these models is adopted, however, the common denominator is that the state remains the ultimate paymaster and the opportunity for private profit is found only in the ability of the contractor to deliver the agreed services at a cost below the negotiated sum.

The problem is that, in matters of public administration, the old adage that he who pays the piper calls the tune has often been whittled away. A key question, accordingly, is whether, in remaining paymaster but delegating service delivery, the state truly does retain control over standards – whether in fact there still is present that degree of public accountability and control that must always be requisite when the state exercises its ultimate power of restraint and punishment over the citizen. To this there cannot be any a priori answer; it will always depend upon precisely how that delegation is structured and supervised. That issue – public accountability – will be the main focus of this book.

Beyond this, it is not proposed to become embroiled in terminological issues. The scope of the following analysis covers arrangements whereby adult prisoners are held in institutions which in a day-to-day sense are managed by private sector operators whose commercial objective is to make a profit from such activities. The phrase 'private prisons' and all related phrases refer to this.

So the book is not directly concerned with related matters such as the role of the private or the voluntary or the non-governmental organization sectors in juvenile corrections or non-institutional adult corrections, nor with private sector involvement in court escort services and the like. Of course, each of these is relevant to a full strategic understanding of prison privatization, so their experience and prospects will be invoked at appropriate points.

The threshold question, however, is whether privatization has yet attained such significance that, for all practical purposes, it is irreversible, at least in the foreseeable future. This in turn raises three subsidiary questions: how many private prisons and prisoners there are; whether these prisons are carrying their custodial weight in terms of the security needs of the total system; and whether the administrative and legal structures inhibit policy reversals by governments.

The numbers of private prisons and prisoners

Over the last decade there has been an exponential increase in the number of private prisons and the prisoners they hold. This has occurred predominantly in the western, anglophone world: the United States of America, Australia and the United Kingdom, with New Zealand irrevocably committed and some anglophone provinces of Canada flirting with the idea. Such developments as have occurred in continental Europe are tentative, described for example in the context of France and Belgium as the establishment of *prisons semi-privées*. In most of Europe such developments have not occurred in any form whatsoever. Intriguing questions which will be addressed in due course, therefore, are why privatization has so far been such an anglophone phenomenon and whether the orthodoxy still prevailing in Europe and the rest of the world is likely to change.

The United States

Evaluating US developments in the 18-month period ending 30 June 1994, the director of the Private Corrections Project at the University of Florida stated that the 'alternative created by correctional privatization has moved well beyond the "interesting experiment" status it had in the mid-1980s to the "proven option" status it now enjoys' (Thomas 1994: 5). The context in which that comment was made was as follows: that in the period under review the number of prisons under contract had risen from 54 to 78; their rated capacity had doubled from 21,771 to 41,514; and the actual occupancy of operational prisons had increased from 16,101 to 23,461.

This rate of increase has subsequently been maintained. By the end of 1994 the number of contracted facilities had increased to 88, ten more in a mere six months. Rated capacity was almost 50,000, whilst actual occupancy had increased to nearly 29,000. Private prisons were coming on-stream at regular intervals.

Throughout 1995 and 1996, this momentum has continued. Virginia, a newcomer to this area, committed itself to four private prisons with a rated capacity of 3800; New Mexico positioned itself by legislative committee hearings to embark upon an increased level of private sector participation; Florida let three more contracts and increased the capacity of existing institutions by 50 per cent; both Tennessee and Texas contracted to add further capacity to already contracted prisons; Alaska, which hitherto had sent some of its prisoners to a Corrections Corporation of America (CCA) facility in Arizona, investigated the possibility of establishing a private prison on its own territory; and, perhaps most significantly of all, the federal government announced that for budgetary reasons the majority of new minimum- and low-security jails and prisons which it henceforth builds will be privately managed. The significance of this lies in the fact that the Federal Bureau of Prisons had traditionally been regarded as something of a standard-bearer in American corrections and, as such, had been resistant to private sector involvement.[1] The pace of recent increase and the position as at 31 December 1995 can be seen in Table 1.1.

Table 1.1 Private prison developments in the USA from 31 March 1993 to 31 December 1995

	31 March 1993	30 June 1994	31 December 1994	31 December 1995
Number of private prisons:				
(a) Operational	54	60	68	75
(b) Procured	18	18	20	17
Total	72	78	88	92
Rated capacity:				
(a) Operational	19,667	23,226	30,821	39,665
(b) Procured	8727	18,692	18,334	17,994
Total	28,394	41,918	49,155	57,659

Source: Calculated from Thomas (1994; 1995a) and Thomas and Bollinger (1996).

In personal conversation a senior executive of CCA – widely regarded as the market leader – had in September 1995 told the present author that he believed the USA market would expand 'almost indefinitely'. This vibrant confidence had been reflected in the tone of CCA's 1994 annual report to shareholders: 'There are powerful market forces driving our industry, and its potential has barely been touched.' From the other side of the fence, the executive director of the Florida Correctional Privatization Commission – the body charged in that state with the function of allocating contracts to the private sector – also expressed in personal conversation his view that privatization is now irrevocably part of the correctional scene.

Support for these views is found in Thomas's estimate (1996: 20) that by the end of 1996 there will be approximately 115 operational or commissioned US private prisons with rated capacity totalling about 75,000 – an accelerating pace of expansion in the passage of only a single year. Of course, even if every one of these facilities were operational, their total number of inmates would still only amount to about 4.6 per cent of the massive US incarcerated population. However, an alternative perspective is that if all of those private prisons were to be closed, US correctional authorities would have to find extra accommodation equivalent to the combined prison populations, of, say, Japan and Malaysia or, alternatively, Australia and South Korea.

In that context, the probability must be that private prisons in the USA are here to stay for the foreseeable future. Indeed, the numbers could well double again in the next five years. Thomas is right: privatization is now a proven option.

Australia

Australia was the second westernized anglophone country to commission and open a private prison. In January 1990 a 240-bed medium-security institution for convicted offenders was opened at Borallon, in Queensland. The contractors are Corrections Corporation of Australia, which is a consortium led by CCA of the United States.

Two other private prisons quickly followed: the Arthur Gorrie Correctional Centre in Queensland and Junee prison in New South Wales. Australasian Correctional Management (ACM) was the successful bidder in each case. ACM is a subsidiary of Australasian Correctional Services, which is a consortium headed by the Wackenhut Corrections Corporation (the second largest player in the USA market).

Table 1.2 (page 6) summarizes the growth of private prisons in Australia. It can be seen that about 20 per cent of the projected Australian prison population could be held in a total of eight private prisons by the end of the twentieth century. This would constitute the highest percentage in any country in the world.

Bearing in mind the threshold question as to whether these arrangements could be unscrambled, it should be emphasized that this high percentage which will ultimately be held in private prisons amounts to only 3600 prisoners – a drop in the bucket by USA standards, though the equivalent of the total prison population of a mid-level state system in Australia as at the year 2000. It is also relevant that one of the four state jurisdictions involved – New South Wales, the largest – only has one private prison and there is known to be some distaste for this development at both political and managerial levels, so that privatization might conceivably be unscrambled there. If so, the counter-balance is that each of the other three jurisdictions not currently committed to privatization has actively considered it already (Harding 1992) and seems to have put a decision on hold rather than rejected the possibility for all time.

On balance, it is unlikely that there will be exponential increase in private prisons and prisoners comparable to that which may occur in the USA. This is primarily because there is unlikely to be the massive overall increase in prisoner populations that has characterized US experience. For all that, private prisons in Australia can at this stage fairly be said to be a proven option, integral to the total system.

The United Kingdom

The UK[2] followed Australia into the privatization field in May 1992 with the opening of The Wolds prison in Yorkshire. The management of this 320-bed remand prison was contracted to Group 4/Securitas, an Anglo-Swedish consortium working in the general security field in Europe and globally.

Table 1.2   Private prison developments in Australia, 1990–99

Date	Prison	Capacity	Cumulative percentage of projected prison population held in private prisons[a]	Governmental commitment; operating company
1990	Borallon (Qld)	240	1.9	Operational – CCA
1992	Arthur Gorrie (Qld)	380	4.4	Operational – ACM
1993	Junee (NSW)	600[b]	8.0	Operational – ACM
1994	Arthur Gorrie Phase 2	+198	9.3	Operational – ACM
1995	Mount Gambier (SA)	125	10.1	Operational – Group 4
1995	Borallon Phase 2	+185	11.2	Operational – CCA
1996	Arthur Gorrie Phase 3	+54	11.5	Operational – ACM
1996	Melton (Vic.)	125	12.2	Contract let – CCA
1997	West Sale (Vic.)	600	14.0	Evaluation completed – contract being negotiated with ACM
1997–98	Laverton North (Vic.)	600	17.3	Site identification completed; bid documentation in preparation
1999	Adelaide (SA)	500	20.3	Intention to replace obsolete plant at Yatala; long-term planning under way; no firm commitment as yet

[a] These percentages are necessarily imprecise. The Australian prison population (convicted, unconvicted, and serving sentences in police lock-ups) was in August 1995 approximately 16,000. Increases ahead of general population increase seem likely to continue in view of the current popularity of 'truth-in-sentencing' laws, though there are some significant counter-currents. The assumption is that by the time Laverton North is opened in 1997–98, the total prison population will be no less than 18,000. No further projection had been made for 1999, so that the cumulative percentage figure if the 500-bed Adelaide prison is in fact opened is based on the same figure of 18,000.

[b] The Junee contract required that the prison be constructed in such a way as to allow for an 80% expansion in capacity to 1080. This has not yet happened, so this possibility has been disregarded in calculating the cumulative percentage.

Other private prisons were soon opened: Blakenhurst (650 beds), Doncaster (770 beds) and Buckley Hall (350 beds). During 1995 contracts were also let for Fazakerley, near Liverpool (600 beds) and Bridgend, Mid Glamorgan (800 beds); these two prisons are scheduled to become operational in late 1997.

Table 1.3 Private prison developments in England and Wales, 1992–2000

Date	Prison	Capacity	Cumulative percentage of prisoners held in such prisons	Governmental commitment
1992	The Wolds	320	0.7	Operational
1993	Blakenhurst	650	2.1	Operational
1994	Doncaster	770	3.5	Operational
1995	Buckley Hall	350	4.0	Operational
1997–98[a]	Fazakerley	600	4.9	Let to Group 4
1997–98	Bridgend	800	6.3	Let to Securicor
1997–98	Lowdham Grange	500	7.2	Invitations to tender
1998–99	Greater Manchester	700	8.5	Site clearance and planning being negotiated
1998–99	Telford	700	9.8	Site clearance and planning being negotiated
1999–2000	DCFM 5	700	11.1	Still with CCG
1999–2000	DCFM 6	700	12.4	Still with CCG

[a] For all estimates after 1995, a prison population of 56,000 has been assumed.

Subsequently, because of urgent accommodation needs in the East Midlands area, another prison (Lowdham Grange) was fast-tracked into the private sector programme. This will accommodate 500 medium-security male prisoners, and it is intended to expedite its development so that it should open at about the same time as Fazakerley and Bridgend. At that time there will be about 4000 private prison beds distributed through seven prisons, housing about 7.2 per cent of the total prison population.

The British government had also announced that it was committed to commissioning at least four more private prisons, with a total capacity of about 2800 beds. The first two of these contracts have reached the site planning and specific needs evaluation stage; the other two are still at the most preliminary stage. Once these are all operational, however, the number of prisoners held in 11 private prisons will total 6800 or about one-eighth of the total projected prison population.[3] The committed privatization programme is summarized in Table 1.3.

A wild card is the outcome of the next general election. The Labour Party is on the record as promising that all private prisons will be returned to the public sector when the present contracts expire:

The privatization of the prison service is morally repugnant . . . It must be the direct responsibility of the state to look after those the courts

decide it is in society's interests to imprison. It is not appropriate for
people to profit out of incarceration.

(Jack Straw, *The Guardian*, 8 March 1995)

The priority, in Labour's view, is to implement the reforms recommended
by the Woolf Inquiry (Woolf and Tumim 1991), and their fear is that
privatization would cut across this primary objective.

On the other hand, the present government seems committed to further
privatization. The original policy announcement of 1993 which provided the
foundation for Fazakerley, Bridgend and the four additional contracts spoke
of 'about 10%' of the UK's 134 establishments being privatized (ministerial
statement, 2 September 1993). Subsequently, the home secretary spoke of the
need to renovate and refurbish 25 of those 134 prisons and of the possibility
of inviting the private sector to participate in this capital-intensive project in
return for long-term management contracts (*The Independent*, 16 August
1995).[4]

Which of these competing scenarios, then, is the most likely? The answer is:
neither of them. Whichever party wins the next election will find its hands tied
and its most radical positions unattainable.

Labour will be somewhat inhibited by the terms of the Deregulation and
Contracting Out Act 1994, which is calculated to impose substantial cost
constraints upon policy U-turns in all areas of the UK's extensive privatization programme. There would be complex legal issues as to whether failure
to renew a renewable contract amounted to 'repudiation' in terms of the Act,
and the expectation of prolonged litigation would be high. Whilst in principle
the statute could simply be repealed, in practice this might well incur too high
a political cost.

In addition, if Australian experience is any guide,[5] the pragmatic nature of
contemporary left-of-centre political parties could lead to a reassessment
once Labour is in office. This reappraisal may well be stimulated by
realization of how costly it would be to renege upon the sort of long-term
commitments which are now coming to characterize these contracts. In
'buying back' private prison contracts, the state would be spending large
sums without adding a single bed to prison accommodation. The rhetoric of
opposition parties seldom matches their practice when elected to government, and in this particular area it would seem rather foolish if it did.

The Conservative government, on the other hand, will find the private
sector somewhat reluctant to pick up contracts to run existing, operational
prisons. The leverage which generally makes running a private prison
financially viable is the opportunity, in staffing and structural terms, to 'start
again': to eliminate old work practices, rigid rosters, sick-leave expectations,
open-ended overtime, and so on. Almost without exception, private operators have taken on prisons where nothing at all has been inherited – no staff,
no prisoners, no programmes, no work practices. Yet employment rights and

conditions at existing prisons are such that no government could deliver a 'clean' industrial situation to new contractors. This could constitute a major barrier to the proposed further programme of privatization; at the very least it would raise the costs of bids.

In summary, privatization is now a proven option in the UK and is integral to the overall system. Even if Labour were to come to office in 1997 and were to attempt to implement its announced policy, private prisons would remain an integral aspect of public administration and penal policy until well into the first decade of the twenty-first century. More likely, however, is a scenario where a degree of private sector involvement is accepted and maintained. A win for the Conservative government would certainly serve to consolidate the present situation and ensure that the momentum continues.

New Zealand

In late 1992 the New Zealand government announced its intention to privatize part of its prison system. In May 1993 this commitment firmed up to the point of identifying the new institutions for which bids would be sought: a 250-bed remand prison in central Auckland and a 350-bed medium-security institution in south Auckland.

It was recognized that legislative amendment was necessary to implement this plan, and in 1993 a Bill was introduced into the parliament. Before it could be passed into law, parliament was prorogued and a general election held. The Penal Institutions Amendment Act consequently did not become law until 8 December 1994. Although expressions of interest had been sought before then and the field of acceptable bidders narrowed to five, the formal processes did not really commence until 1995. However, the first of the contracts is expected to be let by mid-1996, with start-up by late 1997. The second should run no more than a year behind that schedule. There is an expectation, but not yet a commitment, that bids will also be called for a 500-bed multi-purpose prison, though a date has not yet been set for that.

The completion of the first two prisons would mean that some 12 per cent of New Zealand's projected prisoner population would be held in private prisons. The 500-bed facility would take that number nearer to 20 per cent. Despite these high percentages, it is premature to include New Zealand in the list of countries for which private prisons are a proven option. However, they are very much on the drawing board.

Canada

Despite its proximity to the United States, Canada has traditionally been not merely resistant but positively antagonistic to the notion of private prisons (Ericson *et al.* 1987). However, since 1994 distinct signs have emerged that privatization could become an important issue in Canadian corrections. For in that year the New Brunswick government, already committed to the construction and operation of a new secure facility for young offenders, started to explore the possibility of privatization. This process included hiring programme consultants as well as commissioning a thorough literature review within the Department of the Solicitor General. In September 1994, expressions of interest were sought, and on 29 June 1995 the government announced that the Wackenhut Corporation was the favoured bidder with which detailed negotiations would now commence.[6]

Two weeks earlier, Wackenhut – presumably anticipating success – had put together a powerful team of lobbyists whose brief was to try to persuade the Canadian government to start privatizing new federal prisons. The political context for this lobbying was initially unpromising, for the Solicitor General has reiterated that he was not considering privatizing federal prisons (*New Brunswick Evening Times Globe*, 4 July 1995). However, the broader picture reveals some commercial cracks, with Alberta actively considering this development and Nova Scotia apparently toying with the idea of contracting out management of the whole of its (very small) prison system.

Summary

In summary, in the three countries where private prisons have already become operational, they are already integral to the total system. In New Zealand, the current plans if implemented would bring about a similar situation. As for Canada, its place in the jigsaw of privatization should at least be kept under review.

Security levels at private prisons

An early criticism of privatization is that the private sector only took on responsibility for the soft end of the penal spectrum – minimum-security prisoners, posing no unusual behavioural or custodial problems. That being so, how could any sensible comparison be made with the public sector as to costs, effectiveness or anything else? There was some justice in this observation. Of course, it was not potential bidders but government authorities who made the initial decisions as to what kinds of prison with what sorts of regime would be privatized.

When in 1990 the first opportunity arose in the USA for the private sector to compete to operate a maximum-security prison, the bidding was keen. CCA was the successful bidder, and the Leavenworth Detention Centre (Kansas), an institution contracted by the US Marshals Service, became operational in June 1992.

Since then a further four maximum-security private prisons have come on-stream. As at 31 December 1995, the security ratings of US private prisons were as follows: 30 minimum; 45 minimum/medium or medium; 11 catering for all security levels; and 6 maximum (Thomas and Bollinger 1996). The standard contracts do not permit the contractor to pick and choose between prisoners within the stated security rating – for example, by health status such as being HIV-positive or by reason of posing a suicide risk.

The criticism that the private sector might only pick the tastiest cherries possessed some validity in relation to Australia's first private prison, Borallon. At the time of construction, the design and designation of the prison had been medium/maximum; but the prisoners actually sent there by the Queensland Corrective Services Commission (QCSC) were designated medium- and minimum-security. Perhaps the QCSC, treading such new ground for Australia, had understandably been over-cautious, for the contract in fact had been written in terms which permitted the operators to refuse to accept HIV-positive, protection, suicidal or even remand prisoners. Borallon was soon redesignated a medium/minimum prison, thus bringing appearance into line with reality. Experienced inmates, recognizing Borallon's superior ambience, quickly began to make applications for transfer to Borallon (Harding 1992), which thus became one of the few prisons in the world possessing an eager stand-by list! The contract, subsequently renewed for a five-year period from 31 March 1995, still contains the same exclusions.

For all that, the Australian situation has now tangibly changed. The Arthur Gorrie Correctional Centre, operational since 1992, accommodates an inmate mix which includes remand, classification, HIV-positive and protection prisoners – some of whom require maximum security. Junee prison is medium/minimum-security, with the emphasis on medium. Mount Gambier is also medium/minimum, but with the emphasis on minimum; whilst Melton, as the main women's prison in Victoria, will have to manage all security levels.

Further down the track, West Sale will be medium-security, whilst Laverton North will cater for remand and some maximum-security prisoners. The projected 500-bed South Australia prison will, if it eventuates, be multi-purpose, including women prisoners, thus covering all security levels.

Private prisons in Australia thus seem in terms of security levels to be a microcosm of public sector prisons, an observation which is also accurate with regard to the United Kingdom. There, the first private prison, The Wolds, was originally designated for remand prisoners, except the most dangerous; its security rating is thus medium.[7] From the outset the operators have had no right or discretion to refuse to accept those prisoners, such as HIV-positive or known drug users, who may pose management problems. Blakenhurst, opened a year later in mid-1993, is a standard British 'local' prison, designed to hold both remand prisoners and medium-security convicted prisoners from the surrounding catchment area. Doncaster, operational since June 1994, caters for about 60 maximum-security remand prisoners, about 600 other remandees (including young offenders) who are thus medium-security, and about 60 minimum-security convicted offenders. Buckley Hall, by contrast, is entirely minimum-security.

Both Fazakerley and Bridgend will be predominantly medium-security, with some maximum-security accommodation; this is also expected to be the case with the next generation of private prisons. Lowdham Grange will be medium-security.

In summary, private prisons in the USA, Australia and the UK are integral to the total system not merely in terms of the numbers accommodated but also in terms of the custodial responsibilities which they carry.

Financing arrangements and types of contract

Financing and general contractual matters are also important when considering the broad question of the growing significance of private prisons. Easily terminable arrangements clearly would reduce the overall significance of privatization to the total imprisonment system. However, what has now become evident is that financial, administrative and legal arrangements typically constitute in themselves a substantial barrier to policy reversal. Conversely, it could be said that they constitute a real commitment by the private sector operators to this sort of enterprise.

The United States, as so often, has led the way both in creating the problem and in finding a solution. A primary factor driving the initial development of privatization had been the political reluctance or the constitutional or statutory inability of state governments to raise capital to build new prisons at a rate sufficient to keep pace with the exponentially increasing inmate populations held in state or federal prisons and local or county jails (McDonald 1990; 1992). From this it naturally followed that, from the outset, the archetypal contract has been one to *design, construct, finance and manage* new prisons. These 'DCFM contracts' leave the private contractor with the onus of putting together a business consortium to cover the whole range of activities which go into turning a green-fields site into an operational prison. Among the key components are architectural matters, engineering and construction, raising risk capital and prison management skills. Evaluation of the competing bids will look at each of these factors separately, as well as weighing the proposal overall. Typically, each stage in this sequence or at least the overall timetable will be subject to strict completion dates and financial penalties.

An initial drawback to DCFM arrangements was that successful bidders were obliged to borrow at whatever commercial rates were available to them. Obviously, their overall bids reflected their own costs of borrowing, which would thus be passed back to the state. Yet the economic reality was that the state was committing to the expenditure and thus stood behind the successful bidder. That being so, could ways be found in which the borrower, and thus the state, could access the favourable interest rates, as well as the tax advantages, which would be available if the state itself were raising the finance?

The first state to find an answer was Ohio, not in the context of private prisons (there are no such prisons in that state)[8] but rather of public sector prisons (de Witt 1986). Ohio wished to go on building its own prisons but also needed to circumvent statutory limits upon the extent of bond indebtedness permitted for this purpose. The mechanism adopted was that of lease-purchase financing. This was based upon a legal arrangement whereby the state[9] became a tenant of a facility nominally owned by another entity. That entity in turn was typically a trustee company representing all the interested parties. The arrangement was characterized as a lease because the state would only acquire legal title to the facility after all the required capital and interest repayments had been made through the trustee company to the parties providing the finance. Interest would be tax-exempt under the normal US law whereby a limited obligation is issued on behalf of a state.

This mechanism – known as issuing 'certificates of participation' – has now been refined so that the successful bidder for a DCFM contract can be dealt in through the trustee arrangement so as to receive the borrowing benefits of state certificates of participation. This is now standard practice. To illustrate: the pending contracts the present author was able to inspect at the offices of the Florida Correctional Privatization Commission each drew upon this model, for the benefit of Wackenhut and Esmor,[10] respectively. By the same token, recent bids (involving Esmor and CCA) are, like all bids in all states, based on the assumption that this financing arrangement will be available.

In the USA, 69 of the 92 private prisons identified in the census of 31 December 1995 were new institutions, and a further 11 were renovated ones (Thomas 1996). The likelihood is that virtually all of these involve DCFM contracts and that, in turn, most of these also depend upon certificate of participation funding mechanisms. More stakeholders are thus tied into the prison privatization process more closely than would be the case if the contracts were simple bilateral ones involving governments and corporations.

In considering the significance of privatization, it should be emphasized that these sorts of arrangement tie private prisons almost inextricably into the total system. Deferred ownership of real estate and physical plant and long-term financial commitments by way of certificates of participation together constitute real if not insuperable barriers to state policy reversal in this area.

Australian governments first entering this field were not as cash-strapped as their US counterparts, or at any rate not constrained by law from drawing on the public purse. Thus Queensland carried the capital costs of construction of both Borallon and the Arthur Gorrie Correctional Centre. These prisons were designed, constructed and financed under the aegis of the relevant state departments, and only the management was contracted out to the private sector. Of course, this has its drawbacks; private operators almost invariably complain that the management regime they have in mind would best be carried out in a differently designed prison, that there is wasted or unusable space or that the fit-out is inappropriate. The corollary is their almost unanimous belief that construction costs would be less in a DCFM contract. From a governmental point of view, however, the benefit is that the commitment to privatization need not exceed the term of a relatively short contract. Moreover, at some point, depending on the way the contract is written, the original successful contractor has to rebid, rather than simply exercising an option to renew; this keeps the discipline of market forces in play both as to costs and as to performance and acoountability.

In its third foray into possible privatization, a 600-bed institution at Woodford, the Queensland government also undertook to meet the capital costs up-front, but provided that the contract should be DCM – *design, construct and manage*. The construction component of the contract itself was to be fixed-price. As it turned out, the QCSC itself won this contract in a market-testing exercise which will be discussed fully later. In doing so, it put together a consortium which included a construction company upon which would fall the risk of the fixed-price element of the contract.

In New South Wales, the Junee contract was also DCM, with the state meeting the agreed fixed costs of construction. The first South Australian foray into privatization, Mount Gambier, was like Borallon and the Arthur Gorrie Correctional Centre, a management-only contract.

In fact, Victoria is the only Australian state which has so far gone fully down the DCFM track. Each of the three contracts in the pipeline will be of this type. The financing arrangements are at the rather rudimentary stage of the early US contracts, with the successful bidders having to borrow at commercial rates. This will be true also with the New Zealand contracts, each of which will be DCFM.

In Victoria and New Zealand, the legal and financial consequences are quite complex. The chosen model in Victoria is that the land itself will remain in the ownership of the state (which will have selected and acquired the site and arranged any necessary clearances), whilst the buildings will be subject to a long lease arrangement of up to 40 years. It will not be straightforward for the state government to untangle itself from such arrangements.

The United Kingdom has tangled itself up in rather a similar way. Although the first four contracts were for management only, involving quite short though renewable terms, the next raft of seven, commencing with Fazakerly, Bridgend and now Lowdham Grange, are DCFM. In each case the site will be owned by the government, so that the arrangements in relation to the buildings, plant and fittings are complex and long-running. Specifically, ownership of the land remains vested in the government, whilst the contractor will receive a lease of the land and buildings for the duration of the contract. Typically, contracts will run for 25 years.

Provisions do exist for early termination, opportunities occurring at five-yearly intervals. However, the costs of termination would be high. The government would have to pay all outstanding lender's liabilities and costs (including losses on hedging loans and the like) plus a fair market value for the contractor's equity in the project including anticipated profits. Reverting to the question whether an incoming Labour government could realistically attempt to reverse privatization policy, provisions such as these mean that to do so would cost tens or more likely hundreds of millions of pounds, without adding a single extra bed to available prison accommodation. In this context, wholesale policy reversal starts to seem fantastical.

It should be added, however, that to intertwine management issues with the original financing deal in this way potentially affects accountability in relation to management standards. Because the original successful contractor has a long lease, the management component (the 'M' in the DCFM arrangement) has been relegated to an option to renew rather than left as a rebid situation. To put this point another way, the 'finance' component of a DCFM contract will inevitably reduce the flexibility of governments in relation to the management side.

Summary

The threshold question has been whether privatization has yet attained such significance that, for all practical purposes, it is irreversible, at least in the foreseeable future. This in turn raised three subsidiary questions as to numbers, custodial responsibilities and financing and administrative structures.

In each of the three countries where privatization is now operational or irrevocably in the pipeline, the existing arrangements could only be unscrambled with enormous strain upon the prison system as well as major impact upon governmental liabilities. In practical terms, private prisons are here to stay.

Notes

1 Subsequently, in July 1996, the Bureau of Prisons put its privatization plans on hold. The reason given was that 'it was unable contractually to reduce the risk of a strike or walk out' of correctional officers employed by private firms. However, the Bureau has been sending out mixed messages and evidently has not entirely ruled out commitment to a privatization programme (General Accounting Office 1996: 13–14). This is also demonstrated, for example, by the fact that it has sub-contracted custody of some of its prisoners to state or local authorities who in turn have placed those prisoners in privatized facilities.

2 The enabling legislation is the Criminal Justice Act 1991, ss. 84–9, plus Schedule 10. This is applicable throughout the United Kingdom, including Scotland. However, no privatization moves have taken place in the latter jurisdiction. A 1994 amendment to the Criminal Justice Act authorized the contracting out or

privatization of juvenile secure detention centres. In September 1995 expressions of interest were sought in relation to the construction and management of six such centres. At the time of writing, no contracts have been let. The issue is being handled by a group within the Home Office quite separate from the Contracts and Competition Group which handles the privatization of adult prisons.

3 The basis of these calculations is a static prison population of 56,000. However, the Home Office itself has a deplorable record in forecasting prisoner numbers (see, for example, its projection in its 1994–97 Corporate Plan that the population would reach 52,000 in the year 2000–2001 – a figure which was actually reached in 1995). Moreover, the Home Secretary seems determined to drive the population up further, as his speech at the Conservative Party Conference in October 1995 made clear. Notice was given that legislation would be introduced imposing mandatory life sentences on certain types of offender for their second offence and that generally the length of prison sentences could be expected to increase.

4 More recently, a commitment has been made (Home Office 1996) to bringing a further 12 private prisons on stream, that is, over and above the 10 per cent of establishment figure and any refurbishments. This matter is fully discussed in Chapter 6.

5 In Queensland the first moves towards privatization were taken by a (right-wing) National Party government, which in early 1988 had established a Review of Corrective Services in that state (Kennedy 1988). Privatization having been recommended, enabling legislation was passed later that year and bids sought for the management of Borallon prison which was then in the course of construction. The successful bidder was CCA. In December 1989, a month before the prison was scheduled to commence, the National Party was defeated at a general election by the Labor Party which earlier had expressed its opposition to prison privatization. Nevertheless, the incoming Labor government allowed the contract to proceed. Subsequently, in October 1991 the Labor government set in motion the procedures which ultimately resulted in the privatization of a new prison, the Arthur Gorrie Correctional Centre.

6 See the *New Brunswick Evening Times Globe*, 29 June 1995. Subsequently, allegations came forth of some kind of financial impropriety involving Wackenhut's US operations, and the New Brunswick government put the contract on 'hold' whilst the matter was investigated. No impropriety was in fact found, but nevertheless the government took advantage of this *locus poenitentiae* to review its position and slow down the process of privatization.

7 Note that following the first report of the chief inspector of prisons (Tumim 1994a), the prisoner mix was altered so as to include convicted prisoners.

8 Ohio is one of five states where the Attorney General has advised that prison privatization would not be lawful for constitutional or current statutory reasons: see Thomas (1995a: 28–9).

9 Or any other governmental unit, such as a county. This point is relevant as privatization has spread to county jails as well as state prisons.

10 Esmor Correctional Corporation is, after CCA and Wackenhut, the third biggest player in correctional privatization in the USA.

Accountability and the political context of privatization

Given that private prisons are here to stay for the foreseeable future, the central question becomes that of accountability. Accountability is not a unitary idea; its crucial components will vary from activity to activity, from structure to structure. The closed nature of total institutions such as prisons means that there are special difficulties in achieving effective accountability, even within public sector prisons (Maguire *et al.* 1985), and obviously these factors will be no less applicable to accountability within private prisons. However, the further question arises: are there additional factors which make accountability in private prisons even more difficult and illusory?

The controversial nature of prison privatization has in fact stimulated widespread and ideologically sharp debate, different in kind from, say, the debate which surrounded the privatization of garbage-collection services. It is in this political context that many of the key elements which should go towards making up proper accountability have been flagged. By traversing the political context of prison privatization and the issues which the debate threw into high relief, therefore, it is possible to identify a check-list of some of the hazards to be avoided and circumstances to be monitored. Accordingly, it is important to understand both the factors which underlie the growth of private prisons and the moral, historical, penological and political arguments which have been put forward in opposition.

Factors underlying contemporary moves towards privatization

The political, economic and social factors which acted as catalysts for privatization have been extensively discussed in the literature (DiIulio 1988; 1991; Matthews 1989; Ryan and Ward 1989; Logan 1990; McDonald

1990; 1992; 1994; Feeley 1991; Moyle 1994). The main points will be briefly highlighted here and modestly supplemented.

Absolutely central has been the exponential increase around the world in prison populations. In the USA there was in mid-1995 a total of almost 1.6 million adult prisoners incarcerated in state and federal prisons and local and county jails[1] – a rate of 600 per 100,000 population. These numbers were twice as great as a decade ago. Apart from revolutionary crises or the pacification of populations by occupying armies, this is the highest recorded incarceration rate in the history of the world. In Australia and the UK also, increases in prison populations as well as in overall rates and numbers, whilst less dramatic, have nevertheless been substantial. For example, in Australia the rate per 100,000 has increased from about 60 in 1984 to almost 100 in 1995; whilst in the three years to mid-1996 the UK prison population has climbed from 43,000 to 54,000, a rate of about 100 per 100,000, thus maintaining that country's position as having one of the highest imprisonment rates in western Europe.

Such increases have led to overcrowding across the respective systems. Moreover, the run-down condition of much of the available prison estate has meant that conditions for prisoners have become increasingly unpleasant. As a consequence, in the US federal court supervision of prison systems has become commonplace. The basis of this has mostly been the 'cruel and unusual punishment' provision of the Bill of Rights, though the 'privacy protection' clause has also founded some successful law suits. At one time, no less than 37 of the 50 states were subject to federal court orders. These related not only to absolute numbers – which typically were capped – but also to confinement conditions (National Prison Project 1989).

In Australia and the UK, the courts cannot exercise such a role. However, such matters as the destruction of Manchester (Strangeways) prison (Woolf and Tumim 1991), the regular reports of the chief inspector of prisons in the UK, and the Royal Commission into Aboriginal Deaths in Custody in Australia (Johnston 1991; Biles and McDonald 1992), plus the saturation media coverage which such matters typically receive, have ensured that prison conditions have remained prominent in political debate.

Hand in hand with these depressed circumstances have gone deteriorating prisoner health (Paulus 1988) and increasing suicide and self-mutilation rates (Johnston 1991; Biles and McDonald 1992; Hayes 1994; Liebling 1994; Liebling and Ward 1994; Rowan 1994). Staff morale has also deteriorated. This has occasionally manifested itself in quite elementary security lapses (Woodcock 1994; Learmont 1995) and, more importantly, in the growth of widespread cynicism as to the value and purpose of prisoner programmes.

Major refurbishment or replacement of prison plant thus became imperative and innovative approaches to prisoner management urgently desirable. As to plant, in the USA, as explained in Chapter 1, the ability and willingness of governments to outlay capital funds is circumscribed. By involving the private sector in the construction of new prisons, it was possible partially to finesse this problem; and therein lay the origin of the standard DCFM contract.

In Australia and the UK, whilst avoidance of up-front capital outlays has subsequently become an important element in privatization, the original drive was as much ideological as pragmatic. Each of those nations, particularly the UK, went through a phase from the mid-1980s when there was pathological governmental antipathy to the public sector *per se*, accompanied by a largely untested belief that the quest for profits automatically increased the economic efficiency of virtually any enterprise (Vickers and Yarrow 1988).

As to prisoner management, the important point came to be recognized that prisons had for decades been run on an input-based management strategy. Whatever human or other resources happened to be available, some real or imagined use must be found for them. The justification for custodial practices was typically not sought in their efficiency nor for programmes in their objective success. The standing 'joke' of a warder bidding a prisoner farewell at the end of his sentence with the words 'See you soon, son' possessed a chilling reality, one which was not confined to the uniformed officer subculture. When Martinson (1974) coined the phrase 'Nothing works', he was not simply sowing the seeds of future cynicism, nor merely providing an intellectual excuse for the abandonment of rehabilitation programmes; he was also reflecting an existing reality. In the mid-1970s, none of the prison systems with which this book is concerned regarded reduction of recidivism as what we would today call a 'performance indicator'. The existence of the prison system seemed to provide its own justification for everything that happened within it – a classic marker of an input-based organization.

An output-based strategy would, by contrast, have put much more emphasis upon 'success' rates: for example, in terms of reduced recidivism or post-release employment opportunities or positive self-development of offenders. None of these measures is by its very nature beyond the reach of a public sector prison system's aspirations; nor is output-based management generally. For the most part, however, these characteristics have been notably absent in recent times from prison culture.[2] However, involvement of the private sector, for which in its general activities such approaches are routine, highlighted the fact that desired outcomes and agreed means can be specified, indeed *must* be specified, if performance criteria are to be established and written into the contract. From this perspective it can be said that 'privatization is principally an issue of fit between the strategic purposes that society seeks to achieve through imprisonment and the currently available means to do so' (O'Hare 1990: 128).

The discipline in approaching penal corrections in this way should then spill over into the public sector. This notion of *cross-fertilization* will be seen in due course to be one of the most important single justifications for the process of properly accountable privatization. However, in the early dialectic only McConville (1987: 240) seemed to perceive this possibility, albeit in rather abstract terms.

It has been mentioned that, in the UK, ideology rather than pragmatism played a significant early role. One aspect of this, in the view of some commentators (Ryan and Ward 1989; Shaw 1989; Rutherford 1990), was a strong desire to break down the influence of the Prison Officers' Association. For the Conservative government of the time, this of course was an extension of the desire to break down *all* union power. Equally, prison reformers were becoming increasingly concerned at the barriers which the union seemed to be putting in the way of reform (Stern 1993). For a while, therefore, there was a curious, if temporary, juxtaposition of two groups who normally felt more comfortable as antagonists.

In Australia the comparable desire was more pragmatic – to reduce recurrent expenditure on prisons through reducing wage bills, which in turn meant confronting the power of unions. The various unions representing uniformed staff had, in all states, progressively throttled management control over budgets through restrictive employment conditions and work practices (Williams 1983). For example, sick leave had in effect become an entitlement for the healthy rather than a privilege for the unwell; and failure to take such leave was contrary to the prevailing subculture in that it reduced the opportunity for other officers to be called in for highly paid overtime duty. Related to this work practice, rosters had come to contain more officers, particularly static turnkey staff, than were reasonably required for the running of the prison.

Understandably, as prison populations increased and both incarceration and employment conditions deteriorated (for they are inextricably linked), unions became even more protective of their situations and intransigent against change. Management was not blameless, however. The fact that these sorts of practice had been allowed to grow and had been tolerated for so long demonstrated that prison bureaucracies and senior management had indeed come to accept and adopt ways of thinking which were entirely input-orientated.

The primary impact of matters of this sort was financial. But their impact was also felt upon penal policy generally. For example, programme implementation, prisoner movements, out-of-cell hours, leisure-time pursuits, even sometimes decisions as to which professionals should be admitted to prisons upon what conditions, became matters for employee convenience rather than managerial decision. There was even evidence that some programme innovations and changes to custodial practices had been deliberately undermined by union resistance (Harding 1992).

Significantly, senior management in both the Northern Territory and Western Australia backed away from the threat of privatization once the unions had conceded staffing and employment conditions which not only delivered financial savings but also bore upon programme matters (Harding 1995). In these instances, the threat of privatization had served to restore management control. As with the value of cross-fertilization, this rationale had not been explicitly articulated in the first wave of privatization; but if its importance had not been expressed, it had certainly been sensed.

In summary, the precursors to the push for privatization were: burgeoning prison populations; consequential overcrowding and deteriorating conditions; an urgent need for large and continuing capital outlays on new plant; legal inability or political reluctance to commit such funds; low management and staff morale, linked with input-based penal strategies; ideological distaste for public sector enterprises, coupled with a general commitment to privatization; anti-union feeling, both for its own sake and because of the increases in recurrent funding needs that flowed from strong unionism; and a sense, if not an articulate expression, of the fact that penal policy benefits might flow from an alternative form of service delivery.

Moral conundrums and the impact of privatization upon penal policy and practice

Cogent as these precursors might seem, as far as some critics were concerned they simply missed the point. Privatization could never in principle be a proper response to these pressures. Punishment, it was said, is a matter exclusively for the state; devolved, it loses its moral legitimacy. In a letter to *The Times* in 1988, the doyen of modern penology, Radzinowicz, in his only known foray into this debate, stated: 'In a democracy grounded on the rule of law and public accountability, the enforcement of penal legislation . . . should be the undiluted responsibility of the state' (quoted in Shaw 1992). DiIulio (1991: 197) puts the same philosophy more explicitly:

> [T]o remain legitimate and morally significant, the authority to govern behind bars, to deprive citizens of their liberty, to coerce (and even kill) them, must remain in the hands of government authorities. Regardless of which penological theory is in vogue, the message that those who abuse liberty shall live without it is the philosophical brick and mortar of every correctional facility – a message that ought to be conveyed by the offended community of law-abiding citizens, through its public agents, to the incarcerated individual . . . The badge of the arresting police officer, the robes of the judge, and the state patch of the corrections officer are symbols of the inherently public nature of crime and punishment.

Christie (1993: 102) sees the matter rather similarly, as one of communitarian responsibility and democratic participation:

[T]he prison officer is my man. I would hold a hand on his key, or on the switch for the electric chair. He could be a bad officer. And I could be bad. Together we made for a bad system, so well known from the history of punishments. But I would have known I was a responsible part of the arrangement. Chances would also be great that some people in the system were not only bad. They would more easily be personally mobilized. The guard was their guard, their responsibility, not an employee of a branch of General Motors, or Volvo for that matter. The communal character of punishments evaporates in the proposals for private prisons.

These are strongly made arguments, then, with distinguished proponents. There seem to be at least two lines of response, however. The first is that the 'communal nature of punishment', the 'deprivation of citizens of their liberty', is protected and preserved as an essential function of the state by the fact that punishment is imposed or *allocated* by an independent judiciary which represents state authority both symbolically and practically. On this view, the administration or delivery of punishment is a second-level aspect of state authority, delegable in a day-to-day sense, as long as the state itself remains actively accountable for its exercise to its citizens – who are the source from which its own legitimacy derives. The key question thus becomes whether the contractor is effectively accountable to the state, and whether the state in turn is effectively accountable to its citizens. If accountability is structured effectively, then in Christie's terms the guard remains their guard and in DiIulio's terms the message continues to be conveyed through agents who are public in the sense of being ultimately answerable to the state.

The second line of response is quite simply that the public system has such a patchy track record in the administration or delivery of punishment that it is perverse to refuse to explore alternatives. This line of analysis has led to the growth of evaluation literature in which it is sought to establish the superior or inferior performance of one sector as against the other according to a wide range of criteria.

Of course, throughout the history of public prisons it has always been problematical to secure the accountability of the state to its citizens. This is the point where the first response and the second merge. The defective level of accountability is what has facilitated a fairly woeful track record in the public sector. In this area of public administration, the instinct for secrecy is very strong; defensiveness against allegations of incompetence or indifference is second nature (Fitzgerald 1977; Zdenowski and Brown 1982; Grindrod and Black 1989). However, that is hardly a sufficient basis for dismissing at the very threshold proposals for alternative forms of the administration of punishment. To the contrary; the opening up of the private sector may heighten awareness of how sloppy public accountability has often been in the past, leading to the creation of innovative mechanisms applicable to both the private and the public sectors.

However, such arguments will never satisfy purist critics. Sparks (1994: 24), for example, is scathing in his attack. The allocation–delivery dichotomy, he argues, 'tends to sandpaper away the contested and "dismaying" . . . nature of state punishment. In that sense it makes it appear more akin to other spheres of ordinary administrative activity.' He adds:

> [T]he construction of complex input-output models of correctional efficiency . . . bespeaks a dominant form of managerialism . . . which tends to displace older normative concerns and anxieties . . . [T]here is the inherent likelihood that expert systems of punishment, whether 'public' or 'private' and however formally accountable, will tend to escape any public sphere of informed debate and decision.
>
> (Sparks 1994: 24)

Yet the arrival of private prisons has already stimulated a huge literature, including Sparks's own contributions, on prisons and punishment generally. This has not simply been at the academic level but within professional organizations and bureaucracies as well as at widely attended conferences.[3] Sparks's complaint, by its very articulation, has stimulated the process of improving the level of informed debate. The challenge is surely to maintain the level of discussion, analysis and disputation which the privatization process has already spawned.

As to the second response – the quality of previous prison regimes and the unproductive use of resources – the director of the National Association for the Care and Resettlement of Offenders has cogently documented the waste that has occurred since the mid-1950s (Stern 1993: 115–31). Likewise, the director of the UK Prison Reform Trust, himself an avowed opponent of privatization, has acknowledged the force of these points:

> I think that the case against privatization would be that much stronger if there were not substantial evidence that the public system is either squalid or ludicrously wasteful of resources. The opponents of privatization have to be careful not to be defenders of public squalor.
>
> (Shaw 1989: 51)

This comment concedes, in effect, that the purist moral argument is something of an intellectual indulgence. A moral position which is blinkered from the realities which exist on the ground may be self-sustaining and may well comfort its adherents; but it does not take debates about penal policy in any useful direction. Indeed, this is the point at which morality starts to give way to fundamentalism. It sometimes seems as if all the data in the world – even if they showed that private prisons were cheaper, prisoner health was better, recidivism rates were lower, and so on – would not convince some opponents.

Neither does moral or ideological fundamentalism help the people who actually inhabit prisons. The *reductio ad absurdum* of this can be seen in Ryan's analysis of the struggle over privatization in the UK:

> It should be clear . . . that in the main we agree with those on the Left and in the penal lobby who oppose privatizing prisons . . . Turning . . . to the position of prison officers, there are signs that the threat of privatization is helping to bring about a rapprochement between the Prison Officers' Association . . . and the Labour movement . . . Though any alliance will no doubt be a cautious one on both sides, the POA's unmistakable shift to the left, its support for reducing the prison population, and its dislike for being used as a scapegoat by a union-bashing government, all point to another fissure in the supposed monolith of State which the Left would be foolish not to exploit.
>
> (Ryan and Ward 1989: 64, 71)

Prisoners may not be particularly cheered by the knowledge that grandiose strategies about ideological realignment can so readily be constructed out of their predicament. They are left stranded as irrelevant symbols of supposedly greater issues. Their own identities and preferences are of no interest. This is their ultimate disempowerment. A debate which *par excellence* possesses profound human connotations is reduced simply to moral or ideological abstractions.

Penal policy implications

Several critics have put the view that privatization is inherently expansionist. Sparks (1994: 25), for example, has argued as follows:

> If one takes the strong analogy of private provision of health services, the whole strength of the privatization case turns on the notion of an indefinitely large demand which public provision can never in principle satisfy. In examining privatization discourse, the term which routinely arises is *supplement* . . . Private prisons are explicitly conceived as *supplementary* to an existing system which has reached or exceeded even the most permissive estimation of its capacity. They are exceedingly unlikely, for reasons of economic and political logic, to reduce the overall dimensions of any such system. Moreover, there is a powerful tradition of criminological analysis which suggests that *supplementarity* is precisely the mechanism whereby criminal justice institutions are most likely to extend their scale and their sphere of operations.

Dilulio (1991: 199) adds to the debate another expansionist dimension – into wider forms of law-enforcement activity:

Or, suppose that CCA [Corrections Corporation of America] has made it really big. They have proved that they can do everything the privatizers have promised and more. The corporation decides to branch out. The company changes its name to CJCA: the Criminal Justice Corporation of America. It provides a full range of criminal justice services; cops, courts and corrections. In an unguarded moment, a CJCA official boasts that 'our firm can arrest 'em, try 'em, lock 'em up, and, if need be, fry 'em for less'. Is there anything wrong with CJCA?

Nellis (1991: 180) sees the technological innovations of the private sector as almost inevitably driving expansion onwards to the point where investment at last becomes cost-effective. In standard economic terms, the greater the number of 'customers', the lower the unit costs. Thus, net-widening becomes structurally implicit in the adoption of new correctional technology. He argues, for example, with regard to electronic monitoring:

> Although not a consumer good in the same sense [as a motor vehicle], tagging also fits the thrust of contemporary political and economic development in so far as it feeds on the ideologically inspired need to reduce expenditure on public services, whether prisons or social welfare, and also on the need to develop cheaper but none the less effective control over the dispossessed populations – elements of the urban underclass – who are becoming surplus to capitalism's requirements.

That being so, it must in his view be regarded as likely that tagging will eventually be utilized at some of the proposed 'new' control points – upon prostitutes, kerb-crawlers, street children, minor offenders, and so on. Restrictive punishment would thus be targeted upon groups who would not normally, under previous arrangements, have been subjected to restraint.[4]

Both Feeley (1991) and Moyle (1993: 232–3) have documented this same concern in historical rather than futuristic terms. Referring to transportation of convicts to the United States, Feeley points out that 'most of its costs were borne by profit-seeking merchants selling their human cargo and planters who purchased it'. He continues:

> What underlay the entire administrative and economic structure of transportation was reliance upon private enterprise to effect public policy. More precisely, transportation was an innovation promoted by mercantile interests which was only reluctantly embraced by public officials as they slowly came to appreciate its cost effectiveness.
>
> (1991: 3)

Nor was it, in his view, simply a merciful displacement, exile instead of execution:

> It was an innovation of gigantic proportions. It radically transformed the administration of criminal justice. Although it was a merciful

alternative for those few who otherwise would have been hanged, in terms of numbers it had its greatest impact on those who had no risk of death ... [T]he new alternative swept up those who would have claimed benefit of clergy and escaped punishment altogether and those who would otherwise have received an unconditional pardon, a whipping or a small fine. For still others it increased the likelihood of prosecution, conviction and punishment since victims were more willing to prosecute and juries were more willing to convict if they knew the offenders would not be hanged.

(1991: 4)

Feeley constructs parallel arguments with regard to the convict lease system which prevailed in the South after the Civil War and during the opening up of the West. He concludes that 'the most significant feature of private involvement in corrections is the capacity of the private sector to promote new forms of penalty which expand the capacity of the state to apply the criminal sanction' (1991: 8). Like Nellis, he envisions electronic tagging as being one of those new technologies which will end up driving aspects of penal policy rather than passively reflecting agreed correctional needs.

Lilly and Knepper are likewise concerned at the implacable march of technology, whipped along by corporations for whom the social constraints and responsibilities of innovation are completely swamped by the need for global expansion and profitability. They see corrections as representing 'an international market ... closely linked to various sections of the inter-national military industrial complex' (1992: 175). The new electronics market particularly exemplifies the risk (1992: 184). More alarmingly, however, at 'the centre of the international privatization movement are transnational corrections corporations. The future of private prisons abroad [outside the USA] will be determined by what these companies do more than by the transfer of corrections policy' (1992: 183).

This sort of concern is lent some credence by the overtly expansionist tone of the official pronouncements of some of the leading players. Reference has already been made to the 1994 annual report of CCA which stated that 'there are powerful market forces driving our industry, and its potential has barely been touched'. The Wackenhut Corporation, in its 1994 annual report, is more explicit in its aspirations:

In preparing for the third millenium and *the globalization of privatized corrections* [emphasis added] Wackenhut Corrections Corporation has taken a number of important steps. We have established a central corporate infrastructure capable of sustaining global operations with numerous clients. Additionally, we have established two regional offices in the U.S. and have offices in the United Kingdom and Australia.

Baldry (1994a: 125), writing from one of those countries – Australia – where Wackenhut has set up an office and where CCA, the other USA-based 'transnational corrections corporation', has also now gained a strong foothold, echoes Lilly and Knepper. She argues that this aspect of 'U.S. entrepreneurial expansion can be paralleled with the export for profit of nuclear power, health care systems and toxic chemicals . . . and the attempted "colonisation" of those industries in countries outside the U.S.' Her concern is that extravagant claims are invariably made for the benefits of the commodity being 'sold'. She argues:

> Each [commodity] has necessitated the introduction of culturally foreign attitudes and personnel, and each has talked about economic imperatives to the exclusion of argument about social cohesion, well-being and citizens' rights . . . The introduction of the U.S. private prison model to Australia and its ready acceptance has been an exercise in entrepreneurial colonisation hastily invited and given without proper investigation.
>
> (Baldry 1994a: 126)

Baldry fortifies her argument by examination of the probity, ethics and previous *modus operandi* of the actual parties involved, particularly persons associated with the Wackenhut Corporation (1994a: 134–6). 'Do you really want people like this doing any kind of business in your own backyard?' is the thrust of her investigation. In her view, an Australian state government assigning private prison contracts without obtaining probity guarantees has failed its citizens.

Tenets of accountability

This recent history should have facilitated the process of identifying the key tenets of accountability – accountability which the state must require of private contractors and which citizens must require of the state.

(i)   *The distinction between the allocation and the administration of punishment must be strictly maintained, with the private sector's role being confined to administration.*
      If privatization worked in such a way as to enable the private sector to allocate punishment, there would be a profound and irreparable fissure in the balance of the modern democratic state and the corresponding fealty which it could expect of its citizens. As to this the critics are absolutely correct. A key aspect of accountability will thus be whether the administration or delivery of punishment shades into its allocation. It will be seen that this hazard has not been completely avoided.

(ii) *Penal policy must not be driven by those who stand to make a profit out of it.*
      This concern is legitimate and proper. The development of penal policy

should be something for the whole community. Of course, to make such a statement in the context only of private prisons finesses a little glibly the fact that it is not only commercial enterprises who wish to expand their activities and to influence penal policy. Just as financial profit is the reward of commercial success, so enhanced influence, expanded territory and the power to shape organizations is the reward of non-commercial activism. These desires can thus be found with voluntary or non-governmental agencies, as well as within government itself. Yet their places in the correctional harlequinade seem to be uncritically accepted, treated in fact as untainted, by most of the critics of adult private prisons. A better-rounded perspective may be that, wherever such desires are found, they should be viewed with scepticism.

The other perspective to bear in mind is that it is somewhat naive to believe that some kind of purely scientific or abstract development of crime and justice policy generally is any longer attainable at this stage of the late twentieth century. To illustrate: we live in times where, for example, security services or devices constitute an immense, growing and transnational industry; where much advertising, whilst purporting to be informational, is in reality emotional, fomenting fear of crime; and where news coverage of crime (which media operators see as being akin to entertainment) promotes it to a point of prominence which is completely out of kilter with its objective seriousness or frequency.

Penal policy, like it or not, has become everybody's business. Private correctional companies must certainly be scrutinized so that any lobbying they attempt will be recognized and, where appropriate, stigmatized. But in a broad sense they can hardly be quarantined from participation in a debate in which everyone else seems to be participating.

(iii) *The activities of the private sector and their relations with government must be open and publicly accessible.*
This point bears upon the lobbying issue mentioned above. It reflects also the concern that 'deals' may be struck with transnational correctional corporations in disregard of a wider public interest. No accountability structure, in relation to prisons or anything else, can be effective if the relevant activities are hidden from view. This is self-evident. Yet it will be seen that this standard has not been fully met, particularly in Australia and the UK.

(iv) *What is expected of the private sector must be clearly specified.*
Access to contractual arrangements enables measurement of performance to be made openly. The derision expressed for 'complex input-output models of correctional efficiency' (Sparks 1994: 24) fails to acknowledge that objectives *can* be spelt out, measurement criteria *can*

be identified, and that this cannot in itself be a harmful process. Of course, accountability must look to the substance of penal purposes. It should not simply be processual, to see whether the agreed protocols have been met; though it will emerge that there has been more than a hint of this from time to time.

(v)   *A dual system must not be allowed to evolve in which there is a run-down and demoralized public sector and a vibrant private sector.*
        As the origins of privatization are anchored in overcrowding and the need for new plant, plus the constraints upon public sector capital-raising for these purposes, there is a danger that resources will be directed towards the newly emerging private sector to the exclusion of the decaying public prison system. Staff demoralization may then flow from these disparities. Linked to this, there is also the possibility that the private sector may be allowed to operate predominantly at the soft end of the inmate spectrum. Although the discussion in Chapter 1 suggests that this danger has not been realized, it is nevertheless an important factor.

        Unless the two strands of the system operate with broadly comparable resources and in overlapping areas, there cannot be cross-fertilization for the benefit of the total system. Cross-fertilization is an important aspect of the public interest not noticed by most critics, who see private prisons more as a virus invading the public system than as a source of healthy nutrition. An aspect of accountability is to ensure that the total system is structured so as to bring this about.

(vi)   *Independent research and evaluation, with untramelled publication rights, must be built into private sector arrangements.*
        Accountability involves knowing whether we are on the right track. Arrangements made with the private operators must permit and encourage independent research to be carried out. Some contracts will be seen to have enabled the private sector in effect to veto research. A recent Prison Reform Trust (1995) evaluation of Doncaster prison was attempted in the face of denial of access to the prison itself. Of course, the public sector has hardly been a paragon, indeed on occasion has behaved disgracefully (Grindrod and Black 1989) and has itself thus inhibited accountability. The authorities should not be able to suppress research findings, though naturally publication will be subject to the general laws of defamation, privacy and the like.

(vii)   *Custodial regimes, programmes and personnel must be culturally appropriate.*
        Concern about the new style of managerialism is justifiable in corrections, as elsewhere, in that it downgrades difference and exaggerates similarity. Prisons, perhaps above all, are places where subject-matter knowledge is crucial to successful management. Part of

that knowledge relates to prison culture; but an even more important part relates to national culture. To take as an example the thorny question of differential ethnic needs in prisons (and the racism which is often associated), a US prison, with many Hispanic and Afro-American inmates, is different from an Australian prison, with its huge over-representation of indigenous Aboriginals; and a New Zealand prison, with its distinctive Maori and Polynesian populations, is different from a French one, with its large population of north African Muslims. The notion that one could entrust management of any of these institutions to a person or a team which lacks intuitive understanding of the complexities which flow from these differences is ludicrous. Yet, as will be seen, this has sometimes happened.

An aspect of accountability, therefore, is that the state retains an appropriate degree of control over the staffing decisions of the private contractors.

(viii) *There must be control over the probity of the private contractors.*
The critics are right to point to this as a potential problem. There are fast-talking opportunists in every new commercial field. The private prisons area has already seen the demise of some early operators (Thomas 1994: 2). In this respect, market forces should be recognized as a counterpoint to formal probity regulation; this is an area of accountability not generally recognized or understood by critics (Thomas and Logan 1993: 233).

(ix) *There must be financial accountability.*
With all state procurements, whether capital or recurrent, the usual accountability mechanisms which apply will obviously cover private prisons. Beyond that, the crucial area of accountability is to ensure that the agreed services are actually supplied and that this is done to the contracted quality. A corollary of this is that the whole contract, including financial details, must be publicly accessible. There must also be financial sanctions within the contractual arrangements.

Of course, the primary concern in much of the debate has been cost-saving in the sense that costs are actually lower than comparable public sector costs. It will be seen that some states build this requirement into their contractual systems in a way which is quite formulaic and inflexible. But a notion of accountability which required lower costs even if this entailed lower quality would be perverse. It will be argued in this book that, on the financial side, privatization should be about better value for money, with reduced outlays possibly occurring as a desirable by-product.

(x) *The state must in the last resort be able to reclaim private prisons.*
In emergencies or cases of chronic malfeasance, the state must be able to reclaim the private sector and reincorporate it into the public sector. If

accountability is to mean anything, no devolution of the administration of punishment should be irrevocable. In considering this, one should look beyond the formal provisions of the contract to the realities. If the practical constraints – such as compensation costs or legal prerequisites – in fact discourage the state from invoking this power, then a crucial element of accountability will be missing.

Summary

This list of the key tenets of accountability is not exhaustive, though certainly it covers the most important issues. Even at this early stage, the comments of Brown (1992: 34), a prominent critic of prison regimes generally, seem apposite:

> The same difficulty [of simply adopting a crude public–private dichotomy] arises in relation to the argument that private prisons will necessarily be less accountable. Having spent much time showing how unaccountable the public system is, and how the limited forms of accountability have been eroded, . . . it is a little difficult suddenly to trumpet its virtues against an untried challenger . . . [T]he analysis must be pitched at the institutional, technical and discursive conditions under which different penal regimes are likely to operate, rather than assuming that certain effects are necessarily embedded in either public or private operation.

Brown is right; the proper question is how the system is structured and how it actually works. But, having said that, it should be emphasized that, whatever panoply of accountability arrangements is in place, the day will come when the system will in some aspect fail and indeed could fail dramatically. Indeed, as will be seen, there have already been significant breaches of standards. Does this, without more, invalidate privatization? The answer must be: no more than the public system has been invalidated by its manifold and oft-repeated failures. Properly regulated and sensitively administered, privatization provides a unique opportunity to raise standards and increase accountability across the total prison system.

Notes

1 As at 30 June 1995 there were 1,104,074 prisoners held in federal and state prisons (*Overcrowded Times*, 6(6): 4) and as at 30 June 1993 there were 459,804 prisoners held in local and county jails (*Overcrowded Times*, 6(3): 12).
2 Genders and Player (1995: 135), in evaluating quite positively the therapeutic regime at Grendon Underwood prison in the UK, observe that 'the extent to which the entire prison system could be run on the Grendon model is inevitably limited by

the need to preserve the concept of privilege'. In other words, the fact that the bulk of the system is so lacking in clear objectives is a factor which makes Grendon comparatively so successful in eliciting positive responses from prisoners.

3 For example, in the USA the American Correctional Association has debated this issue widely, and passed various resolutions which broadly accept privatization as long as the standards conform with the Association's accreditation requirements. In the UK, a special issue of the *Prison Service Journal* was devoted to the issue in 1992. In Australia, a special issue of *Socio-Legal Bulletin* (No. 12, Autumn 1994) covered the various issues. These are merely examples of extremely wide debates getting well beyond the academic and managerial levels (where these sorts of matters are usually discussed without really intersecting) to practitioner, activist and even prisoner level.

4 These kinds of concern turn out not to be vindicated so far. Far from expanding in scope, electronic monitoring has failed to take root in any of the jurisdictions in which it has been trialled.

3

Accountability, monitoring and capture

Accountability, then, sounds straightforward. Evidently, all one has to do is identify the areas of an activity that require supervision, specify them in sufficient detail, establish an appropriate regulatory structure, and let the responsible organization and persons get on with it. In the particular case of private prisons this would seem to involve setting up, in addition to all the general accountability mechanisms applicable to public prisons, a special mechanism to monitor or audit contract compliance. In this way, the body responsible for letting the contract would have an open window through which to view the standards being applied in the private prison. Unfortunately, the organizational and human realities are liable to be very different.

The basic theory of 'capture'

Putting aside the occasional reality of the corrupt or disillusioned or maverick regulator, the more routine problem in this area of public administration is that of 'capture', sometimes called 'co-optation' (Bernstein 1955). This notion is used to describe situations where 'regulators come to be more concerned to serve the interests of the industry with which they are in regular contact than the more remote and abstract public interest' (Grabosky and Braithwaite 1986: 198). The theoretical basis of capture is such that predictably it will be a relevant factor in structuring and managing a suitable accountability system for private prisons. Moreover, it will be seen that capture has already become an actual, not merely a hypothetical, problem. In this regard accountability in private prisons accords with the dilemmas arising in the public administration field generally.

Dealing, then, with general theoretical considerations, there are numerous factors predisposing regulators to capture (Bernstein 1955; Sherman 1980; Grabosky and Braithwaite 1986). They include: being recruited from the same sort of professional background as the persons being regulated or even having worked on that side of the fence previously; working in an environment where the disparity between the resources of the regulator and the size of the job to be done means that short-cuts must be found and discretions must be exercised; and working in a culture where there is little organizational support for a firm approach towards regulation. Of course, these are overlapping, not discrete, factors, and in any given case study they will frequently merge into each other.

Examples of capture in regulatory areas other than prisons

The mining industries are a good illustration of the first predisposing factor. The technical nature of mining operations is such that only a qualified mining engineer can really make meaningful checks on the safety of engineering practices at a mine. This means that the inspector/regulator will tend to be as much part of the specialist mining subculture as he is part of the generalist regulatory subculture. There is a danger that he will come to over-identify with industry needs, coming to share the values and the priorities of the regulatees rather than focusing on the 'abstract public interest', as befits a regulatory agent.

An Australian example relates to a coal-mine disaster at Appin, New South Wales, in 1979. In that case an underground gas build-up led to an explosion when a spark from a defective electric fan escaped into the atmosphere. The ensuing fireball killed 14 miners. The official inquiry which followed established that the mine inspectors habitually tolerated gas levels more than twice the statutorily permitted limits, on the basis that it was 'not practical' to enforce the required levels. Hopkins (1989: 170–1) comments:

> The mines inspectors are . . . employed by the government and would appear to have no vested interest in allowing safety violations. However, over time they undergo the process of 'co-optation' to which those who work in regulatory agencies are so often prone. When confronted with a problem such as excessive gas they have a choice. One option is to stop mining until the problem is rectified, with the consequent loss of thousands of dollars of company profit and the loss of workers' productivity bonuses. Such a choice would generally be opposed by management and workers alike. Alternatively, they may request management to do something about the problem but allow mining to continue, knowing very well that the chances are minimal that any particular violation will lead to death or injury. The pressure to choose the latter course is overwhelming, and since such situations arise routinely on mine inspections a pattern of non-enforcement arises . . .

[T]he co-optation of safety inspectors to company viewpoints seriously undermines their capacity to enforce the law.[1]

In most industrialized countries, occupational health and safety issues epitomize the second predisposing factor – inadequate resources for the task required. Two Australian examples bring this out, each of them also shading into the third factor – a non-supportive culture. They both relate to air safety.

In 1993–94 two major crashes occurred in the commuter sector of the civil aviation industry. In the first, a plane flew into high ground as it approached an airport; in the second, the airframe broke up in flight. Different as these immediate causes are, they each came back to issues of regulatory competence and the apparent capture of the responsible agency by the industry. This happened as follows.

In the first case, the airline had been on the verge of bankruptcy. This fact was known to the agency (the Civil Aviation Authority) though not to potential passengers. The agency was structured along lines that combined the promotion of industry with its supervision – a not uncommon confusion of purposes. However, to be both huckster and sheriff creates intolerable strains. In a context where government deregulation policies were starting to take effect in the commuter sector, the agency culture was to keep airlines flying; the safety function was thus demoted, to the point where the agency had been instructed to recover the cost of its safety function from industry – 'affordable safety', as the agency itself described it (Gration 1994). In the event, a detectable mechanical defect went undetected, contributing to the fatal crash (Bureau of Air Safety Investigation 1994).[2]

In the second case, the type of equipment involved – an Aerocommander – had six months earlier been the subject of an air-worthiness directive from the USA Federal Aviation Authority. This directive related to the precise cause of the subsequent crash – excessive aileron flutter at certain speeds placing intolerable strain on the wings and airframe. According to one version of events, that directive had never been passed on by the safety division of the agency to the airlines. The explanation offered was that the literally hundreds of such directives received each year simply could not be checked out and actioned by the small and over-stretched number of available personnel.

Another version was that the message had been passed on, but that no checking of flight data or logs or indeed any genuine enforcement attempts of any kind had followed. If so, this might well have been a classic case of capture. For to retain their certificated status, air safety inspectors must keep up their own flying hours; but facilities and resources available within the agency for this purpose were extremely limited. However, the company in question had been making its aircraft available gratis for use by inspectors.[3]

This third predisposing factor – a non-supportive internal culture or an antagonistic macro-political scene – is also well illustrated by two case studies: the development of the North Sea oil rigs (Carson 1982; Clarke

1990) and the disaster which overtook the *Challenger* space shuttle (Vaughan 1990; Kramer 1992).

As to the first, Clarke documents how acute time pressure to get North Sea oil into production was exacerbated by the oil crisis and the concomitant stock market crash of 1973–74 so as to produce a climate in which it became acceptable (at least to the government of the day) to delay the development of a regulatory regime. During this hiatus, the fatal accident rate far exceeded those found in other hazardous industries such as quarrying, construction and terrestrial mining. When at last in 1980 a regulatory agency was established, it was to be under the control of the Department of Energy – the body promoting the commercial aspects of the industry – rather than the Health and Safety Executive, which existed to coordinate safety standards across workplace situations generally. Once more, the huckster was to get to wear the sheriff's badge. And once more the safety performance of the industry as a whole, culminating in the 1988 Piper Alpha explosion with the loss of 188 lives, was not up to standard.

The second case, the explosion in January 1986 of the space shuttle *Challenger*, was seen by half the world through television news coverage and replays. At first blush this might not seem to have much to do with the notion of capture but rather, as the subsequent technological witch-hunt established, with the inadequate expansion capacity on a cold morning of rubberized O-rings which were intended to seal the field joint of a solid rocket booster. However, as Kramer (1992) has shown, it was a classic case of persons who should be pursuing distinct objectives coming to share a single objective – to get the shuttle launched at all costs on a particular day. Why that day? Because it would enable President Reagan, in his State of the Union address that evening, to refer to the mission and the presence on it of a young female school teacher.

Capture came about as follows. Both NASA and the rocket manufacturer had safety teams working for them. And each of these teams knew of the danger posed by the O-rings. But in each case they had been placed under the management control of the flight development and scheduling teams, the very offices whose activities they were supposed to monitor. This time it was a case of the sheriff working to the huckster. In disputes during the countdown period as to whether a launch should be made in the light of the known hazards and the prevailing weather conditions, the safety engineers either let themselves be captured (that is, stopped objecting) or were simply overruled. Kramer (1992: 239) summarizes the case thus:

> The *Challenger* space study provides general support for the hypothesis that criminal or deviant behaviour at the organizational level results from a coincidence of pressure for goal attainment, availability and perceived attractiveness of illegitimate means, and an absence of effective social control.

Less dramatic as the effects of regulatory capture may be in the area of private prisons, the same hypothesis is valid.

Refining the theory of capture

Black's (1976) theory of law enforcement posits that the greater the relational distance between regulator and regulatee, the greater the tendency to use formal sanctions. Endorsing this theory in the light of their empirical study of almost 100 Australian regulatory agencies, Grabosky and Braithwaite (1986: 207) highlight the obverse implications:

> [W]e would predict that an agency with a high percentage of staff drawn from the industries which they regulate would prosecute less than one whose staff were recruited directly . . . Similarly, we would predict that agencies which regulate a relatively small number of companies, or companies drawn from a single industry, would resort to less formal means of achieving compliance than those which regulate a relatively large number of companies from diverse industries. Moreover, agencies whose inspectors have frequent contact with the same firms may be expected to use less formal sanctions than those characterised by more impersonal contact.

In this sense some categories of capture can be said to be normal rather than abnormal. For as regulators become more and more involved with an industry, they come to perceive the dilemmas and share the values and priorities of their regulatees. This understanding then starts to work its way into how they carry out their tasks, and law enforcement as a means of regulation tends to give way to what they perceive as co-operative compliance. These observations will be seen to be apposite to the accountability mechanisms applicable to the private prisons industry.

The final theoretical point to be made at this juncture is that commercial organizations must be expected to carry out tasks, if they can, in ways which are most convenient and financially advantageous to themselves. To say that is not to imply that they have no moral constraints, no sense at all of public service. But it is to acknowledge an absolutely normal aspect of reality. Where there is *self*-regulation, the regulatee can expect the regulator to see his point of view, to treat his dilemmas sympathetically! That is why external regulation and accountability are necessary whenever a function bears upon the public interest.

In this regard, it can be anticipated that external accountability mechanisms which are statute-based will tend to be more effective than those which are contract-based. The existence of a statute can be seen as indicating some level of governmental faith in the culture of external regulation, some commitment to ongoing accountability according to industry-wide standards, some willingness to confer appropriate status upon the regulatory organization and its employees. Whilst it does not follow that contract-based accountability is the complete antithesis of these values, nevertheless such arrangements will tend to be perceived in any given industry as much more a negotiated 'deal' between two equal parties than a manifestation of the broad public interest. By the same token, statute-based accountability mechanisms do not *per se* guarantee that there will be no capture; but they do give the agency and the individuals stronger ammunition with which to resist.

Private prisons and the question of statute-based or contract-based monitoring arrangements

The present concern, as indicated at the outset of this chapter, is with the special and additional mechanisms created to ensure that both contractual and generally applicable penal standards are met – mechanisms calculated to compensate for the fact that the private sector is not under the line management of the normal public sector agency. In most states, this additional mechanism is the creation of a 'monitor', alternatively known as a 'controller' or 'liaison officer'. What is not being discussed at this stage is the whole panoply of regulation and accountability generally applicable across the prisons area: for example, ombudsman oversight, freedom of information laws, board of visitor arrangements, the opportunity to litigate for breach of prisoners' rights, accreditation processes, and so on. Of course, such matters naturally constitute a backdrop against which the special monitoring mechanism can be seen; they will accordingly be examined in detail in the next chapter.

In the United States, two main patterns are found. One approach is that taken by Texas – which in terms of numbers of prisons and prisoners is the largest participant in this industry. The statutes which authorize privatization[4] are written in the broadest terms, with very few matters specified for mandatory coverage by the applicable contract. The question of monitoring is not in fact mentioned at all. It so happens that Texas contracts do make provision for monitors working for the Ministry of Justice (the department responsible for public prisons) to supervise contract compliance. However, this is a matter of choice, not obligation.[5]

The second approach is epitomized by Florida, another major player in the private prisons industry. In that state the authorizing statute specifically requires that the responsible state agency (the Correctional Privatization Commission) provide in the contract for the appointment of a monitor:

> [The contract] shall require the selection and appointment of a full-time contract monitor. The contract monitor shall be appointed and

supervised by the commission. The contractor is required to reimburse the commission for the salary and expenses of the contract monitor. It is the obligation of the contractor to provide suitable office space for the contract monitor at the correctional facility. The contract monitor shall have unlimited access to the correctional facility.[6]

This sort of provision certainly cements a special regulatory mechanism into private prisons in a way which the first approach does not. But even so, its efficacy is very much dependent on the current negotiating priorities of the body letting the contract and the governmental culture in which it operates. For example, in Florida itself the present salary package covered in the contract may well be too low, at $50,000, to attract experienced prison administrators; moreover, the complete absence of provision for administrative assistance or relief cover potentially erodes the on-the-ground efficacy of the monitor's position. The Commission perceives the importance of these matters (personal interview, 14 September 1995), but there is governmental reluctance to fund that body to an effective level (Thomas 1995b). Similar issues arise in the other US states adopting this model.

It should perhaps be made quite explicit that even those US states which statutorily require that the contract provide for the appointment of a monitor, fail to specify by statute what duties the monitor should have or to confer upon that person an autonomous status to carry them out. In the USA monitors and their duties are the creatures of contract, nothing more. Looking ahead, contrasting situations will be found in the UK, New Zealand and two Australian states.

Dealing first with Queensland, however, the situation there mirrors that of Texas – legislation authorizing privatization but without any specific reference to special mechanisms of accountability.[7] The first contract, that relating to Borallon, provides that the Corrective Services Commission *may* (not must) appoint a person 'to monitor the performance of the Contractor and/or to undertake any audit of any aspect of the Centre or its operations' and that this person 'will be the official liaison between the [Commission] and the Contractor on all matters pertaining to the contract'. This sort of optional mechanism, lacking statutory support or status and evidently seen by the supervising agency mainly in terms of liaison, is precisely the sort of situation which invites capture.

The Queensland enabling legislation was passed in 1988. Although New South Wales passed its laws only two years later, the climate was much different. This was because the discussion of privatization had widened considerably and the concept was becoming more familiar.[8] The developing ethos was one where it was considered that monitoring arrangements should be accorded greater status, as well as some autonomy within the correctional hierarchy. Accordingly, the 1990 Prisons (Contract Management) Amendment Act provided that a monitor *must* be appointed, that this person would derive standing not merely from the Prisons Act but also from the Public Sector Management Act applicable to public service positions generally, that the appointment should be for two years and be renewable, and that the monitor should make an annual report to the commissioner of the Department of Corrective Services as to any findings with regard to the operation of the contract, which report the commissioner would be obliged to incorporate into the annual report relating to the Department as a whole.

That structure appears to be a strong one. The UK statutory arrangements are also strong, but in different ways. Under the Criminal Justice Act 1991, there shall be appointed in relation to each 'contracted out prison . . . a controller who shall be a Crown servant appointed by the Secretary of State', i.e. nominally the home secretary, but in reality the director-general of prisons. In practice, controllers were to be governor-grade employees of the Prison Service. The controller has an overview function in relation to the running of the prison and a matching duty to report upon this to the secretary of state. In addition, the controller has a duty to investigate and report upon allegations against custody officers in relation to the performance of their custodial duties. The latter provision, unique in privatization legislation, takes the whole relationship with the private contractor beyond that of contract. It promotes such matters as brutality or neglect above the level of a mere employment relationship into the realm of public administration.

Even more important than this, however, is the fact that all disciplinary complaints against prisoners must be heard and adjudications made by the controller. The private contractor thus possesses no direct disciplinary powers in relation to prisoners, beyond laying charges.[9] Discipline is the single most important managerial function in the prison subculture. It not only possesses great symbolic significance in setting prisoner–staff relations but also is the pulse of practical prison operations. 'Directors' (i.e. governors or wardens) of the UK private prisons have expressed to the author a sense of great frustration that this function is not theirs to exercise. Their frustration is increased, doubtless, by the fact that each of them has come from a governor-grade position in the public prison system, and has thus previously been exercising the adjudicatory function as a matter of course. They regard it as crucial that the controller understands their own dilemmas and is sympathetic to their own views about such matters. Yet clearly the distribution of power is such that the controller – the external accountability agent – should be able to call the tune, should in fact be secure from capture, not only in this but in all his other functions. However, it will be seen later that in practice UK controllers have not been immune from capture in this 'contract compliance' aspect of their role.

The UK arrangements amount to the strongest statute-based accountability structure currently in existence. Neither Victoria nor New Zealand has gone as far as to confer disciplinary powers upon the monitor. They each adopt the standard approach whereby the contractor's officers possess disciplinary powers, with the monitor's duties extending only to general overview that they are being exercised lawfully in terms of the general law and legitimately in terms of the contract itself. In New Zealand, the monitor's general reporting duties specifically include a duty to report on these matters, including major disciplinary matters. In Florida the monitor has no formal role in disciplinary matters. However, discipline is exercised with the authority of Department of Corrections classification officers posted to private prisons; actions recommended by the contractor's officers are taken in the name of these officers who may, exceptionally in practice, thus decline to approve them.[10]

In Victoria the appointment of monitors is authorized by statute. They are to be responsible to the director-general of the Office of Corrections for 'the assessment and review of the provision of services by contractors and [to] have any other functions as may be prescribed by the Director-General'. As in New South Wales, they must report annually on their activities and that report must be included in the Department's own annual report.[11]

In New Zealand, the status and responsibilities of the monitor are more explicitly spelled out by statute.[12] Status derives from the State Sector Act as well as the Penal Institutions Act. The monitor's general duty of assessing and reviewing the management of the private prison is fortified by a duty to report to the secretary of the Department of Justice at least once every three months on general management matters, as well as a string of specified matters. These include prisoner transfers and, as already mentioned, major disciplinary matters. The secretary, for his part, is obliged to publish only summaries of the monitor's reports in his own annual report.

The most flawed regulatory structure of all – weaker, certainly, than the Texas model – is found in South Australia. This is because privatization has been allowed to go ahead outside a framework of authorizing legislation. Legislatively thwarted in the upper house of the state parliament, the government took the view that, as nothing in the Correctional Services Act positively prohibited the delegation of custodial functions, reliance could be placed upon the general power of the executive arm of government to delegate or contract out. This position has yet to be tested in Australia and is by no means settled, though there is some case law in both the UK and the USA to lend some credence to it.[13] Inevitably, in these circumstances any monitoring arrangements the government enters into with the private contractor lack appropriate status.

In summary, to the extent that the status and autonomy of monitors' positions are factors in the capture of the regulatory process by the regulatees, one can construct a vulnerability ranking as follows: (i) South Australia; (ii) states following the Texas and Queensland model; (iii) those following the Florida model; (iv) New South Wales, Victoria and New Zealand; (v) the UK. It is still too early in the history of private prisons for a comprehensive picture of actual practice to have emerged. However, the following examples will illustrate that aspects of capture have already occurred and that even the strongest structures do not always completely avoid this hazard.

The process of capture and private prisons

Queensland

Queensland commenced the monitoring process in relation to Borallon with great gusto. A monitor working to the deputy director-general of the Queensland Corrective Services Commission (QCSC) visited the prison daily and stayed for long hours. She was available to hear complaints from prisoners, and was particularly vigilant where disciplinary sanctions had been imposed. Thus, although the monitor possessed no direct authority in relation to discipline, this function was rightly perceived as a crucial one in relation to which active monitoring and reporting were appropriate.

But rather soon the time she spent at the facility began to diminish. Interviewed in 1991, just over a year after Borallon became operational, she herself explained:

> 'I'm responsible for five centres for audit purposes . . . Originally we were supposed to have an on-site monitor five days per week, but that isn't how it has worked out . . . There have been very few incidents of significance that have occurred here.'
>
> (Moyle 1992: 118)

Attendance was reduced to one day a week. Moyle estimated that, after dealing with paperwork and other administrative matters during that weekly visit, the monitor was thus spending just one hour per week actually auditing contract compliance – the very purpose for which the position was nominally created in the first place.

Not surprisingly, the operators had no complaints about these arrangements. The general manager of the prison stated:

> 'I had some concerns about the contract monitor's role when I first started here. Big Brother watching over us and interfering and being a de facto manager. We have had two contract monitors since we started and we have had an excellent relationship with both of them. *They haven't been intrusive at all.*'
>
> (Moyle 1992: 118; emphasis added)

This tone was replicated by CCA's programmes manager at Borallon:

> 'It is not the responsibility of the QCSC contract monitor to monitor the quality of our programs. There is not a great deal being done through

the contract monitor other than I know she is aware we have programs here and reports that fact back to the QCSC.'

(Moyle 1994: 56)

In fact, the terms of the management contract clearly authorize direct monitoring of these activities if the QCSC chose to do so.

What this illustrates is an absolutely classic case of capture – or perhaps more accurately *surrender*. The organizational culture was not at that time sensitive to or supportive of the need for monitoring; consequently, the resources made available were inadequate, forcing the monitor to spread her efforts very thinly across multiple tasks. Indeed, despite the terms of the contract itself, the monitor was not even directly involved in the 1992 Borallon operational audit.

The latter seems to have been a rather peremptory affair. Six head-office persons were sent to the site, each with discrete areas of activity to inspect. Judging on the basis of the resulting document, it would appear that the check was processual and formulaic rather than qualitative or evaluative. Boxes were ticked, very brief observations made, and the six mini-reports in effect stapled together into an audit report. No overview was offered, no 'feel' for how the institution actually works was detectable.

Other manifestations of capture quickly emerged, particularly with regard to the failure of the QCSC to supervise the contractor's personnel selection policies at the Arthur Gorrie Correctional Centre and also with its ready acceptance of the view that the contract itself should remain secret as being 'commercial-in-confidence'. These things will be discussed more fully in Chapters 5 and 6. Suffice to say for now that the Queensland legislature, in relegating this mechanism of accountability to contract rather than statute; the QCSC, in not encouraging a culture of external accountability or allocating adequate resources to it; and the various monitors, in understand-ably allocating their time so as to reflect corporate needs and pressures, were each to some degree captured. The operators can hardly be blamed for this; they have behaved absolutely predictably in seeking to carry out their commercial obligations in ways which best accord with their own priorities and standards.

Florida

Reference has already been made to the somewhat scant resources currently available for monitoring. In more detail, just one monitor is available for each contract site. Recalling that one of those institutions will house 1318 prisoners and two of the others 750 each, and bearing in mind that there is no provision for relief coverage or administrative and secretarial assistance, this could be somewhat inadequate. There will be a danger that the monitor will have to tailor his work to the time available and that, in making choices, he will inevitably be influenced by the priorities of and possible assistance from the contractor. However, that is not inevitable. Much will depend on how much time is spent on-site, exactly how on-site time is allocated, and what culture evolves.

In this regard, it should be noted that each Florida private prison will have an additional external accountability mechanism. Classification officers from the Florida Department of Corrections will be present to deal with transfers in and out of the institution and also to oversee disciplinary functions. The impact of these officers will be indirect, for they will work to a different line of command – the Department rather than the Correctional Privatization Commission. Nevertheless, their presence should help create a culture where the contractor expects and becomes accustomed to accept external accountability, and where capture (either of the monitor or of the classification officers) may accordingly be somewhat less likely.

Certainly, the Commission behaves as if it is aware of the danger. The very first private prison in the state – Gadsden Correctional Institution, contracted by the Department of Corrections before the Commission was established – was monitored in July 1995 on the Department's behalf by a private monitoring agency. Its personnel went into the prison after the event – a far weaker accountability model than having an employee of the public agency build upon continuous prior presence and knowledge. Not surprisingly, therefore, that first Gadsden monitor's report is very much 'tick-a-box' in format, with no overview or sense of the practical functioning of the institution – akin, in fact, to the QCSC audit of Borallon. For future audits, the prison now falls within the jurisdiction of the Commission, which has firmly rejected this model.

So Florida, with a statutory structure akin to that of Queensland, seems to be much more sensitive to the risk of capture, indicating that the issue is no less one of organizational culture than of legislative arrangement.

New South Wales

Despite the statutory status of the monitor at Junee prison, the Corrective Services Commission assigned a low value to the position from the outset, as shown by the appointment of a person much junior to those whose prison she was to monitor, and by the early redesignation of the post as that of 'liaison officer'. Consonant with this, the Commissioner of Corrective Services spoke of 'working hard to build a completely open relationship with' the contractor, and stated his view that a strong on-site presence would only be required for the first six to twelve months (Harding 1993; Vinson and Baldry 1993). After that period,

> it has not been considered necessary to have the contract monitor located at the [prison] on a full-time basis. The monitor does, however,

carry out regular monthly inspections and reports to the Commissioner who chairs the Junee Correctional Centre steering committee meetings.
(Downes 1994: 2)

These arrangements evidently came into existence and continued despite an early riot and a death in custody. The monitor's subsequent performance review noted that 96 per cent of the operational standards specified in the contract were being fully met. But, as with Borallon, one gets no 'feel' for the working of the institution; the review is predominantly processual in tone rather than interpretative or agenda-setting. A major riot subsequent to this review did not really come as a great surprise (Harding 1993; Vinson and Baldry 1993). The second performance review report (Sneddon 1995) was just as processual in tone and content as the first, an observation exemplified by the fact that it contained no reference at all to the riot which had occurred within that review period.

Rather as with Queensland, and once more bearing in mind an apparent reluctance of the Commission to supervise personnel appointments,[14] capture by the operators was painless and almost effortless. In each instance this may have been attributable to organizational naivety in relation to a novel activity; possibly the lessons will eventually be learned. But the operators could be forgiven for imagining that the regulators have surrendered much of their role, leaving them free to move into the unoccupied territory.

The UK

The disciplinary and adjudicatory functions of the controller, already described, have in no sense been captured by the contractors. Indeed, most of the directors of private prisons have a strong sense of grievance about the denial to them of this function. In interview one director asked: 'If the home secretary thinks I am responsible enough to be appointed to run a large prison, how come he isn't prepared to trust me with adjudications?' Another referred to the fact that he met the controller once a month to discuss trends or problems in adjudications, but he did not consider that 'this was an adequate substitute for actually conducting them' (personal interviews with author, 14 and 21 February 1995). Quite evidently, then, there has not yet been the faintest suggestion of capture in this important area. However, the matter is the subject of regular lobbying by contractors. Statutory amendment would be needed to alter this system. Any such change would be a reliable indicator that highly strategic capture was taking place.

Adjudications are very time-consuming. In all of the new private prisons the daily average had initially been much higher than in a comparable, established public sector prison. For example, in its early days Doncaster prison averaged 28 a day; and although a year into its operation this figure had fallen to about 16, this duty still took up more than half the time of a controller.

There are normally two controllers posted in each private prison in the UK. Secretarial and administrative assistance is also available to them. By international standards, monitoring is indeed resource-rich. For all that, as mentioned above, it seems that the contract compliance side of monitoring has been nowhere near as effective. The chief inspector of prisons, who has general oversight of all prisons, public and private, in the UK, identified this weakness in his report relating to The Wolds (Tumim 1994a: 2, 31). In his view, this flowed partly from the fact that the monitor was of much lower prison governor equivalent status than the director of the prison and partly from the fact that inadequate arrangements had been made to cover for the senior controller when absent.

The chief inspector's second private prison report related to Blakenhurst. During a visit in September 1993, the present author had observed that the controller had been prepared to let the contractors develop their on-site protocols at their own pace with a view to eventually identifying the key control points which would merit the most intensive monitoring. At that time it seemed that, 'pragmatic and sensible as this [was] from one perspective, it [was] not from the point of view of accountability the optimum arrangement' (Harding 1994a: 74). The chief inspector evidently observed something similar during his May 1994 inspection, and echoed this view. He stated:

> As at The Wolds, our principal concern over the effectiveness of the controller centred on the monitoring of contract compliance. There was no current copy of the contract with approved amendments to hand . . . Not all parts of the contract were in operation when Blakenhurst opened. The deputy controller told us that in many respects the contract was not capable of being monitored for several months after the prison opened because systems were not in place. Understandably in these circumstances, the controller saw his role as providing active help to UKDS [the contractors] in setting up some of the systems . . . In his written briefing to us the controller described a wider managerial role for himself than we had anticipated. There may be a fine line between 'monitoring' and 'assisting', but in our view the amount of assistance which can appropriately be given to the contractor by the controller should be defined clearly. In our judgement the Home Office, as the Authority, should have been tougher in enforcing compliance with the contract at the earliest stages.
>
> (Tumim 1995: 21–2)

What all this goes to show is not necessarily full-blown capture but certainly a degree of over-identification with the regulatee's problems. This, of course, is a predisposing factor to capture. The Contracts and Competition

Group within the Prison Service, which allocates contracts, is aware of this and believes that the two aspects of monitoring – disciplinary control and contract compliance – probably need different approaches or structures or personnel. It is hoped that new procedures will be in place in time for the opening of the next private prison in 1997 (personal communication, 6 November 1995).

Acknowledging the risk of capture: a new theoretical paradigm for private prisons

Even the most robust monitoring system, then – the one possessing the greatest resources and the strongest statutory structure – has not been completely immune from the hazards of possible capture, whilst the weakest system examined – that of Queensland – seems readily to have succumbed. Wherever there has been capture, the public interest is potentially at risk and the state, as protector of its citizens, is powerless to forestall problems. Indeed, it would not normally become aware of them in any detail until after the event. For example, in Queensland at the Arthur Gorrie Correctional Centre there were five deaths in custody over a short period; several of these cases were such that they should never have occurred. However, in a captured system they were unable to be headed off by effective external control; it was only when the contractors themselves decided to deal with the matter that decisive steps were taken (Harding 1994a: 76).

As has been seen, many of the factors associated with the theory of capture have been present in actual cases which have already occurred. But there is one factor which is quite distinct from those identified in the previous theoretical literature. It is this. Almost invariably in other areas of public administration, strong regulatees capture weak regulators. There is an initial power imbalance which in turn feeds the other predisposing factors. Typically, for example, vibrant mining industries are lined up against over-stretched inspectorates; the rampant financial services sector against a rump of accountants and lawyers; and so on. By contrast, in the prisons business the public sector is still overwhelmingly stronger, numerically and in terms of financial and human resources, than the private sector. The lion, it would seem, does not need to lie down with the lamb.

What, then, differentiates capture in this area of public administration? Black's (1976) theory of relational distance, referred to previously, takes us somewhere along the road towards an answer. Grabosky and Braithwaite's (1986: 207) commentary that 'agencies which regulate a relatively small number of companies' tend to resort to less formal means of seeking to achieve compliance has a clear relevance, as does their observation that 'agencies whose inspectors have frequent contact with the same firms may be expected to use less formal sanctions than those characterised by more impersonal contact'. Each of these factors is present with private prisons. Paradoxically, their minority status brings their regulators closer to them.

Sherman (1980: 487) takes the theoretical point a little further: 'The more social control agencies depend upon their subjects to accomplish their formal goals, the more likely it is that organizational corruption will arise . . . through co-optation of the subjects of control.' In the case of prisons, the way privatization so far has mostly been structured is that the public sector operator itself allocates contracts to the private sector contractors whose responsibility becomes, in effect, that of carrying out custodial and programmatic tasks which the public sector operator itself would otherwise be obliged to carry out directly.[15] As the Tennessee Select Oversight Committee on Corrections (1995: 64) succinctly put it when discussing the monitoring of a private prison by the public Department of Corrections: 'The fact is that the South Central Correctional Center [the private prison] is a facility *in the family of Tennessee prisons*' (emphasis added). This is quite different from most regulatory structures, where the regulator is not itself actually an operator in the business. Thus, it is not simply that the agency, in Sherman's (1980) terms, 'depends upon [its] subjects to accomplish [its] formal goals'. Rather, it is a case of the agency delegating the accomplishment of its formal goals and the discharge of its responsibilities to others. Failure by the delegates is tantamount to failure by the agency itself. All criticism is akin to self-criticism. The regulator, as the principal operator, thus has a vested interest in its delegates appearing to be doing a satisfactory job. The Tennessee Select Oversight Committee (1995: 64) drew attention to this role confusion:

> The Tennessee Department of Corrections [TDOC] central office was placed in an awkward role by being contract and compliance monitor, while trying to assist CCA in the understanding of policy, TDOC system issues, compliance requirements, etc. . . . [The state] should establish an independent contract monitoring and operational compliance capability for corrections contracts . . . The potential conflicts and the complexities require a separate contract monitor.

It is possible, therefore, to posit a theoretical proposition arising out of this examination of private prison accountability structures, one which is also applicable to public administration generally. That proposition is that whenever the principal operator in a public service industry is empowered to contract out or delegate to others some part of its own operational responsibilities, and in so doing it takes on the role of regulatory agency in relation to the activities of those delegates, there is a high risk that some degree of capture or co-optation will occur.

Subsequent chapters will analyse in detail arrangements relating to the letting of private prison contracts, how their terms and conditions are set, staffing requirements, the maintenance of the distinction between the allocation and the administration of punishment, financial accountability, contract compliance procedures generally, prisoners' rights, broad accountability to conform with legal requirements and appropriate custodial standards – in fact all the crucial areas of accountability. Their effectiveness must be evaluated against the principles of capture, especially the one identified above.

Before this, however, normal accountability mechanisms applicable to public sector prisons must be described, both from the point of view of evaluating their scope and efficacy and, more particularly, so as to ascertain the manner in which they also impact upon private prisons. Once more, a thematic concern will be that of capture. In this way it will be possible to start building a model of accountability for the future.

Notes

1 Braithwaite (1985) shows that the bulk of coal-mine accidents in the USA follow upon breaches of the applicable safety laws. Gunningham (1989: 220) shows that the James Hardie Industries group, a large mining company and the only major employer in the town of Grafton, invariably received advance notice of health inspections, and took advantage of this fact to clear up asbestos dust so that the inspection readings were always misleadingly low.

2 The official report (Bureau of Air Safety Investigation 1994: 54) states: 'The activities of the [Civil Aviation Authority's Safety Regulation and Standards] Division appeared to be biased towards promoting the viability of the operator rather than [. . .] promoting safety. In the case of Monarch [the airline in question] this was evidenced by the seeming reluctance of [the Division] to take early and decisive action to ensure compliance with the required airworthiness and operational standards. This was despite consistent breaches of those standards by the company, and the fact that the company was carrying fare paying passengers throughout this entire period.'

3 These allegations emerged, without denial or contradiction, from contemporary newspaper accounts of the matter. Subsequently, the broad accuracy of each was confirmed and the diagnosis of agency capture confirmed by the report of a Commission of Inquiry (see generally Staunton 1996).

4 Local Government Code, s. 351.101; Government Code, s. 495.001.

5 Whilst, as will be seen in Chapter 5, it is now the invariable practice for contracts to incorporate ACA standards, the references to monitoring (§§3.4018, 3.4019) do not mandate that it should be external nor do they define more precisely the role of monitors.

6 Florida statutes 1993, ch. 957.04(1)(g).

7 Corrective Services (Administration) Act 1988, ss. 19(2)(f), 19(3) and 19(4).

8 The NSW government had commissioned a merchant bank/management consultant company, Kleinwort Benson, to examine the matter and report back: see Kleinwort Benson (1989).

9 Criminal Justice Act 1991, ss. 85(3)(a) and 85(4); Prison Rules: Contracted Out Prisons, ss. 48–50.

10 The question of discipline and the imposition of punishment is discussed more fully in Chapter 6.
11 Corrections Act 1986, s. 9D, as amended by the Corrections (Management) Act 1993.
12 Penal Institutions Amendment Act 1994, s. 3, inserting new sections 4G, 4H and 4I into the Penal Institutions Act 1954.
13 See *Carter* v *Carter Coal Co.* (1936) 298 US 238, and *R.* v *Lord Chancellor* ex parte *Hibbit* (*The Times*, 12 March 1993), each of which provide some support for the contracting-out notion. However, in a slightly different context there are also some US views that such contracting out is *ultra vires* and void: see the opinion of the attorney-general of Maine with regard to the 'Aroostook Contract' made between the state and Pricor Ltd for the operation of a county jail and subsequently cancelled. Four other jurisdictions in the USA subscribe to the view that such contracting out is void.
14 See further Chapter 6.
15 In the UK, as in most jurisdictions, it is the responsible government minister who formally allocates the contracts. But in reality this is invariably done according to the recommendation of the Prison Service itself. Similarly, the minister nominally appoints the controllers at private prisons; but again in reality this is done by the director-general of the Prison Service. That person's choice was in turn on the recommendation of the quasi-autonomous Contracts and Competition Group which meant that the line of command was not part of the main management hierarchy. However, in 1995 the director-general conferred this function upon the area manager. It is to that office that the controller now works, thus diminishing the slight independence which previously had attached to the position.

4

Accountability mechanisms in public sector prisons and their applicability to private prisons

When comparing the accountability of the public and private sectors of the prison industry, there are three main possibilities: that public prisons are more accountable; that private and public systems are equally accountable; and that private prisons are more accountable. Wherever privatization has occurred, monitoring mechanisms have been created as a putative add-on to general accountability mechanisms which apply to the public sector prison system. Undoubtedly, the objective has been to make the private system more accountable than the public system, not less. Learmont (1995: 106), reporting on the escapes from Parkhurst prison, certainly saw it that way:

> Such arrangements [monitoring] raise the question of whether the problems at Whitemoor and Parkhurst would ever have arisen if the Prison Service had the same monitoring and audit arrangements as are compulsory for the private sector. Through this mechanism, performance standards in private prisons are kept under review, with the result that they are maintained at a high level. In comparison with the public sector prisons, private prisons demonstrate the advantages of . . . continuous audit on site.

However, Learmont's task was not to review private prisons as such, and this view is a little simplistic. As has been shown, organizational capture may and does erode that notional extra accountability. So the question remains: is there any substantial difference between the accountability of the two parts of the system? To answer that question, it is necessary to describe in outline the standard mechanisms of accountability found across the public systems.

These fall into three main categories: constitutional and parliamentary; legislative and judicial; and inquisitorial and administrative.

Constitutional and parliamentary mechanisms

With regard to constitutional aspects, the Eighth Amendment of the US Constitution, proscribing 'cruel and unusual punishment', is relevant. As is well known, this provision has underpinned an enormous volume of litigation as to the functioning of federal, state and local prison systems. Being constitutional in nature, there is absolutely no way in which the device of privatization could circumvent this aspect of accountability. The same comment can be made also of the other Bill of Rights provisions which have underpinned prison litigation – the Fourth Amendment relating to un-warranted search and seizure and the Fifth and Fourteenth Amendments relating to due process and equal protection before the law (Morgan and Bronstein 1985; Fowles 1989; Branham and Krantz 1994).

As for parliamentary scrutiny, this may be one of the grand self-delusions of democracy, but at least with prisons it is something more than a rhetorical flourish. In fact, in Australia and the UK, it is almost an obsession – the fugue to which the 'law and order' debate is the coda. The standard of debate may not always be very well informed, but debate there is. For example, the initial introduction of the law authorizing privatization 'was at least debated in Parliament and in that formal sense is beyond constitutional criticism' (Richardson 1993: 78).

Of course, the executive arm of government does not always feel at ease with this. The decision to extend the UK legislation, initially restricted to private *remand* prisons, to all kinds of prison was 'vulnerable to criticism'. A promise to return the question to Parliament for any such extension of power 'if, and only if, the remand centre . . . proved to be a success' was broken (Richardson 1993: 78). Only a few months after The Wolds had been opened and before any evaluation had been made, the power was extended by administrative order. In a comparable way, it is instructive to note that the recommendation in the Woolf Report (Woolf and Tumim 1991: 11.133–11.149), initially accepted by the government, that Parliament should be informed each time a prison's population exceeded its certified normal accommodation was later rejected by the home secretary (*The Independent*, 24 June 1991).

The parliamentary history of privatization moves in Australia and New Zealand has been mixed, though on balance somewhat more connected than in the UK. Vinson and Baldry (1993) have drawn attention to the fact that, in a five-year period after privatization was first mooted in New South Wales, only two parliamentary questions were asked about the Junee prison arrangements – each contemptuously dismissed by the responsible minister.

But that was in the early days. Since then, in South Australia and New Zealand, and to a lesser extent in Victoria, there have been long parliamentary debates about the enabling legislation – debates which actually affected outcome. Indeed, in South Australia the proposed laws were defeated, whilst in New Zealand the government was forced to accept an amendment which required contracts to be made public – a crucial aspect of accountability and thus an uncharacteristically valuable parliamentary input.

Legislative and judicial mechanisms

As far as legislative input into accountability is concerned, the terms in which statutes are drafted crucially affect litigation-based accountability. In other words, this aspect is inextricably linked with judicial mechanisms of accountability. The group with the keenest incentive to see that custodial standards are maintained, the one which would be the natural guardian for keeping the bureaucrats on their toes is, of course, prisoners. Yet the legalistic view, and the legislative starting-point, has historically been that, on becoming prisoners, criminals forfeit virtually all their rights.[1] Traditionally, in all of the jurisdictions under consideration, prison laws have accordingly denied prisoners standing to activate accountability mechanisms directly, for the attainment of their own objectives. Prison laws were predominantly a deal between the state and itself.[2]

In relation, for example, to the Prison Rules (UK), which constitute in effect the handbook as to the conditions prisoners can expect to receive, it has been said that they are 'justiciable' but not 'actionable'. Absence of 'actionability' means that they cannot form the basis of an individual claim for breach of statutory duty. 'Justiciability' means that, in abstract principle though seldom in practice, breach of the Rules may possibly support a public law remedy, such as a declaration or an injunction – small consolation for an inmate seeking rectification of or compensation for a tangible grievance (Richardson 1985b; Livingstone and Owen 1993). Australian legislation is drafted from the same starting-point with much the same consequences. The most notable inroad into this approach is found in 42 U.S. Code §1983, which will be explored more fully later.

The UK has, however, slowly been drawn into a more 'rights-orientated' approach. The first stage of this development has been processual, with judicial decisions superimposing 'natural justice' requirements upon disciplinary hearings conducted before boards of visitors and governor's adjudications.[3] Livingstone (1994: 100–1) has summarized prisoner's procedural rights as follows:

(i)   prisoners should normally be allowed to call witnesses;
(ii) if the authorities are aware of a relevant witness that is unknown to the prisoner, they should inform him/her;

(iii) prisoners should also be entitled to cross-examine witnesses for the prosecution;
(iv) they may apply for legal representation at hearings;
(v)   where there is ambiguity in disciplinary charges this should be construed in favour of the defendant . . . ;
(vi) tribunals are not entitled to acquit a prisoner on one charge and then convict on a less serious offence where no charge in respect of that less serious offence has been laid; and
(vii) the criminal burden of proof (i.e. beyond reasonable doubt) applies to disciplinary charges against prisoners.

This summary focuses on disciplinary proceedings before boards of visitors. The case law indicates that these standards, although similar in their abstract formulation, apply 'rather less rigorously' to governors' hearings (Livingstone 1994: 102). Yet governors' hearings have always predominated, constituting on most estimates about 96 per cent of all disciplinary proceedings. In 1993, following the recommendation of the Woolf Report (Woolf and Tumim 1991: 14.395), boards of visitors lost their disciplinary jurisdiction. Thus, a rather less rigorous version of the above standards is now applicable to all disciplinary hearings.

There are two immediate points which arise from this. The first is that, whatever are the current procedural contents of these standards at any given time, they are no less applicable to controllers in private prisons than to governors in public sector prisons. The second is that the government could have legislated all these safeguards, either directly or by ratification and adoption of the European Prison Rules; however, it has chosen not to do so.

In this context, and still focusing on the position in the UK, it should be noted that judicial inventiveness has not really been able to circumvent legislative intransigence with regard to prisoners' conditions. These remain, as stated above, a deal between the state and itself. Richardson (1994: 80, 83) summarizes the current position as follows:

> The formal rules governing the management of prisons, whatever their constitutional status, . . . do not, either singly or in combination, purport to provide a code of directly enforceable rights in prisoners . . .
>
> The failure of the primary legislation to provide any enforceable rights to minimum physical conditions is compounded by the courts' attitude towards the Prison Rules . . . Some [of them] are phrased in mandatory and relatively unambiguous terms, referring, for example, to the provision of a separate bed (Rule 24) or the provision of toilet articles (Rule 26). None the less the courts have denied that the Prison Rules vest prisoners with any special rights.

That will also be the case with regard to private prisons; prisoners will be no better off, but no worse.[4] Just as the state's self-imposed standards are not actionable, so too the terms of the contract between the state and the private prison operator will not provide the basis of action for the prisoner who believes that the terms of the contract are not being met. Contracts are written in terms that do not confer rights upon prisoners, but merely set a contractual relationship between the agency and the private operator. There is, as lawyers say, no privity of contract between the contractor and the prisoners. Once more, a legislative choice has been made in this matter, manifesting a reluctance to move away from the historical starting-point of disfranchised inmate/citizens.

For all that, the spread of private prisons, because of the controversy it has excited and the additional attention it has drawn to imprisonment issues generally, might just possibly give some extra impetus to the debate as to why the UK has not adopted and enacted into domestic law such international instruments as the United Nations Standard Minimum Rules for the Treatment of Prisoners, the European Prison Rules and the United Nations Rules for the Treatment of Juveniles Deprived of Their Liberty.

In the USA, judicial intervention in relation to total prison systems, particular prisons and individual prisoner rights is far more developed (Branham and Krantz 1994). It is axiomatic that a private prison is no less susceptible to an Eighth Amendment court order (or a suit under the Fourth, Fifth or Fourteenth Amendments) than is an individual public prison or a total public system.[5] It should be noted that litigation of this sort is almost invariably in the form of 'class actions', so that a successful suit brought by or in the name of one individual will affect the rights and conditions of all prisoners within the system which has been challenged.

With regard to individual rights, 42 U.S. Code §1983, enacted in pursuance of the Fourteenth Amendment to the Constitution, has been the fount of litigation. This section provides as follows:

> Every person who, under color of any statute, ordinance, regulation, custom, or usage, of any State or Territory or the District of Columbia, subjects, or causes to be subjected, any citizen of the United States or other person within the jurisdiction thereof to the deprivation of any rights, privileges or immunities secured by the Constitution and laws, shall be liable to the party injured in an action at law, suit in equity, or other proper proceeding for redress.

The operation of this section is such that a defendant who has allegedly acted in such a way as to deprive someone of their civil rights must be shown to satisfy both the 'state action' test (that is, to be acting on behalf of a state entity rather than privately or on behalf of the federal government) and the 'color of law' test (that is, in purported reliance upon a state or local law or an administrative practice which in fact contravenes constitutionally protected rights). The state action criterion has been fleshed out by the doctrine of 'fair attribution', which means that in certain circumstances private parties whose activities have been facilitated or encouraged by the state may be found to be in breach of §1983. Thus, it has already been held, in the context of private medical services provided within a public prison by way of contract between the prison authorities and the medical practitioner, that the latter can be liable to an inmate.[6]

It naturally follows from this that individual custodial or other officers employed by companies operating private prisons will potentially be liable for any category of rights infringement covered by §1983. Their actions are 'fairly attributable' to the state, since they could not happen at all without there first being a contract between the state and the employer company to carry out services which the state would otherwise be constitutionally obliged to carry out for itself. The judicial accountability of the public and private prison sectors can thus be seen to be at least equivalent.

However, Thomas (1991) has argued that private sector vulnerability to litigation actually exceeds that of the public sector. His argument revolves around the nature of the Eleventh Amendment, which has been construed so as to protect the state itself from vicarious liability for the actions of individual defendants. However, no such immunity is extended to corporations in similar circumstances; the Eleventh Amendment is simply irrelevant. That being so, in §1983 circumstances a prisoner may sue not only the employee (who is quite possibly a 'straw man') but also the employer corporation (which certainly is not, its financial strength having been thoroughly tested during the bidding process). Whilst, admittedly, the state will as a matter of practice usually stand behind an employee who is successfully sued for breach of §1983 for acts committed in the course of his employment, a private corporation will be liable to be sued directly. Judicial accountability is thus greater in the private than the public sector.

Apart from these special US rights, all jurisdictions under consideration now accept that prisoners are owed a duty of care. This includes a duty by the authorities not to expose prisoners unreasonably to the risk of assault by other inmates and also a duty in relation to the maintenance of prisoner health. However, Richardson's (1994: 81) UK observation that 'courts appear reluctant to find a breach of duty on the part of the authorities' seems applicable to Australia and the USA.

Inquisitorial and administrative mechanisms

Inquisitorial mechanisms refer primarily to special inquiries following extreme or unusual incidents. These may be by way of royal commissions (Nagle 1978; Johnston 1991), ministerial inquiries or judicial inquiries under general inquiries legislation (Woolf and Tumim 1991; Logan 1993; Learmont 1995), inquiries under the relevant prisons legislation (McGivern 1988), coronial inquests (Hallenstein 1989), gubernatorial commissions or special grand jury proceedings (Dinitz 1981; Weiss 1991). But whatever form they take, the common feature is that outsiders – non-Prison Service people – conduct wide-ranging inquiries, with powers to call witnesses and often to compel answers, into prison crisis situations which evidently have gone well beyond 'normal' administrative, custodial, management or human rights problems. Moreover, the findings of such inquiries will typically be made public, with consequent parliamentary and media discussion and debate.

In all those states which have adopted privatization, these inquisitorial mechanisms remain applicable. If Blakenhurst or Doncaster were to be torched and ransacked, there is no greater impediment to setting up a judicial inquiry than when this fate befell Strangeways. Similarly, if one of the projected new private prisons in New Mexico were subjected to riot, rape and murder, an inquiry equivalent to that which followed the Santa Fe disturbances of 1981 could likewise be set up by the state. Moreover, the findings of such inquiries might well lead to the contractor's loss of the right to continue operations – a sanction which the state never imposes on itself in relation to its own prisons.

With regard to administrative mechanisms of accountability, there are numerous ones applicable to the public prison system. They include: for Australia and the UK, general ombudsman overview; for the UK, as from 1994, and for several states of the USA, specialist prison ombudsman jurisdiction; for the UK and Australia, the activities of boards of visitors and official prison visitors; for the UK, reports of the chief inspector of prisons; and within the USA the accreditation procedure involving reviews by the Commission on the Accreditation of Corrections set up by the American Correctional Association (ACA). The defining characteristic of these administrative accountability mechanisms is that they are governmentally created (or, in the case of ACA accreditation, governmentally sanctioned), partly external, to a degree autonomous, and designed to operate as ongoing safety valves in relation to 'normal' or non-emergency problems. These mechanisms designed for public sector prisons will be found to be none the less available, indeed sometimes more so, in relation to private prisons.

The jurisdiction of the general ombudsman

The ombudsman movement arose out of a growing recognition that administrative organs of the modern state could affect citizens' rights adversely without their decisions necessarily being judicially reviewable. They could be both technically lawful and yet procedurally unfair or oppressive. Accordingly, the archetypal ombudsman model empowers that office-holder to examine 'matters of administration' or 'maladministration' involved in any particular decision made by a government department or agency. The particular government departments to be covered by this will be specified in the enabling statute; usually prisons departments, unlike police departments, are included on the list. Most states require that possible remedies within the administrative system should be exhausted before the ombudsman's intervention can be sought.

The ombudsman's role has never been to second-guess or overrule administrative decisions, but merely to see whether the decision-making body has abided by the rules, conformed with the due processes, and taken account of the relevant factors in decision-making. On the substantive matter of complaint, therefore, the findings are recommendatory only, not self-executing or binding upon the executive. However, an ombudsman office which has defined its own role shrewdly and realistically can expect the bulk of its recommendations to be adopted.

Ombudsman jurisdiction links naturally to parliamentary scrutiny, for the archetypal ombudsman model requires that annual reports be tabled in parliament (as opposed to merely being sent to the responsible minister) and that special reports on individual cases may likewise be tabled. Indeed, in some states – notably the UK – a complaint originally could only be forwarded to the ombudsman through a member of parliament.[7]

It is evident from the above description that general ombudsman jurisdiction was always unlikely to be a significant source of external accountability for what happens in prisons. Most of the real or imagined injustices are very much practical matters of day-to-day management – transfers, mail censorship, visiting arrangements, classification, suitability of food. Seldom do such matters qualify as system-based maladministration. In practice, the number of prisoner complaints which have been investigated (that is to say, not filtered out on a jurisdictional basis or because they are 'trivial, frivolous or vexatious') has been low in the UK and New Zealand. In the Australian states, whilst prisoner complaints constitute a significant proportion of the ombudsman's postbag, in practice the only matters which seem to survive the filtering mechanism are minutiae rather than systemic or structural matters. Moreover, complaints are only upheld fairly infrequently (Anderson 1981a; Birkinshaw 1985; Johnson 1989).

The ombudsman's presence has hardly been felt in public prisons over the years, therefore. Possibly, this jurisdiction is a worthwhile symbol for prisoners that the prison system is not entirely closed. To the extent that it possesses any symbolic or practical value, however, it is no less applicable to private prison administration. This is because formally such prisons remain part of the state system, so that the relevant state department (in the UK the Home Office, in Australia various departments of justice or corrective services) remains within the ombudsman's jurisdiction.

The prisons or corrections ombudsman

Given that one of the problems of the general Ombudsman is his inability to be on the spot and deal with day-to-day complaints, and perhaps also an inability to develop an expertise in the day-to-day running of a prison . . . , there has been much support, internationally, for the concept of a Prisons . . . Ombudsman.

(Johnson 1989: 131–2)

The earliest examples are found in the USA: Minnesota (1972), Connecticut (1973) and so on (Anderson 1981b). Unfortunately, this did not become a universal pattern in the USA, and is not for the most part found in the states where private prisons are most prominent.

In the UK, Woolf recognized how widespread was the sense of injustice amongst prisoners, and considered that this was a key underlying cause of the April 1990 riots in British prisons (Woolf and Tumim 1991: 9.24–9.37). He recommended that reasons should be given to prisoners for decisions which affect their conditions or life-style – for example, transfer, mail censorship, visits, and so on – and that a 'Complaints Adjudicator' should be appointed to recommend, advise and conciliate consequential grievances. That proposed office-holder should also constitute an appellate tribunal in relation to disciplinary proceedings (Woolf and Tumim 1991: 1.207–1.209; 15.83).

A prisons ombudsman – the title preferred by the Home Office – was appointed from October 1994 with powers broadly reflecting Woolf's views. His jurisdiction extends to both private and public sector prisons and prisoners. This office and its *modus operandi* were created by administrative fiat – an Instruction to Governors issued by the director-general of the Prison Service. It thus required no statutory basis or even an amendment to the Prison Rules. The power is recommendatory only, to the home secretary via the director-general of the Prison Service. The status of the office is, therefore, questionable, its autonomy from government and the bureaucracy not being readily apparent.[8] Indeed, already only 18 months after its establishment the prisons ombudsman has been publicly complaining that he is being frustrated in his task by the withholding of documents and other relevant material by the Prison Service itself (*The Independent*, 25 February 1996; *The Guardian*, 26 February 1996). For what it is worth, however, its jurisdiction covers not only public but also private prisons.

Boards of visitors and official prison visitors

A board of visitors is constituted in relation to each UK prison. Until 1993 the UK model had combined an inspectorial role with a disciplinary one. These functions were mutually contradictory; inspections must involve prisoner contact, indeed positive availability to prisoners to receive complaints and to act upon them equitably. How could this be reconciled in the eyes of prisoners, or anyone else, with handing out punishments to the same people at the behest often of those against whom their complaints may lie? Moreover, there was a distinct feeling amongst boards that if the governor had referred the matter to them at all, it was because he considered that his own powers (28 days' loss of remission at maximum) were insufficient. That being so, they would be letting down the prison administration if they failed to find the charge proved and impose a higher punishment (Woolf and Tumim 1991: 14.377).

The Woolf Report was the latest in a series going back to 1975 which recommended that the disciplinary function be stripped away from boards of visitors (Maguire 1985; Woolf and Tumim 1991: 14.395), and this has at last been done. That leaves the inspection role, which is formulated in wide terms. The duty of boards is 'to satisfy themselves as to the state of the prison premises, the administration of the prison and the treatment of prisoners' as well as to hear prisoner complaints (Prison Rules 1964, s.94(1)). In carrying out these functions, they have rights to enter the prison without notice at any time, to interview prisoners confidentially and to inspect records. They are also required to report annually to the home secretary on their activities, though their reports are not entitled to individual tabling in Parliament. As with the ombudsman, however, their reports are recommendatory only.

Maguire and Vagg (1983) have investigated in detail the inspectorial performance of boards of visitors. Their findings were not encouraging; many boards seemed to have been captured by the prisons' establishment. Vagg (1985: 136–7) states that '[M]uch of the criticism levelled at Boards of Visitors . . . has rested on assertions about the conservatism . . . of individuals who happen to constitute the membership of the Boards'. Acknowledging this, the Woolf Report specifically endorsed the suggestions of Maguire and Vagg (1983) for more representative membership. Previously, membership had been dominated by magistrates and the white middle class, and they argued that there should be a wider socio-economic and ethnic distribution. Some changes are now under way. Their benefits should start eventually to become apparent in relation to public sector prison inspections.

However, Vagg (1985: 137) also emphasized that the defects of the boards of visitors scheme are partly structural:

> [W]hile many of the problems identified by critics are correct, they are aimed to some extent at the wrong target; the problems are systemic and likely to affect any inspectorial group which occupies the ground and assumes the functions given to Boards.

It is likely, therefore, that changes in selection procedures will only improve the efficacy of the inspection role up to a certain point.

The present relevance of the foregoing discussion is that boards possess exactly the same role in relation to private as to public prisons. Indeed, the boards of visitors appointed to overview the first two private prisons can already be seen to have been thorough in making prompt and perceptive reports.[9] It is evident that the private sector prisons have been subject to special vigilance in terms of the frequency of visits, the extent of consultation with the directors and so on. Some strong criticisms have been made – for example, as to the extent of substance abuse by prisoners at The Wolds and as to cash transfer and wages accreditation practices at Blakenhurst. However, the majority of the adverse comments related to matters which are driven by general Prison Service policies and priorities – for example, inadequate provision for vulnerable prisoners at Blakenhurst and failure to explore the possibility at The Wolds of opening up adjoining land for exercise purposes. These private prison boards also shared and expressed the frustration of other boards that, however well they did their jobs, no one was actually listening to them in the Home Office or the Prison Service – a function doubtless of the fact that their role is advisory and recommendatory only.[10]

In summary, then, boards of visitors take their roles very seriously in relation to the private prisons. Their comparative impotence arises out of the fact that there are systemic defects in board structure generally, plus political and managerial reluctance to pay heed to outsiders, not out of the fact that the prisons for which they are responsible are private rather than public ones.

Australia has not adopted this more formal board of visitors mechanism, but each state does have a system of official prison visitors. Their rights and role are akin to that of UK boards. But of course individuals must inevitably spread their efforts more thinly than groups. They will thus tend to have less influence, to be more overborne by management considerations, and to be even more vulnerable to capture. Nevertheless, the system is better than nothing.

Interestingly, the nearest that Australia has come to a British-style board of visitors is in relation to the affairs of a private prison, Junee, in New South Wales. The enabling legislation specifically created a Community Advisory Council to overview issues relating to the running of the prison. The Council's task is 'to assist in the monitoring . . . and to encourage community involvement in the oversight of its management' and it is required to make quarterly reports in writing to the responsible minister.[11] There is no equivalent arrangement in relation to any of the state's 24 public sector prisons. Whilst the Council's *modus operandi* and impact are somewhat unclear and do not really become apparent from the public record,[12] the very fact that such an arrangement has been statutorily entrenched indicates an apparent commitment to the value that there should be greater accountability rather than less in the private sector.

Her Majesty's chief inspector of prisons

The position of chief inspector came into existence in the UK on 1 January 1981. Before then prison inspections were generally in-house affairs conducted by senior Prison Service staff, their findings for internal consumption only. The 1979 May Committee, however, had recommended that an inspectorate be established independent of the Prison Service, though within the Home Office; it would be answerable to the home secretary, and its reports would in due course be made public. Its quasi-autonomous status would be enhanced if it could make unannounced visits to prisons and also report on the general policies and performance of the Prison Service, not being confined therefore to the minutiae of prison operations. However, it would have no direct power, being advisory and recommendatory only. In this way its efficacy could be bedevilled in the same way as that of the ombudsman, the prisons ombudsman, boards of visitors and official prison visitors.

Morgan (1985) has described the early development of the office. In the last decade its resources have grown and its self-confidence burgeoned. The reports it makes are punchy, colourfully written, shrewdly evaluative, and leave the reader very much with the 'feel' of any given prison. After reading one, it is as if one has spent the last few days in the prison oneself. Consequently, the importance of the office has increased. As this has happened, its *de facto* independence has also grown even though its formal position is unchanged. Part of its success is certainly attributable to the personality of the longest-serving (1987–95) chief inspector, Judge Stephen Tumim, and his capacity to deliver timely 'one-liners' and gain widespread media coverage.[13] As mentioned, the chief inspector's recommendations are not self-executing, but must run the gauntlet of departmental filtering and prioritization. Nevertheless, governors of public prisons and directors of private prisons alike have told the present author that they await the release of an inspection report with trepidation.

From this it may be gathered that the inspection system is as applicable to the private as to the public sector. In fact, in a sense it has been even more active in the former. The chief inspector sets his own schedule of inspections. Most of the 134 prison establishments can anticipate one scheduled and at least one unannounced inspection every five or six years. However, the first two private prisons were pushed to the head of the queue. The Wolds, operational from April 1992, was inspected on 17–26 May 1993; Blakenhurst, opened in May 1993, was inspected on 22–27 May 1994. Each inspection report had some strong criticisms to make, whilst also containing much that was laudatory.

But for present purposes the point is not whether the reports were laudatory or adversely critical. Rather it is the fact that the inspections were made at all. Experienced prison administrators would argue that a year's operation is not sufficient to allow the regime to settle down, and that therefore an inspection at such a time comes too soon. Newly opened public prisons have not been inspected so quickly. The chief inspector has now taken some account of that view in relation to Doncaster, which is likely to have been operational for two years before its first full-scale inspection. He was not unaware of the early difficulties at that prison (Prison Reform Trust 1995) and indeed commented publicly on them only four months after its opening.

Nevertheless, he considered that a slightly longer-term view of it should be taken than had been the case with The Wolds and Blakenhurst. However, the point is that the type of prisons whose existence heralds a new policy development – privatization – have been treated as more in need of prompt supervision and input than standard prison regimes. In that narrow sense, therefore, private prisons have been subjected to a greater degree of accountability.

From this description, looking ahead momentarily to Chapter 12 and the search for a model of accountability, the chief inspector system seems to be the least 'capturable' of the various mechanisms so far discussed. It may well be that it should form a building block in constructing such a model.

Accreditation

Neither Australia nor the UK has formal prison accreditation protocols – though in a sense the findings of the chief inspector have been tantamount to this, exposing for all to see any shortcomings in conditions and practices. In the UK, the Woolf Inquiry (Woolf and Tumim 1991: 1.186–187; 15.5.6.) specifically recommended that such a system should be instituted, based on precise standards and regimes within particular prisons. The implementation of such a system should be tied in with the role of the chief inspector, whose reports would henceforth culminate with a recommendation to the home secretary as to accreditation. Woolf's views have not so far been implemented. In Australia, a comparable debate has surfaced over the years at the regular meetings of correctional ministers and administrators, but the proposal has never gained the kind of credence that Woolf has now conferred upon it for the UK.

In the USA a national accreditation process was established in 1978. It now covers about 80 per cent of adult correctional institutions across the nation. The system was developed by a voluntary association of high-level correctional professionals, the American Correctional Association, and is administered through its Commission on the Accreditation of Corrections. National accreditation was a response to the fragmentation of prison standards in that country. In a real sense the USA does not possess a prison *system*. Rather, it has a multitude of mini-systems: a dispersed federal system, 50 state systems, innumerable local or county systems, a plethora of police jails, and some limited-purpose prisons such as those run by the US Marshals Service and the Immigration and Naturalization Service. In these circumstances some unifying standards were desirable; and the only feasible path was voluntary.

Accreditation works as follows. Standards have been developed over the years through experience and discussion, failures and successes. They are published in a comprehensive handbook. Those applicable to adult correctional institutions are now in their third edition (January 1990).[14] Any correctional system or institution seeking accreditation requests an audit, and at an agreed date a team of three or four will visit the institution(s). If the inspection is initially unsatisfactory, the team will identify the deficiencies; once they are rectified, an accreditation certificate will be issued. This is valid for three years. At the end of that period, the process must recommence. A fee is payable to the ACA in relation to each accreditation audit.

Because it is voluntary, some states have naturally chosen to stay outside of the system. There has almost been a self-defining process whereby those who would not measure up anyhow are also those who do not embark upon the process. But the interesting thing is that those very same states, when letting private prison contracts, now impose a requirement that the operator obtain ACA accreditation within an agreed time and continue to meet those standards during the period of the contract. The accreditation clause now, quite literally, appears in every private prison contract; the private operators have, unlike those in the public sector, no element of choice about compliance. Even if the abstract law does not mandate this, private prisons are subjected *de facto* to a greater degree of external regulation.

An example is the state of Louisiana, the whole of whose prison system came under federal court order in 1975 because of overcrowding and poor conditions. The accreditation process became available, it will be recalled, in 1978, but Louisiana at that time would have none of it. Yet, letting a private prison contract in 1990, the state authorities inserted a term requiring the operators to obtain ACA accreditation. This was done. Encouraged, an incoming director of the State Department of Corrections decided to seek accreditation across the whole public system. Before risking audit, real efforts had to be made to lift standards. Conditions were markedly improved; and in due course accreditation was granted for all but one prison (the maximum-security penitentiary) in the state. As a by-product the court order was lifted (Keve 1996: 119–20). This saga will be referred to again when the crucial issue of cross-fertilization between the private and public sectors is being considered.

The process of accreditation by the ACA has, however, attracted some criticism. First, it is said that the audit is too much a paper audit – an examination in the prison offices of procedures manuals, official records and the like. Qualitative contact with staff and inmates comes as something of an afterthought. In this regard audits seem to be less searching than those conducted by the UK chief inspector. Second, there is concern that the visits are scheduled well in advance. Moreover, no unannounced visits are made during the three-year accreditation period. Again, the UK chief inspector's practice seems preferable. Third, the ACA is dependent on audit fees as its primary source of income. To fail an applicant might be seen as biting the hand that feeds one.

In summary, critics such as the American Civil Liberties Union (ACLU)[15] claim that the ACA is in acute danger of being captured by, or even surrendering to, the bodies whose standards it monitors. The ACA itself believes that its own professionalism effectively protects it (Keve 1996: 133–7). Despite that belief, both the theory of capture and the case studies described in Chapter 3 lend credence to the critics' concern. However, the danger of capture would seem to be no greater in the private than the public sector; if anything, it may be marginally less. This is because the private sector *must* acquire ACA accreditation to meet its contractual obligations and maintain its contractual benefits. Unlike the public sector system, it cannot opt out of the accreditation system if it does not like the outcome (Keve 1996: 132).

Summary

The question was posed whether, in relation to the standard accountability mechanisms applicable to public sector prisons, private prisons are more or less accountable. Whilst it is apparent that the public accountability mechanisms themselves are frequently defective, it must nevertheless be said that in none of the situations considered was the private sector less accountable. Indeed, in significant ways it already seems either *de facto* or *de jure* to be more accountable. These ways include: parliamentary attention; inspectorial activity of boards of visitors; scrutiny by the chief inspector; ACA accreditation requirements; and judicial supervision under 42 U.S. Code §1983.

There is already some evidence that this enhanced accountability may be starting gradually to permeate into the public sector. The impact of privatization upon an area of public administration that has traditionally been passive and 'closed' could be to enliven and expose it.

Notes

1 For the US position, see *Ruffin v Commonwealth* (1871) 62 Va. 790; Fowles (1989); Branham and Krantz (1994). For the UK, see Richardson (1985a) and Livingstone and Owen (1993).

2 The UK Prison Operating Standards, promulgated by the Prison Service to governors on 12 April 1994, contains as a preamble the following statement: 'Meeting the Operational Standards will be a line management responsibility . . . The standards are not entitlements for prisoners . . . Nor are [they] intended to be legally enforceable, and the introduction contains specific caveats to make this clear.'

3 See *R. v Board of Visitors Hull Prison*, ex parte *St. Germain* [1979] QB 425, and *R. v Deputy Governor of Parkhurst*, ex parte *Leech* [1988] AC 533.

4 The Prison Rules: Contracted Out Prisons 1992 are identical in substance to the Prison Rules applicable to public prisons, the only differences being the

substitution of appropriate terminology such as 'director' for 'governor', and so on.

5 An intriguing possibility is that, just as a whole state system can be mandated, so may a whole company's activities, even if spread over several states, be mandated.

6 *West* v *Atkins* (1988) 108 Supreme Court Reporter 2250.

7 This provision of the Parliamentary Commissioner for Administration Act 1967 was repealed in 1978, belatedly bringing the UK into line with other states.

8 In a letter to *The Times*, 28 February 1996, the chairman of the British and Irish Ombudsman Association revealed that the prisons ombudsman has not sought membership of that organization 'because the terms of his appointment do not fully meet our requirement of independence'.

9 See the annual reports of the boards of visitors of The Wolds (1992 and 1993) and Blakenhurst (1993).

10 The first report of the Board of Visitors of Doncaster prison, for the period 20 June 1994, remains unpublished. This is because the board evidently assumed that the home secretary, to whom all such reports are submitted, would automatically publish it. He did not do so, nor does the board appear to have published it directly itself as other boards often do. This report would have been of particular interest because of the fact that Doncaster got off to a difficult start (Prison Reform Trust 1995). The only impact – an ephemeral one – that the board's report accordingly had was through its press release of 12 June 1995. Where accountability is at stake, all participants have to understand their own role in the process.

11 Prisons Act 1952, ss. 31E(7) and 31E(8), as enacted by the Prisons (Contract Management) Amendment Act 1990.

12 For example, there are no specific references to its activities in the annual performance reviews (Downes 1994; Sneddon 1995) nor in the annual reports of the Department of Corrective Services nor even in the major evaluation of Junee carried out by the Department's Research Unit after one year's operation (Bowery 1994).

13 Judge Tumim's appointment was not extended. It was widely assumed that the very qualities described in the text made him unpalatable to the then home secretary. An ex-military man was appointed in his place. If it was considered that he was less likely to be a loose cannon, demanding accountability, than his predecessor, the government must initially have been very disappointed. Virtually the first inspection he carried out after taking office resulted in his team's walking out of the prison in question (Holloway, a women's prison) on the basis that it was too disgusting even to be inspected (*The Guardian Weekly*, 7 January 1996). The office of chief inspector clearly has developed a culture which is likely to survive the departure of its most charismatic leader.

14 The ACA has developed 19 other standards documents, applicable across the correctional spectrum – juvenile institutions, parole, community corrections, boot camps, and so on.

15 In the *Criminal Justice Newsletter* of 15 July 1991, the ACLU accuses the ACA of selling out its integrity by not seeking *amicus curiae* status in a brutality suit being brought against a prison in a state which was seeking accreditation.

5

Letting the contract and setting the terms

Inputs and outputs

The argument so far has been that with privatization there must inevitably be fuller specification of outputs. These will be negotiated between the agency and the contractor and be reflected in the contract. Performance can then be measured against something more tangible than is the case with the input-orientated systems historically exemplified by public sector prisons. The substantive terms of the contract are thus crucial. Contract compliance is a central element of accountability. It follows from this that the less prescriptive the contract is, the looser will be the accountability which it underpins, and vice versa. For example, the Junee contract provides with regard to education that 'the Correctional Centre is to provide access to, and encourage offenders to undertake, a range of educational and vocational programs'. This is exactly the kind of non-prescriptive obligation that an input-orientated organization might impose upon itself. But dealing with a private sector company which needs to know exactly what is expected of it, this clause led to several major disagreements (at last resolved) between the parties (Downes 1994; Sneddon 1995). Donahue (1989: 82) puts the proposition as follows: 'the fundamental distinction is between competitive output-based relationships and non-competitive input-based relationships rather than between profit seekers and civil servants per se'.

At this stage, however, a refinement needs to be made to the strict input–output dichotomy. 'Output' emphasizes ends, the means being flexible. 'Input' emphasizes means, the ends being by-products which are not exactly unplanned but are certainly subject to redefinition and retrospective rationalization. However, there is a point, relevant to current contractual practices, where these two concepts meet and merge. This middle ground could perhaps be characterized as a category of 'output-driven inputs'. An alternative way of conceptualizing it would be to speak of 'intermediate outputs' (as opposed to final outputs). For purposes of consistency, the first of these alternative terms will be used hereafter.

This merger occurs, for example, in relation to the specification of prisoner programmes. The desired output in relation to, say, remedial literacy classes is that participants should develop their reading skills up to a certain level. Even in a non-institutional setting, professional educators would baulk at binding themselves to precise targets: x per cent of participants reaching attainment level y in z months. The task is simply too difficult, involving too many human variables. So outputs tend to be defined not as absolutes but by reference to the desirable level of inputs which predictably ought to produce something resembling the desired ends. The Glades County, Florida, contract, for example, is as follows:

> The primary purpose of the education program is to provide a comprehensive program that is structured for the individual and is designed in an open entry, open exit format . . . The special education teacher will provide approximately 85 contact hours daily.

Evidently, the negotiating parties have made some calculation of eligible prisoners, likely participation rates, desirable class sizes and number of classroom hours that a teacher can handle in a day's work. The reference to '85 contact hours daily' is thus an input definition related to output objectives.

Much the same approach is found in relation to health services – specification of the extent of human and medical services calculated to maintain a satisfactory level of prisoner health (the input) rather than attempted prescription of an acceptable level of physical or mental illness within the prison (the output). Once more, the human variables are too volatile for any contractor to be expected to stand or fall by outputs alone, so 'output-driven inputs' replace or supplement them. Of course, the precise manner in which these inputs are made is a decision for the contractor, and in this sense the fundamental dichotomy remains intact.

This preliminary analysis needed to be made at this point, because, as was seen in Chapter 2, there exists some cynicism as to whether these concepts are useful in a prison context or simply mimic the jargon of the desiccated 'new managerialism' (Sparks 1994). Once it is understood that there is an area of overlap between input and output, it becomes evident that claims made for the privatization process are nowhere near as grandiose as they might otherwise be represented. Nevertheless, contract specification has become increasingly complex – the 1995 New Zealand invitation to tender (ITT), for example, running to 700 pages. Comparable trends are apparent in the USA, Australia and the UK. The objective has been to tighten the accountability of the contractor to the agency.

Secrecy

But accountability to the agency is not in itself enough, because of the risk of capture. In the public interest, contract specifications should be on the open record. That way prisoners themselves, members of legislatures, academics, the media and above all ginger groups, such as civil liberties and prisoners' support organizations, can bring pressure to bear on the contractor as well as on the contracting agency whose duty it is to monitor compliance.

In the USA general procurement laws in virtually all states require that such contractual arrangements be publicly accessible. Thus, in formal terms, public accessibility is the norm. In addition, Securities and Exchange Commission rules require that the procurement contracts of publicly listed companies be lodged for inspection. The three major players in the USA – CCA, Wackenhut and Esmor – are each listed on a stock exchange.

However, it is not always easy in practical terms to access the full agreement. Apart from the usual daunting difficulties of identifying where exactly one goes, at what times and with whose permission, there are often several voluminous documents to be rounded up. Increasingly, for example, contracts incorporate by reference clauses set out in the original Request for Proposals (RFP – US terminology for an invitation to tender or ITT) and the final contract contains long schedules. Also, as explained in Chapter 4, American Correctional Association (ACA) accreditation standards are invariably picked up. In practice, therefore, several documents must be cross-referenced, interleaved and reconciled to identify a meaningful contract. We are perhaps approaching the stage where some kind of summary document should be available as a first resort if the nominal openness of the US system is to remain a reality. Nevertheless, the basic guarantee of accessibility is an important symbol of accountability, a commitment which could give the notion teeth.

By contrast the position in Australia and the UK is quite unsatisfactory. For example, the first Australian contract – that between the Queensland Corrective Services Commission (QCSC) and CCA relating to Borallon – was treated as being 'commercial-in-confidence'. The QCSC was captured by, or perhaps surrendered to, the argument that, as performance criteria and contractual obligations were intimately bound up with pricing, as pricing itself was bound up with company profitability, and as knowledge of the margins of the successful bidder would become known to rivals bidding for future contracts, every aspect of the contract should be withheld from public access.

This first foray into contractual ethics seems unfortunately to have set a cultural norm in the Australian correctional community. As recently as 1995, both the South Australian authorities, in relation to Mount Gambier, and the Victorian, in relation to Melton, have taken the line that every aspect of the respective contracts will remain confidential. This gravely undermines accountability. Ironically, as the late-comers have jumped aboard this bandwagon, Queensland itself is about to jump off it. In evidence to the Australian Industry Commission in May 1995, the deputy commissioner of the QCSC stated as follows:

> Under the original contracts that we had entered into, the contracts were essentially treated as a commercial-in-confidence document. However over time it has become apparent that . . . there would be no commercial liability and it would be appropriate to make significant aspects of the contract available. So the latest model of contract that we have available is the one that has just been signed with Borallon [a three-year renewal as from 1 April 1995] . . . [T]he confidentiality provisions have been reduced dramatically [and] now only relate to a very small number of commercial aspects . . . Certainly in relation to those performance specifications, we would now treat those as a public document.

What remain confidential are the financial provisions. However, total outlays per annum would be readily discoverable from state budget papers, so that all that is left is precisely how the gross amounts payable are calculated. That is a great improvement, significantly enhancing account-ability.

Since the inception of privatization, the UK has officially maintained an unyielding commercial-in-confidence posture with regard to all elements of the contracts. The *reductio ad absurdum* of this stance occurred when the Contracts and Competition Group would not permit researchers com-missioned by the Home Office itself to evaluate The Wolds access to the contract documents (Bottomley *et al.* 1996a: 1). However, the House of Commons Public Accounts Committee, by dint of its Parliamentary privilege, and the National Audit Office, by dint of its overriding statutory authority, have each demanded and been supplied with various financial details. This was particularly so in relation to The Wolds and its start-up costs (National Audit Office 1994; *The Times*, 16 June 1994).

Another circuitous way in which contract information may be obtained relates to US stock exchange and SEC requirements, mentioned above. If a successful bidder for a UK contract is a subsidiary of or partly owned by a publicly listed US corporation, then the beneficial procurement contracts of that corporation become open to inspection in the USA, but not in the UK! In the case of Doncaster prison, the contractor – Premier Prison Services Ltd. – is partly owned by the Wackenhut Corporation. It is thus possible, as the present author has done, to obtain a copy of the contract (Prison Reform Trust 1995: 9–13). But in relation, say, to The Wolds – whose operator, Group 4, is not listed on a US stock exchange – no comparable loophole is open.

It is evident that these devices are no substitute for openness and full accountability. Access to contract information is fragmented and fortuitous. What is required is routine entitlement to inspect and copy contracts. In this regard, New Zealand is set to become an exemplar. As mentioned in Chapter 1, the enabling legislation had a rough parliamentary passage. The government, which had hitherto unquestioningly adopted the Anglo-Australian approach, was obliged to make the concession that all such contracts should be tabled in the House of Representatives 'within 12 sitting days after [being] entered into'. A similar provision is applicable to variations or renewals of such contracts.[1] This is preferable even to the standard US practice, for it enables interested parties readily to locate, examine and copy the relevant document(s). If there turn out to be problems with accountability in New Zealand, at least it will not be because contractual secrecy has impeded it.

Evaluating bids

The discussion of secrecy assumes that terms have been set and a contract let. However, it is necessary to backtrack a little and see exactly how this comes about. There are important public interest aspects here, as to both penal policy and administration, as to the final specification of the terms with which the contractor must comply and as to general probity. As DCFM deals have now become the norm, this kind of contract will be used as an example. However, in principle, identical considerations arise in relation to management-only contracts, CM contracts and DCM contracts.[2]

The need for a new prison

The very first stage, of course, is a governmental decision that a new prison of a certain size and security rating is needed. The second stage relates to whether it shall be a private prison or part of the public system. The legitimate concern of those who fear that the private sector may come to have an undue influence on penal policy by lobbying for high imprisonment rates must be met at this stage. Possibly, some open mechanism, such as a standing parliamentary committee, should be set up to scrutinize each of these stages. Its purpose would not be to second-guess the ministers and agencies whose job it is to carry out these very tasks, but to ensure that procedural proprieties are seen to have been met. Opening new prisons is serious business. If decisions to do so are properly scrutinized as a matter of course, the chances of penal policy being driven by private sector commercial interests, or indeed any other sectional interests, are thereby reduced.

The Woolf Report (Woolf and Tumim 1991: 11.133–11.144) recommended the obverse of this: that whenever a prison exceeds its certified normal accommodation for more than seven consecutive days the home secretary should be obliged to report this fact to Parliament so that its implications might be debated. Initially this recommendation was accepted; but subsequently the government reneged (*The Independent*, 24 June 1991).

The location of the new prison

Quite clearly, technical matters relating to catchment areas for prisoners and current and projected accommodation deficiencies should drive this decision. Traditionally, proposals to build prisons in a neighbourhood have been marked by community resistance – the well-observed NIMBY (not-in-my-back-yard) effect. However, it has recently begun to be accepted that prisons may well be good for a community, bringing short-term jobs at the capital works stage and permanent ones thereafter, with all the usual multiplier effects upon the local economy (Carl Vinson Institute of Government 1993). Moreover, there is no evidence that inward investment to the area by unrelated enterprises will be adversely affected (Home Office 1993; HM Prison Service 1995).

In this context, there may paradoxically start to be strong competition to be selected as the location for a new prison. In the westernized world, this may be particularly so in rural areas as urban clustering continues and regional economies decline. In New South Wales, for example, the announcement that the government would be opening what in the event became Junee prison initially attracted 70 'bids' by 62 separate local government areas, eager to trade land, fast-track or even by-pass planning procedures and offer other incentives in return for the supposed economic benefits that would flow (New South Wales Public Accounts Committee 1993: 127). In the event the successful bidder was Junee – a former railhead town which was losing population and whose economy was in steep decline. But Junee is some 600 kilometres from Sydney, which is the main catchment area for the prisoners who are now accommodated there. Visits to prisoners are thus problematical, a situation exacerbated by the fact that Junee now exists in a public transportation limbo (Harding 1993). It was predictable that the prison would have problems going beyond the normal start-up tensions, and this is in fact what has happened.[3]

At least the decision to locate the new prison at Junee was taken, wisely or unwisely, in the normal bureaucratic way. Only *after* the decision had been made were invitations to tender for the construction and management of the prison sought. However, in the USA it has now become almost universal practice for siting or location to be an integral part of the bid for a DCFM contract. In some cases, such as Florida, one of the statutorily mandated bid evaluation criteria specifically relates to the ability of the bidder to find a site and obtain clearances. In others, such as Virginia, it is implicit that the bidder must identify a suitable site and obtain clearances, and RFP practices have developed on this basis. In yet others, such as Texas and Tennessee, the enabling legislation makes no specific reference to this factor, but *de facto* the practice has grown up of requiring the bidder to include siting as part of the bid. In other words, in virtually all private prison situations bidders must select a site, make provisional arrangements to purchase it, and go as far as they can in obtaining the necessary planning and environmental approvals. Inevitably, in the course of doing these things they must enter into negotiations with local community representatives as to hiring policies, mutual incentives and so on.

Under all these pressures, it is likely that siting decisions relegate what one might call 'penal appropriateness' to a rather low point on the totem pole. If the public interest is to be met, the agency which allocates the contract must inject this criterion back into the equation. Otherwise there is a danger of overall prison accommodation policies becoming distorted. However, the public correctional authorities in the USA increasingly have no taste for making and implementing siting decisions themselves. Almost invariably, therefore, they will accept the siting recommendation put forward by the successful bidder. This is an example of surrender: letting oneself, with regard to a matter which above all should reflect the broad public interest, be captured by the private sector – for which, naturally, commercial convenience is the most important single consideration.

Operational standards

As already explained, contracts emphasize outputs, though there is a large area where inputs and outputs cannot sensibly be disentangled – 'output-driven inputs'. The broad point to stress is that there is a far greater degree of specification in these contracts than has hitherto been the case with public sector prisons.

Implicitly conceding this point is the provision in the New South Wales enabling legislation that, as part of the contractual process, the Corrective Services Commission was required to prepare a minimum standards document for incorporation into the contract.[4] It is remarkable that such a document was evidently not already in existence. Three years later, the Victoria enabling legislation contained an identical provision.[5]

In the UK there is such a document: the Prison Rules. As mentioned, those Rules have been extended in identical form to private prisons. However, they are simply a backdrop to the much more detailed specifications that are found in all private prison contracts. Much the same is true in the USA, where ACA accreditation is required which in turn involves meeting certain minimum standards. However, in many respects, the contracts themselves are far more specific and detailed; the greater includes the lesser.

These operational standards are initially developed by personnel working within the letting agency. Typically, the contract team includes agency finance and management personnel as well as experienced prison administrators. Increasingly, however, finance and management experts are brought in specially for the privatization exercise to contribute to these deliberations. Of course, bidders themselves also contribute. This may occur before the letting of the contract or after the favoured bidder has been identified.

Before the letting of the contract, it may well be that 'non-conforming' bids are received. Such bids are a means by which potential contractors let the agency know that they believe that the specifications are unrealistic or could be improved. This occurred, for example, in relation to Bridgend and Fazakerley in the UK; the specifications were amended in response. After selection of the favoured bidder, the process of finally settling the terms commences. The RFP or ITT process will never have brought the parties absolutely together, and this is the time when detailed consensus should be achieved. The second bidder is usually kept on stand-by in case the final negotiation with the first bidder falls through.

Selecting the successful bidder

There are two questions here: first, who chooses; and second by what criteria. As to who chooses, there are three basic models: the public sector agency as part of its normal management process; the public sector agency with some kind of quarantine or 'Chinese wall' system in place; and a separate agency not directly involved with the day-to-day management of any part of the public system. The closer the selecting body is to the operational public sector prison system, the greater the danger that the choice will simply reflect existing approaches and the subsequent monitoring process will be captured.

The first model is epitomized by the situation in most states of the USA (but not Florida) and by New South Wales and South Australia. Public agency officials control the bidding and selection process and make final recommendations to ministers or governments. Queensland also fell within this category for its first two privatization exercises, but since 1994 has exemplified the 'Chinese wall' approach. This change came about because that state's third privatization exercise – not previously referred to – involved 'market testing', that is, permitting the public agency itself to enter the bidding. In such circumstances, obviously, the public agency should not both be a contender and also make the evaluation. Yet public agency expertise was needed for each of those processes – to formulate its own bid and to assess bids generally. Accordingly, by administrative arrangement a Chinese wall was erected between those personnel within the QCSC who were formulating a bid and those who would assist with the assessment. A not dissimilar arrangement was made in New Zealand with regard to the first DCFM contract, not because the public agency itself was competing (it had been prohibited from doing so) but because of a belief that the values and assumptions of personnel directly involved in the day-to-day management of what would become a competing element within the total system should not play a key role.

The third model is illustrated by several jurisdictions, notably the UK and Florida. In the UK, the contract process is administered by the Contracts and Competitions Group. Although nominally part of the Prison Service, it works to a different line of command than those involved in prison operations. In fact, the director of the Group reports to the director-general and no one else. This differentiation is now so well established that it is probably not unreasonable to characterize it as a separate agency rather than one sheltering behind a Chinese wall. The Group has its own staff, separate premises, budgets for hiring its own consultants and a developing subculture. Against this, it should be said that personnel who work for the Group are liable to be posted back into the mainstream Prison Service, for it lacks any statutory autonomy and cannot offer a long-term career structure. The first two directors were in fact brought back into the mainstream as they grew in seniority and were required for higher responsibilities.

The arrangements in Florida more clearly fit within the third model. A brief history will facilitate understanding of how this has come about. From 1985 onwards the Florida Department of Corrections had been statutorily authorized 'to enter into contracts with private vendors for the provision, operation and maintenance of correctional facilities and the supervision of inmates'.[6] In the same year, county governing bodies were likewise authorized[7] to implement privatization initiatives. Quite soon three counties actually did so, with what they considered to be satisfactory outcomes. However, the Department of Corrections was reluctant to utilize its new power, and only one such contract was entered into over the period of almost a decade. Impatient with this diffidence, in 1993 the legislature stripped the Department of this power and established a new organization, the Florida Correctional Privatization Commission, whose sole function was to take charge of private prison arrangements not just at state institutional level but also with regard to counties. The Commission is functionally responsible to the director of the Department of Administrative Services, and possesses no line responsibility for or accountability to the public sector agency, the Florida Department of Corrections. The Commission is beholden to no set of values, no correctional subculture, and its operations, including subsequent monitoring of contract compliance, truly are at arm's length from the public agency (Thomas 1995b).

Selection criteria

In virtually all systems, potential bidders are filtered at the 'expression of interest' stage. For example, there were 53 expressions of interest in the first New Zealand contract, of which only six led to invitations to tender. After this filtering process has occurred, the difficult question is how to evaluate bids and bidders. The approach which has now become commonplace is to assign a fixed weight to various factors – design, known previous performance of the construction company associated with the bid, financial arrangements or 'bankability', quality of proposed prisoner programmes, health service delivery, ability to conform with the mission statement or performance objectives of the public agency, and so on. For some bids and in some jurisdictions, special criteria are introduced – for example, in New Zealand, innovative penological approaches to dealing with Maori prisoners. Some states, such as Florida, go out of their way to emphasize innovative approaches as a statutory criterion.[8]

Some contracting authorities break down their fixed weight categories into numerous very small ones – for example, Florida has quite literally no less than 18 scoring areas, subdivided into 107 different possible marks. The main areas may provide as few as 2 per cent of the total score and subdivisions as little as 0.25 per cent. The Glades County contract was awarded to Wackenhut ahead of CCA on a difference of 0.25 per cent; this was how the sums added up and that was the end of the matter.

Virginia, on the other hand, has larger and looser scoring categories. There are only nine, the last of which is 10 per cent based on interview of the final contenders. Even then, however, the arithmetic does not, as in Florida, settle the issue. The selection protocol provides as follows:

> Selection shall be made of two or more offerors scoring the highest. After negotiations have been conducted with each offeror so selected, the Department shall select the offeror which, in its opinion, has made the best proposal and shall award the contract to that offeror, contingent upon its being able to get all the necessary local approvals for the project.

Thus Virginia circumvents the tyranny of arithmetic, recognizing that the total can indeed be greater than the sum of the parts. The scoring system is treated as a cogent guide and provides important signposts for the assessors; but the proposal which is best overall (for example, because of its congruence with plans for the total prison system or because some proposed innovation seems so exciting) may not necessarily have been the top scorer.

The UK bidding system achieves much the same flexibility via a slightly different route. European Community rules relating to competition cover the bidding process, so that the assessment criteria must be spelled out in the ITT, thereby made known to bidders, and adhered to by the Contracts and Competition Group when making its recommendation to the minister. However, a 'soft' criterion, the one which enables value judgements to be made and arithmetical scores to be circumvented, is that of 'deliverability'. This permits the assessors to ask themselves whether, however excellent the highest-scoring proposal may seem on paper according to the abstract criteria, it realistically can be achieved, and also whether in the light of broad penological developments and needs it is what they really want.

Most assessment processes – not just those of Virginia and the UK – are more flexible than that of Florida. In the context of accountability, the argument can cut both ways. The authorities, it could be said, are more accountable if they must go unquestioningly where the scoring system leads them; or, alternatively, they are more accountable if they are permitted and indeed obliged to make the final decision using the scores not as a determinant but as a guide to ascertain what proposal is qualitatively best and fits overall needs.

Nevertheless, fine as this sounds, the starting-point these days is that the cheapest conforming bid should normally succeed.[9] The problem with this is that companies are thought to 'low-ball' bids (bid a price at which they cannot make a profit if they meet their contractual commitments properly) to get their foot into the door of new markets. If such a bid is accepted, one of two things will subsequently happen. Once ensconced in a position where the public agency is dependent upon a company for the delivery of services which it cannot deliver itself, the company may seek to renegotiate the terms; one of the significant players in the field is notorious amongst its competitors for this supposed practice, though the evidence is blurred. Alternatively, attempts may be made to deliver the services below contract standard. Either way, the efficacy of state accountability mechanisms is a key factor.

One example where low-balling was alleged related to the US Immigration and Naturalization Service (INS) detention facility at Elizabeth, New Jersey.[10] The DCFM contract was let to Esmor Correctional Services Inc. in August 1993; Esmor's bid of $54 million was approximately $20 million lower than that of the next lowest bidder, Wackenhut Corporation. At the time Wackenhut protested, saying that Esmor's proposed pay scale for guards ($8.02 an hour) was 'unrealistically low . . . , thereby materially increasing the risk to the contracting agency of non-performance'. Such a low pay scale would, it was argued, guarantee high staff turnover – something which is antithetical to control in any hierarchical institution. The INS dismissed this protest, reiterating that Esmor's proposal offered 'the lower price and higher technical value'. Accordingly, the contract went ahead, and in August 1994 the facility was opened. In June 1995, the inmates staged an uprising; this was followed by an internal INS inquiry, which found that the 'level of salary was not realistic and could not . . . ensure the availability of well-qualified applicants. It is obvious that many . . . of the guards hired by Esmor did not meet the requirements of the contract or were only marginally qualified.' As a result there were various malpractices in the treatment of inmates. A month after the uprising which these malpractices occasioned, Esmor's contract was cancelled.

One cannot be sure that the INS would have made a different procurement decision if its brief and its culture obliged it to look beyond cost consider- ations – encouraged it in fact to let in the 'softer' criteria, such as 'deliverability'. But on the basis of this evidence, it would certainly seem to be desirable that it should do so.

However, the lesson that this story also illustrates is the fundamental importance that the contracting agency, when making an RFP, should have an absolutely clear vision of its own policies, objectives and standards. Accountability is the obverse of contractual clarity. In this particular case, the INS sought proposals for the construction and management of a facility to hold illegal immigrants for a maximum of 30 days. To be blunt about it, it was looking for a hygienic and decent human warehouse, not a programmatic correctional facility. But in the event, because of its own mismanagement of its overall resources, the INS left detainees in the Elizabeth facility for many months; indeed, some of the rioters had been confined there virtually since the day it opened. The types of physical arrangements and management regimes required for a medium-stay facility are quite different from those required for a facility which inmates and staff understand from the outset is for very short-term stays. Esmor had some basis for feeling aggrieved; it had been awarded the contract on one basis, complied with its formal terms, and yet made accountable on another basis. The *Wall Street Journal* (11 July 1995) commented:

> The real lesson from the riot is that the federal government isn't any better at managing private contracts than it is at the many other things it does poorly . . . Previous riots involving I.N.S. detainees at facilities managed by the federal government have been far more destructive, and they led in part to the I.N.S. deciding to hire private companies to jail detainees. But privatization can be done badly, and the I.N.S. could write the book on how not to write the contract.[11]

Checking probity

Fraudulent or malevolent contractors can circumvent the best-designed accountability systems or at the very least push them to the extremes of their tolerance. Better to screen such companies from the outset, however apparently attractive their bids.

The Victoria legislation specifically requires that a probity check be conducted of all 'relevant persons'. This means the bidders, company personnel, anyone who has voting rights in the company, and anyone who is employed by the contractor – custodial and other staff. The check is to be made by the police department and refers to 'the character, honesty and integrity'. In police parlance that means criminal record, and is unlikely to extend further.

Rather surprisingly, this sort of provision is uncommon in the enabling legislation of other jurisdictions. Presumably, the responsible authorities do make inquiries of this sort with regard to bidders who make the short-list. But the fact that there is multinational participation in private prisons means the process is not entirely straightforward. In particular, previous malfeasance as a company director – the sort of information held in the UK by the Department of Trade and Industry, in the USA by the Securities and Exchange Commission and in Australia by the Australian Securities Commission – is less readily available through inter-agency transfer than straightforward criminal record information through Interpol.

However, there is a further level of probity, the kind to which reference was made in Chapter 2 and which so much concerned Baldry (1994a; 1994b: 14). This relates to general reputation, whether as a bad employer, an anti-democratic corporate citizen, someone insensitive to local cultures, and so on. For example, with regard to Wackenhut Corrections Corporation – the dominant company in the consortium put together for the Junee contract and earlier the successful bidder for the Arthur Gorrie Correctional Centre – Baldry refers to the findings of a US House of Representatives Committee on Interior and Insular Affairs which indicated in relation to the policing of the trans-Alaska pipeline that Wackenhut Corporation – associated with Wackenhut Corrections Corporation – could have been involved in various matters which at the very least were unethical and could well have been illegal. They included: conducting a 'sting' against a damaging witness who wished to give evidence to the Committee; obstructing the Committee's investigation by withholding and possibly destroying and altering key documents; obtaining telephone usage data without permission; obtaining private credit and financial reports under false pretences; and so on.

The point of this is not to say whether the allegations were right or wrong, true or false or indeed whether alleged wrongdoings of the mother company would in any case have spilled over into the running of the Wackenhut Corrections Corporation itself. It is simply to point out that no process existed in New South Wales for investigating these matters and possibly bringing them into the equation. Quite the contrary; the minister responsible for allocating the contract had already announced, before the ITT stage, that he was quite satisfied that the main US companies (including Wackenhut) met any reasonable probity test (Baldry 1994a: 134). Once more, we see almost indecent surrender, not merely struggle followed by capture. From the point of view of accountability, there is an important hiatus in testing probity.[12]

Take-overs and amalgamations

In 1995 Virginia issued an RFP for a 1500-bed medium-security prison. The successful bidder was Corrections Partners Inc. (CPI), a relatively small operator running three prisons in Kansas, Mississippi and Oklahoma. After the decision had been made but just before it was announced, it became known that CCA had taken over CPI. Thus CCA took on the mantle of successful bidder, even though, bidding in its own right against CPI, it had been unsuccessful.

The question is not whether CCA will or will not do the job effectively.

Rather, the point is that there does appear to be a hiatus in accountability in that a state can set out to contract with one company and find itself subsequently dealing with another. Some contracts refer to the maintenance of corporate identity as a condition of the contract. Victoria goes so far as to require by statute that the contractor notify the agency 'of any change in the management or control of the contractor'.[13] But the sanction for breach of both these contractual and statutory constraints is left rather hazy. Clearly, the implications of these situations have not yet been thought through. Yet, in a context where, as Thomas (1996: v, 28), has pointed out, 17 companies are currently involved in the private prisons industry in the USA and 11 of these share a mere 10 per cent of the business, 'the probability of further consolidation within the industry remains high'.

Summary

Public accountability of the private prison sector is symbiotically related to contract specification. A loose contract will tend to have loose accountability; a tighter one should facilitate accountability. Public authorities are undoubtedly honing their skills as they gain in contractual experience.

Even the best contract must be public if all the levers of accountability are to be made to work. Because of the demonstrable danger of capture, this cannot be left to the public authority alone. Unfortunately, an almost obsessive secretiveness still characterizes some jurisdictions, though there are clear marks of improvement.

The processes for evaluating bids and bidders are becoming increasingly sophisticated. In places they are a little too rigid to enable the broad public interest always to be reflected by the decision-making process; but this too seems to be improving. Probity checks and the way in which changes in the ownership of the contractor should be dealt with are two areas of structural weakness. Each potentially bears upon the effectiveness of accountability.

On the whole, however, these aspects of privatization – letting the contract and setting its terms – are working adequately and continuing to be improved with experience.

Notes

1 Penal Institutions Act 1954, s. 4L, as enacted by s. 3 of the 1994 Penal Institutions Amendment Act.
2 These terms were first used in Chapter 1 and will appear frequently hereafter. 'DCFM' is code for design, construct, finance and manage; 'DCM' for design, construct and manage; 'CM' for construct and manage; and, of course, the last possibility is management only. The practitioners are not always consistent in the use of these terms, either within a single organization or across jurisdictions. But it

is usually self-evident which type of contract they have in mind, whatever their own adaptation of this terminology.

3 The Woolf Report (Woolf and Tumim 1991: 11.49) perceived the importance of the relationship between siting and prisoner welfare, recommending that 'where this is practical, prisons should be community prisons sited within reasonable proximity to, and having close connections with, the community with which the prisoners hold their closest links'.

4 Prisons (Contract Management) Act 1990, s. 31B(2)(b).

5 Corrections Act 1986, s. 9E, as amended by the Corrections (Management) Act 1993, s. 4.

6 Florida Statutes, 944.105.

7 Florida Statutes, 951.062.

8 Florida Statutes, 957.03(4)(b).

9 This issue is more fully discussed in Chapter 7. An important example of the lowest bid not succeeding relates to The Wolds.

10 The account which follows is derived principally from a long article in the *New York Times*, 23 July 1995, and the earlier coverage in *The Wall Street Journal*, 11 July 1995.

11 The postscript to this story is that in May 1996 the Elizabeth facility was reopened pursuant to a management contract between the INS and CCA. The contract has been written in terms which reflect much more clearly the obligations of each party.

12 Wackenhut, a successful bidder in Victoria, has also been the subject of probity challenge in that state. Once more the point is not whether those allegations are or are not sustainable, but rather that there was apparently no established procedure by which the state could test the allegations. The matter simply fell, therefore, into the realm of political point-scoring. See *The Australian*, 9–10 December 1995.

13 Corrections (Management) Act 1993, s. 9(2)(h).

6

Prison personnel, the administration of punishment and the impact of privatization upon penal policy

Three of the key elements of accountability identified in Chapter 2 were as follows:

- that custodial regimes, programmes and personnel must be culturally appropriate, from which it followed that the state must retain some control or at least be able to make some effective input into the staffing decisions of the private contractors;
- that the distinction between the allocation and administration of punishment must, for profound constitutional and political reasons, be strictly maintained, with the private sector's role being confined to administration;
- that penal policy must not be driven by those who stand to make a profit from it.

These issues, starting in the workplace with employees and going right through to the boardroom on policy matters, will each highlight something of the private sector's approach to being regulated and the public agencies' commitment to ensuring accountability.

Personnel

Prisons are a human service; the quality of the employed personnel is crucial. In all states, private prison personnel derive their status and coercive legal powers from the enabling legislation. If these personnel are ill trained or poorly managed, however, even the most robustly constructed accountability system will not be able to prevent the particular prison regime from starting to wobble or even toppling to the ground. Examples of this have already been seen, most notably in the collapse of the custodial regime at Esmor's Immigration and Naturalization Service (INS) detention centre. An element of an accountability system, then, is the extent to which the supervising agency can influence or control the appointment or the dismissal of custodial staff selected by the contractor to work at the private prison.[1]

The legalistic pattern that will emerge ranges from no agency control or influence upon any level of custodial appointee, on the one hand, to complete power of veto upon the appointment or continued employment of all levels of employee, on the other. The practical pattern stops short of these two legal extremities, however.

Legal arrangements

In the USA the fundamental approach is that the contractor has the responsibility to provide the custodial workforce and thus the untrammelled right to select, hire and fire employees. Their status and authority derives directly from their appointment by the employer. The contractor must live with bad decisions here, as in all other areas of promised service delivery. But it is only if those bad decisions adversely affect contract performance that the matter becomes one for the supervising agency. This was the case, for example, with the cancelled Esmor contract. But even at that advanced stage of breakdown the agency possessed no legitimate role or direct authority in relation to individual employees, merely a contractual remedy against the contractor.[2]

At the other extreme is the UK position. The enabling statute designates all employees involved in the custodial regime, from the governor or director to base-grade officers, as 'prison custody officers'. All such personnel nominally derive their status and authority not from their employment contract but from a certificate granted by the home secretary:

> In this Part 'prison custody officer' means a person in respect of whom a certificate is for the time being in force certifying –
> (a) that he has been approved by the Secretary of State for the purpose of performing . . . custodial duties . . . ; and
> (b) that he is accordingly authorised to perform them.[3]

The statute then sets out the qualifying criteria and the circumstances of revocation. The main criteria are that the person is 'fit and proper' to perform the relevant functions and that he has received training of an appropriate standard. It is not known overall how often potential custody officers have been refused a certificate or on what precise basis; however, no less than 21 persons were vetoed during the recruitment stage for Doncaster prison (Prison Reform Trust 1995: 29). This would seem to indicate the function is being taken seriously.

Revocation of the certificate by the home secretary can occur on the basis that the person is not a fit and proper person; an intermediate stage is suspension by the controller on identical grounds. This ties in with the unique UK provision, mentioned in Chapter 3, that the controller is empowered to investigate and report on allegations of misconduct committed by prison custodial officers.[4] One would naturally expect that this role would be relatively exceptional and that revocation would be a less frequent recourse than denial of certification in the first place. Whilst no comprehensive figures are available, it is known that on at least one occasion the Blakenhurst controller conducted such an inquiry and the prison custodial officer was dismissed (Tumim 1995: 20–1). The import of this statutory scheme is to symbolize that it is the state, not the employer, from which the status and authority of custodial employees in private prisons derive.

Most other jurisdictions fall somewhere between these two extremes in their legal arrangements. The Queensland Corrective Services Commission, for example, possesses a power of veto over the contractor's choice of a general manager of a private prison as well as power to authorize, and by implication to refuse to authorize, the appointment of custodial correctional officers.[5] What is not so clear is whether the QCSC could withdraw authorization, once granted (Moyle 1993: 237). This possible hiatus leaves the Queensland model short of the UK scheme.

In New South Wales, the law is very similar to that in the UK – prior authorization or veto of custodial staff from the highest to the lowest on specified grounds, plus the power of revocation. In fact, the parameters of the latter power are broader than the UK equivalent, taking in 'any other reason which the Director-General thinks is a sufficient reason, in the public interest, for revocation of the authority'.[6] However, no authorization can be revoked 'without affording the person concerned a reasonable opportunity to be heard' – a formula which, by opening up the full panoply of administrative law principles, including judicial review, would tend to inhibit the exercise of such a power. The Victoria enabling legislation is virtually identical in its intended effect with that of New South Wales.[7] It can be seen, therefore, that each of the Australian states is at the UK end of the spectrum of potential control over custodial personnel working in private prisons.[8]

New Zealand – perhaps surprisingly in view of its statutory fastidiousness in other matters relating to privatization – falls towards the US end of the spectrum. Personnel matters are covered by a statutory requirement that the contract must address the issues of the employment of suitable staff and the provision of suitable training. This is reinforced by a requirement that the private prison superintendent report regularly to both the monitor and the secretary of the Department on each of those matters, such as the use of force or of the power to search, which are at the cutting edge of institutional disciplinary practices. Beyond that, hiring and firing practices at a private prison are a matter entirely for the contractor.[9]

Personnel issues in practice

In practice, the US legal position does not give the contractor a free rein. In some states – for example, Florida and Kentucky – there are specific statutory requirements as to the qualifications of staff. Florida's requirement relates to the training of custodial workers: the contractor must provide initial and in-service training which 'meets or exceeds the requirements for similar employees of the department' itself.[10] Kentucky echoes this notion of equivalence for uniformed staff, and goes on to specify that the administrator or manager must have at least five years' correctional experience and five years' administrative experience.[11] Of course, in neither case can there be agency veto of qualified personnel.

Even those states, such as Tennessee, Texas or Arkansas, which do not statutorily specify training standards or management qualifications in practice incorporate personnel standards into their arrangements. This may be via 'soft' statutory requirements (for example, that the successful contractor must be able to demonstrate that it possesses 'the qualifications, experience and management personnel necessary to carry out the terms of the contract') or because of mandatory statutory or *de facto* contractual incorporation of American Correctional Association (ACA) standards.[12] As explained in Chapter 4, incorporation of these standards is now the invariable practice, and they can be quite rigorous.

In relation to wardens or administrators of institutions, for example, the ACA standards provide:

> The qualifications for the position of warden . . . include at a minimum the following: a bachelor's degree in an appropriate discipline; five years of related administrative experience; and demonstrated administrative ability and leadership.[13]

In much the same way, the ACA standards are detailed and prescriptive with regard to pre-employment suitability of all levels of custodial officers and the training which should be available to them.[14] The incorporation of these standards provides the contracting agency with an arsenal of ammunition to keep the contractor in line. But, as stated previously, they do not enable the agency to decide for itself whether any particular individual is suitable or unsuitable for employment, nor do they permit the agency to dictate training requirements in detail. A clear distinction is maintained between what must be done (the agency's concern) and how it is done (the contractor's prerogative).

In Queensland and New South Wales the respective corrective services commissions – agencies, it will be recalled, with statutory mandates to involve themselves directly in the appointment or removal of a manager or warden – have treated this issue as pre-eminently one for the contractor. Empowered under UK-style legislative structures, they have nevertheless taken a US approach to their own responsibilities and rights. The importance of this matter, previously referred to in Chapter 3, should be reiterated; it is indicative of a degree of capture.

Prisons are as much a function of national culture, identity, priorities and problems as are schools or sports or systems for the care of the elderly or eating habits or religion. A Japanese prison regime – in the broadest sense of attitude towards confinement, acceptance of authority, expectations of privileges, participation in programmes, relations with other prisoners, and so on – could never be mistaken for a British one, or vice versa; nor could a New Zealand regime for a French; nor even an Australian regime for an American one. Working assumptions are different and an understanding of what one can take for granted varies, whilst ability to anticipate problems before they arise depends on familiarity with and an almost intuitive 'feel' for the prison culture. In other words, prison management is not simply a generic skill but one that is to some degree culture-specific. In what is inevitably an introverted institutional atmosphere, to misread the culture can have quite disproportionate effects. To say this is not to be xenophobic, merely realistic.

That being so, when the contractors for the Arthur Gorrie Correctional Centre proposed to put an American prison administrator, completely lacking in any Australian background or experience, in charge as the first manager, warning bells should have sounded within the Queensland Corrective Services Commission (QCSC) – the body with the power to veto this suggestion. This was not because there was any doubt as to that person's competence or suitability in a US setting. But in a prison system with a significant Aboriginal population and a recent agonized history of deaths in custody, no career American prison administrator could possibly be suf-ficiently sensitized to Australian issues. Of course, from the point of view of the American operators the choice was understandable. It brought Arthur Gorrie within the 'career structure' of their own senior management personnel; and it meant they would be dealing with someone they already knew and trusted. But the task of the QCSC was not to 'understand' the contractor's point of view, but rather to safeguard the public interest.

In mid-1992 the American manager took up his post. By the end of the year there had been two suicides – one of them after prisoners allegedly taunted the inmate to kill himself whilst prison officers stood by laughing and the other of an inmate who was in the process of suing the prison authorities after allegedly having been raped twice within the prison. The first of these suicides led to a protest, which was allegedly dealt with by stripping prisoners naked and leaving them locked up. A subsequent riot involving about 30 prisoners, after being suppressed, was followed by the laying of criminal charges of 'mutiny' under the Prisons Act. This is something quite alien in the Australian correctional culture, escalating a problem which could normally be expected to have been dealt with by standard disciplinary procedures.

In March 1993 the manager was posted back to California to take charge of another Wackenhut institution. The most revealing aspect of this decision was the reaction of the QCSC. All new institutions, said the director-general, went through 'teething problems' and the departure of the manager was 'a matter for his private employers'. The point had still not been understood; the appointment of the manager and the question of subsequent removal were *par excellence* matters for the regulatory authority, which seemed to have failed in its responsibility. Capture, or rather surrender, was evidently complete.

In New South Wales, the same scene was being repeated. As one American manager left Queensland, another was taking over responsibility for Junee private prison, which was run by the same private contractor. As already mentioned in Chapter 5, the location of the prison was quite unsuitable, and trouble could have been anticipated (Harding 1993). Within three months of its opening, tear gas had to be used to quell a riot of about 100 prisoners. Shortly thereafter a prisoner committed suicide. It is, of course, quite true that all new prisons do have start-up problems and these cannot fairly be attributed to an American rather than an Australian style of management. However, the real lesson of this is that the supervising agency, like the QCSC before it, evidently could not perceive that this might be a problem. Bringing in an American, it was said, was simply a way of 'importing the best in American correctional practice' (Harding 1994a: 76).[15]

From the above it can be seen that Australian practice has drifted towards that of the USA despite the contrasting legal framework. A legitimate lever of accountability has so far not been pulled.

The UK position is quite different. Every director so far appointed to run a private prison has been a former governor-grade employee of the Prison Service. On the basis of conversations with the majority of them, the present author would say that their common characteristic is a desire to be allowed actually to run an institution of which they are nominally in charge. Frustration at the suffocating structures based around the directives of area managers and head-office protocols (Woolf and Tumim 1991: 12.71) has drawn many of the best performers out of the public system. The power of veto over appointments has evidently not been an issue to date.

However, there is some suggestion that, not overtly but subtly and indirectly, the existence of the power of revocation has been used as a lever. It will be recalled that both the chief inspector of prisons and the board of visitors made early reports on the operation of Blakenhurst. The board commented adversely on the state of the prison in September 1993, about three months after it became operational. The chief inspector also commented on these matters, and referred to the fact that the foundation director had been sent to a Kansas facility of the parent company in August 1993 and was then formally replaced in October (Tumim 1995: 16). He also observed that the controller seemed almost to have crossed the line between monitoring the operations and assisting the contractor (Tumim 1995: 22). In conversation with the present author, one of the Blakenhurst controllers suggested that the regime would have been in deep trouble had that course not been taken. There was the distinct suggestion that the controller had in fact been quite interventionist in relation to the change of personnel at the top. If so, it was his formal statutory authority which underpinned any informal behind-the-scenes involvement.

Finally, in this section, a word should be said about training requirements. This is the expensive end of the labour market, involving as it does outlays without immediate returns. The public prison systems have been apprehensive of their newly trained staff being 'poached' by the private contractors. This factor has underpinned the 'equivalence' philosophy which is broadly reflected in statutes and contracts. At this early stage of privatization, there is some evidence that the private contractors may be falling a little short of their commitments (Downes 1994: 7).[16] By the same token, the supervising agencies have evidently tolerated deficient performance. The chief inspector of prisons noted in his review of The Wolds, for example, that certification after the completion of training 'did not include any checks of competence' (Tumim 1994a: 38). Once more, a degree of tolerance bordering on capture manifests itself.

In summary, active participation in personnel policies and practices certainly constitutes a useful aspect of accountability. There is no uniform practice in this regard, nor do the formal legal structures and entitlements faithfully mirror actual practice. None of the agencies lacking formal powers is quite as non-interventionist as might be thought. And none of those with formal powers is quite as interventionist as it could be. Corrections professionals still seem to be trying to work out mutually advantageous arrangements on this matter.

The allocation of punishment and its administration

Radzinowicz's view that 'the enforcement of penal legislation . . . should be the undiluted responsibility of the state' (quoted in Shaw 1992), and thus that prison privatization was unacceptable in any form and whatever the safeguards, was expounded and discussed in Chapter 2. In response it was argued that this view was simplistic, failing to distinguish between the *allocation* of punishment and its *administration*. The former was, and with privatization still is, the responsibility of the independent judiciary; whilst the latter was a matter for the executive. As with many of its functions, the executive might delegate this task. Indeed, delegated administration of criminal punishment, as well as other forms of involuntary institutionaliz-ation, has been and remains commonplace. Examples include: community-based corrections, juvenile corrections including detention, psychiatric services, and drug treatment centres (McDonald 1992: 362–3). As long as it is understood that the state remains responsible for how that task is then carried out by its delegate and ensures that it is done according to the proper standards, there should be no objection of principle.

Of course, practice and principle do not always equate. Historically, it must be said, the distinction between allocation and administration has not always been strictly maintained, indeed has sometimes been abandoned (Moyle 1993: 232–3). The question is whether modern accountability systems are, or will be, more effective in maintaining this distinction. In this regard, there are three areas where the distinction may become blurred and which should accordingly be subjected to particular scrutiny. They are: disciplinary decisions and penalties; classification, sentence planning and transfer; and release decisions, such as parole or work release.

Disciplinary decisions and penalties

A preliminary point which should be made is that the disciplinary code in private prisons is in all states identical or equivalent to that which is operative in the public prison system. There is no question of private prisons developing their own private code of discipline. This fundamental point is secured variously by enabling statutes and the terms of the contract. For example, Florida provides that 'a contract . . . does not authorise the contractor to . . . formulate rules of inmate behavior, violations of which may subject inmates to sanctions, except to the extent that those rules are accepted by the [correctional privatization] commission'[17] and contracts then go on to provide that such rules must be consistent with those of the Department of Corrections. Arkansas more succinctly provides that a contractor may 'impose discipline upon inmates only in accordance with applicable rules and procedures'.[18]

Technically, of course, sanctions for misconduct within prisons are not the allocation of punishment for offences against the criminal law. In abstract terms the distinction is not breached. However, these punishments can only be imposed because of a person's status as one who has breached the criminal law and been sentenced to imprisonment in the first place. The state has placed the person in a situation where he is subject to more sanction-backed regulation than other citizens. That being so, new deprivations of liberty (such as loss of remission/good time) or stricter levels of incarceration (solitary confinement) or restrictions upon privilege (loss of visits or telephone privileges) are arguably tantamount to the allocation of pun-ishment. Even if the dichotomy is not flagrantly breached, it certainly starts to become blurred.

Formal disciplinary charges

The greater the input or the overview which the state has in relation to this function in private prisons, the less vulnerable to criticism will the arrangements be. In this respect the UK system is optimal. A public official, the controller, deals with adjudications of all disciplinary charges laid in the private prisons; the status of custodial personnel once the charge has been laid is simply that of witnesses. It was noted earlier that the directors of private prisons find this arrangement frustrating, because they see the imposition of discipline as symbolic of their own control over their prison. In his report on Blakenhurst, Tumim (1995: 59) stated quite simply: 'We preferred the safeguards offered within the present arrangements.'

This is surely the correct position. Charges have run at a considerably higher rate, at least initially, in private prisons than in comparable established public ones. The temptation would obviously be strong for a director to tend to support his staff by upholding charges, whereas the controller should be able to be completely objective. In terms of the process, the controller system must be seen – particularly by inmates – as more equitable. The Woolf Inquiry (Woolf and Tumim 1991: 9.24–9.37), of course, had emphasized that a sense of injustice is a significant contributor to an unstable prison environment. As previously mentioned, there has been active lobbying against this arrangement. However, present information suggests that the Home Office will stand firm on this matter. Any change would require legislative action.

This model has not been adopted by any of the Australian states. The common position is that discipline is a matter for the contractors, whose personnel have the day-to-day responsibility for running the prison. The monitor's broad responsibility includes checking whether this function is being discharged lawfully, in terms of the general law, but it does not go beyond this. Naturally, the other mechanisms of accountability discussed in Chapter 4 are also available; but, short of major abuse, they cannot be activated in most disciplinary situations. The point that administration of punishment begins to merge into its allocation has simply not been perceived, it seems, in Australia.

The New Zealand model is slightly preferable, for it elevates the imposition of disciplinary penalties to the level where at least they must specifically be reported to and by the monitor. However, that person possesses no direct authority even if, for example, it seems that there has been some misuse of power or miscarriage of justice. The contractor sets the tone, and as long as there is no contractual breach there is no remedy.

In the United States, the normal position is that the contractor is also the disciplinarian. As to the substance of the rules, it should be reiterated that there will always be equivalence to the state system. As to procedures, the ACA standards, incorporated by cross-reference into all contracts, are quite detailed in their attempt to secure a reasonable degree of due process.[19]

Florida, however, is exceptional in that it circumscribes the role of the contractors. The enabling statute provides that a contract does not authorize the contractor to 'take any disciplinary action against an inmate'.[20] The manner in which this provision is operationalized is to have discipline administered by the contractor's custodial staff subject to confirmation or veto by the Department's on-site classification officer. A typical contract provides as follows:

> Disciplinary hearings will be conducted by Contractor staff who will make recommendations to the Department of Corrections classification officer. The . . . classification officer shall either accept those recommendations or prepare a written statement in which good cause for the rejection of those recommendations are established. In the event that a recommendation is rejected by the . . . classification officer, the Contractor shall have a right of administrative appeal to the Executive Director of the [Correctional Privatization] Commission.

This provision is the nearest approximation to the UK model to be found in the USA. Whilst it seems rather cumbersome, it is a clear acknowledgement of the importance of not blurring the line between the allocation and the administration of punishment.

In summary, the arrangement by which the contractors are also the disciplinarians is probably in a literal sense not destroying the dichotomy between administration and allocation of punishment. But it does become blurred. The preferable arrangements, ensuring a higher degree of accountability, are those found in the UK and Florida.

Other disciplinary matters

The approaches to disciplinary discretions, such as the temporary segregation of prisoners, parallel formal disciplinary sanctions. The UK assigns these matters to the controller 'except in cases of urgency'.[21] Florida seems to regard the matter as an aspect of formal discipline, and thus subject to the formula set out above. Other US states for the most part leave it to the contractor, subject to the constraints of the ACA standards.[22] The positions in Australia and New Zealand likewise parallel those set out above.

Managerial decisions

The whole range of minor impositions upon an inmate's quality of life, such as temporary suspension of visiting rights or withdrawal from a programme, are matters simply for the contractor's staff. It could hardly be otherwise if daily routines are to be maintained. The private sector is no different from the public in this regard.

Classification, sentence planning and transfer

Assessments made at initial reception into the prison system affect crucially the type of regime an inmate will have to endure. Even if it is accepted that one goes to prison *as* punishment, not *for* punishment, it could be said that wherever the sentence is served the custodial authorities are merely administering the already allocated punishment. Yet the reality in the perception of most prisoners is certainly that it is a greater punishment to serve time in a maximum-security institution than in a minimum-security one. If that initial decision is made by the private contractor rather than by the state, the line between allocating and administering punishment starts to become blurred.

Most states have finessed this problem successfully. In the UK, the question has not really arisen, for initial classification is virtually automatic by criteria developed under the Prison Rules. In most states of the USA, this is also true; initial classification depends on sentence length and type of conviction. However, some states, such as Florida, go further by specifically prohibiting private prison operators from becoming involved in classification matters.

In Australia one state – Queensland – has taken the opposite course, however. In letting the Arthur Gorrie contract, the Queensland authorities specified that one of the tasks of the private contractor would be to receive and classify all newly convicted prisoners. In that state initial classification is associated with sentence planning as a whole – the procedure by which the prisoner can anticipate the course of his progress down through security ratings, into various programmes and so on for the duration of his sentence. Of course, that plan is not immutable. But to the extent that it sets the reality of the prison experience, it is almost tantamount to the allocation of punishment rather than its administration.

This arrangement was surely a mistake not only in accountability terms but also in terms of the ability of the public authorities to control the engine-room of their whole correctional system. Classification and sentence planning decisions *par excellence* should be made by the public authorities. It does seem to be missing the point to state, as did the responsible executive within the QCSC (Macionis 1992: 4; emphasis added), that:

> This contract *breaks significant new ground* by contracting the management of the reception function to the private sector. As the [QCSC's] main reception centre, the Arthur Gorrie Correctional Centre performs the initial assessment and classification of offenders and is thus *a key part of the Commission's management process*.

The novelty of this arrangement would hardly seem to compensate for its penological inappropriateness.

As for the difficult question of transfer, around which so much prisoner angst revolves, an initial problem which emerged in the UK has now been overcome. The public sector unions, such as the Prison Officers' Association, have not gained industrial coverage of custodial workers in any state in which privatization has been introduced. The first reaction to this disappointment was accordingly to declare 'black' any prisoner who had at any previous time in his current sentence been detained in a private prison. By thus treating the private sector as self-contained, all kinds of transfer – from emergency dispersal to long-planned treatment programme – became impossible (Tumim 1994a: 61). Fortunately, this posture soon faded away, and as far as transfers are concerned the private and public sectors are now integrated.

This seems to be the position in all the other states. Transfer itself seems to take place within the normal administrative mechanisms and has been no more troublesome an issue in or out of private than public prisons.

Decisions related to release

Parole decisions in all states are made by autonomous authorities. However, personnel of the prisons where the applicant's sentence has been served may have the opportunity to make an input. This is because the Parole Board may well seek information as to his custodial conduct. Indeed, this practice has recently come very much back into fashion as parole decisions increasingly are supposed to take account of whether the prisoner has 'confronted his offending behaviour' whilst detained and what degree of future risk he poses to society. Whatever view one takes as to the appropriateness of these criteria, obviously it is sensible and appropriate that in such cases the managers of whatever prison he has been detained in should be consulted – whether that prison be public or private. But by the same token, it would be inappropriate for prison management – public or private – to seek to overbear the Parole Board by making a committed recommendation as to release or non-release. The Florida legislation recognizes this, and expresses it in terms which to date probably represent common practice with regard to private prisons:

> A contract entered into under this chapter does not authorise, allow or imply a delegation of authority to the contractor to:
> . . . recommend that the Parole Commission either deny or grant parole; however, the contractor may submit to the Parole Commission written reports that have been prepared in the ordinary course of business and shall respond to any written requests for information received from the Parole Commission.[23]

This formula certainly represents also the current practice in Australia (Harding 1992: 4).

As for day release, work release and other variants of release to facilitate a prisoner's reintegration into the community at the end of his sentence, private prisons are universally subject to whatever are the prevailing rules and practices in the particular jurisdiction. As long as the threshold eligibility criteria are met, many states permit a high degree of decision-making at a devolved level; others maintain tighter central control. Private prisons fit within the general pattern.

Penal policy and the profit motive

It was seen in Chapter 2 how strongly many critics feel about the intrusion, as they see it, of the profit motive into the running of prisons. Of course, they understood that there were already numerous people and interest groups who made a profit from imprisonment: construction companies, service suppliers ranging from electricians to teachers and medical practitioners, caterers, purchasers of prison industry products, and so on. However, the difference, it was said, was that none of these made a *sole business* out of their prison trade. They were also in general business, and thus not totally dependent upon prison trade as such. By contrast, private prison operators were in the business of running prisons; they could not switch the focus of their business at short notice. Without prisons – conveniently filled up by the state with prisoners – there would be no business for them. Accordingly, it was argued, private prison operators had a business or profit-making incentive for the continuation of, and preferably an increase in, high imprisonment-rate policies amongst governments. Privatization thus spawned a penal lobby which could only distort penal policy.[24]

The main problem with this argument is that it seems oblivious of the recent history of penal policy. In the USA there have been exponential increases in imprisonment rates and numbers for the last 15 years. Yet it is really only since the mid- to late 1980s that privatization has become a visible aspect of the adult imprisonment scene. Recently, several states have decided to accelerate this increase by adopting 'three strikes' laws. The state which led this trend – California – accommodates fewer than 1.5 per cent of its 100,000 or more prisoner population in private prisons. One could be forgiven for thinking that the private prison industry has a great deal of public imprisonment slack to take up before it becomes dependent for its survival on the adoption of even more oppressive penal policies.

In Australia much the same picture emerges. For example, in 1988 a conservative government was elected in New South Wales on a 'law and order' platform which included 'truth in sentencing' – which means no parole, reduced remission or good time. Over the next three years the prison population increased from 4003 (a rate of 70.7 per 100,000 population) to 5919 (100.2). This was the highest rate since 1907. Yet to that point privatization was not definitely on the political agenda. What put it there was the increase in prisoner numbers which in turn had been a function of deliberate governmental policy. Prison population increase drove privatization, not vice versa.

In South Australia the government has not even waited for an increase in its prison population. In effect, it first announced that it intended to bring about such an increase by means of 'truth-in-sentencing' legislation, and then moved straight into privatization to cope with the anticipated results of its policies.[25] So privatization commenced, at least in a pilot sense, with one small prison. The companies had not expected this and, with such a small base population of prisoners to draw upon, did not particularly relish getting involved in what was likely to be a marginal operation. However, once the commitment had been made they were drawn in on the toe-in-the-door principle.

In Victoria, too, 'truth in sentencing' will go hand in hand with privatization. If, as seems likely, the prison population increases by some 50 per cent over the next three to five years, it will not be because of privatization but because of penal policy.[26]

The UK is going down the same path. The mean rate of increase in the prison population between December 1992 and December 1995 was 9 per cent per annum. This followed the introduction of harsher sentencing policies in the 1991 Criminal Justice Act – legislation passed at a time when privatization was only just getting on to the practical agenda. Five years later, the government announced (Home Office 1996: 55) that it would adopt a whole raft of policies which on its own estimate would cause an increase of 10,800 in the prison population over the next decade. This would require 'some 12 new prisons which would come on stream at a rate of one or two each year from 2001–02 onwards . . . It is envisaged that the new prisons would be provided through the Private Finance Initiative'. This is the clearest example yet of a government first deciding upon a penal policy which will drive up the prison population and then looking to the private sector to finance it.

The fundamental point which emerges, then, is that governments do not need to be pushed; they jump of their own accord when it comes to introducing policies which will increase imprisonment rates. The evidence to date is that it is *as a consequence of those policies* that pressure for privatization arises. Of course, it could be said that the fact that the private sector comes to the party lets governments get away with not having to confront fully the impact of their own policies. That may well be true, but is hardly to the point. Given that governments are determined to implement such policies and offer private sector contractors opportunities to participate, it is hardly realistic to expect that each and every one of them would boycott the bidding process on a point of liberal principle.

The other point to emphasize is how much slack there is to take up. In Chapter 1 were set out the projected percentages of the total prison population which will be held in private prisons once 1995 commitments have been met. When those figures are read in conjunction with the fact that a large percentage of the prison estate or plant in each of the main countries is substandard and in need of capital-intensive refurbishment, it is evident that

there is an immense amount of room for additional private sector participation. In fact, that would still be so if the pie began to shrink, that is, prison
populations began to diminish.

Of course, this is not to say that the private sector will not make its views
about penal policy known to ministers and government officials. As noted in
Chapter 2, it is commonplace for a whole variety of 'non-expert' inputs to be
contributed to criminal justice policy development. However, the structural
realities are such that the impact of any private prisons lobby is, for the
foreseeable future, likely to be peripheral at best. The suggestion in Chapter 5
– that decisions as to the construction and siting of new prisons and whether
they should be public or private should be broadly overviewed by some sort
of standing parliamentary or legislative committee – would help ensure that
no such distortion of penal policy as the critics fear occurs in the future.

To complete this chapter, a case study will be described (Harding 1992)
which epitomizes exactly what critics fear about the distortion of penal policy
as a consequence of lobbying. The irony is that it relates to the detention
of juveniles, not adults, by the voluntary sector, not the for-profit private
sector. In other words, it illustrates the point made in Chapter 2 that
non-commercial activism may distort criminal justice policy no less than
commercial activism. This came about as follows.

From 1984, for just over a year, the Sydney City Mission – a charitable
body concerned with homelessness, the plight of street kids, domestic
violence and the like – ran a residential Wilderness programme, modelled on
the America Vision Quest scheme (Greenwood and Zimring 1985), at
Tallong, near Goulburn, New South Wales. Non-government money got the
programme to the pilot stage, but once operational it depended on funds
allocated by the state Youth and Community Services Department. To be
cost-effective and to utilize human resources optimally, the programme
required that a total of 160 youths should participate in the four-stage,
year-long programme. In other words, as 40 'graduated' at stage 4, a further
40 should enter at stage 1, and so on.

Youths entered the programme via the Juvenile Court, as a condition of
probation or a bond. However, before such a condition would be imposed,
the youth had to undergo an assessment by the operators of the Tallong
programme. A key aspect of this was willingness to sign a so-called 'contract'
to participate in the programme for the full scheduled period of one year. The
assessment process also screened out youths whose offences involved
premeditated violence or drug use. In other words, the participants were
mostly low-risk offenders who would otherwise probably not have been
incarcerated in the public system at all or at any rate for a far shorter period
than one year.

How did it come about that the courts were prepared to use their
sentencing powers in this way? The answer is that they were persuaded by the
infectious enthusiasm and misplaced good intentions of those responsible for

the programme that it would be in the youths' best interests. The very existence of the programme thus had a direct bearing upon the allocation of punishment. Effective lobbying had brought this about – lobbying by people of goodwill but whose programme depended for its survival upon state funding which in turn seemed to depend upon their being able to demonstrate full usage and optimal cost-effectiveness.

It should be stressed that there was no statutory basis for the Tallong project and no externally ascertainable standards. To all intents and purposes, there was no public accountability. After three separate inquiries, funding was withdrawn in 1985, leading to the immediate closure of the program (Harding 1992: 3).

What this saga of deeply flawed privatization illustrates is how far regulation and accountability of the private sector have now come. It is highly improbable, indeed almost inconceivable, that anything similar could happen today with regard to adult detention. The statutory and administrative structures governing the privatization of prisons paradoxically constitute a genuine constraint upon measures which might lead to 'private' justice.

Summary

This chapter has examined three key areas where the private sector must, in the public interest, be properly accountable to the public authorities. In the most important of these – driving penal policy for purposes of profit – there is no evidence that this has become a problem. With regard to the second most important – ensuring that the private prison operators only administer punishment and do not allocate it – some blurring has occurred in practice, even though the abstract position is legitimate. As for the matter of control over personnel, the position varies considerably from state to state but, overall, some tightening of accountability would be beneficial.

Notes

1 The concern here is with custodial workers rather than with professional, programme-delivery or visiting staff, since the former are at the cutting edge of order and equity within the institutional environment.
2 Of course, if there is a breach of the general criminal law, that is a matter for the police in the usual way.
3 Criminal Justice Act, ss. 85(1), 89(1).
4 Criminal Justice Act, s. 85(4).
5 Corrective Services (Administration) Act 1988, ss. 19(2)(f), 19(3).
6 Prisons (Contract Management) Act 1990, s. 31C, particularly 31C(3)(c).
7 Contracts (Management) Act 1993, s. 9A.

8 This comment excludes South Australia which, as explained in Chapter 3, has gone down the privatization track in the absence of enabling legislation.

9 Penal Institutions Act 1954, ss. 4B(4)(b) and (c), 4F and 6(2), enacted by ss. 3 and 4 of the Penal Institutions Amendment Act 1994.

10 Florida Statutes, 957.05(2)(a).

11 Kentucky Statutes, 197.510(19).

12 Arkansas Statutes 12-50-106(c)(1); Tennessee Statutes 41-4-140(a)(1).

13 American Correctional Association (1990: 3-4009).

14 American Correctional Association (1990: 3-4053; 3-4081).

15 In 1995 Wackenhut recruited an experienced Australian prison administrator to manage Junee.

16 Note also that American trainers were flown in to conduct an intensive, shortened preliminary training course at Blakenhurst for custodial staff just before that prison was opened.

17 Florida Statutes 957.06(3).

18 Arkansas Statutes 12-50-106(e)(3).

19 American Correctional Association (1990: 3-4214–3.4236).

20 Florida Statutes 957-06(4).

21 Criminal Justice Act, s. 85(4)(b).

22 American Correctional Association (1990: 3-4214–3-4261).

23 Florida Statutes, 957.06(6).

24 This perfectly respectable argument has sometimes taken on a rather far-fetched form. For example, it has been asserted in relation to Australia (George 1989: 57) that private prison operators 'will be in a position to publish lurid descriptions of violence in prisons, reinforcing a perceived need for increased facilities. This will feed the imagination of the media creating an environment of fear in the community. Such tactics will support policies that ensure that beds are full.'

25 See the feature article by Colin James in the *Adelaide Advertiser*, 21 January 1995.

26 Freiberg and Ross (1995) have argued to the contrary that the 'truth-in-sentencing' legislation has been structured in such a way as to maintain reasonable stability in the prison population. If their view turns out to be correct, it could be said that the presence of private prisons in Victoria demonstrably has not driven increases in the prison population.

7

Financial accountability and control

Many commentators see the main justification for privatizing prisons as lying in cost reduction. For example, the General Accounting Office of the USA stated in a 1991 review that, so far, 'empirical studies have not shown a clear [financial] advantage of private prisons over publicly-operated ones *and, therefore, a clear-cut recommendation favouring them cannot be made*' (author's emphasis) (General Accounting Office 1991: 29). It will by now be evident that such a conclusion is, in the author's view, something of a *non sequitur*. The hypothesis of this book is that privatization, properly regulated, can operate so as to bring about improvement across the whole penal system, and although as a by-product of this process there will usually be some worthwhile reduction in outlays, the alternative form of service delivery does not stand or fall simply by this expectation.[1]

The crux is *value for money*, penological and regime accomplishments as well as effective financial accountability being integral to this concept. As was apparent from Chapter 5, financial accountability starts with the terms of the contract itself. A contract which unambiguously sets out precisely what services must be provided to what standard for what payments facilitates accountability; a loose contract leaves the operator room for discretion, and thus the temptation to exercise it to the benefit of its own balance sheet. Similarly, a contract which identifies the amount and manner of payments for breach enhances accountability over one which leaves the matter to the general uncertainties of the law of contract and thus potential litigation.

No less important are the processes for achieving financial accountability. Are they ongoing or retrospective, internal or external, regular or random? Questions such as these bear upon the effectiveness of accountability arrangements.

Capital outlays in DCFM contracts

Public authorities are becoming much more experienced at letting construction contracts. The naivety epitomized by 'costs plus' contracts – which, for example, added about $15 million to the anticipated $75 million construction cost of the public sector Casuarina prison in Western Australia (Harding 1992) – has given way to the understanding that it is the construction company, not the government, which must carry the unforeseen risks, by way of a fixed-price contract. Moreover, penalty clauses for late completion are now normal. This symbolizes a long-overdue understanding that a delayed start is not somehow a 'benefit' in that recurrent outlays are thereby deferred to a later accounting period, but a cost because of the knock-on effects on planned organizational and financial changes.

In the USA, as previously explained, successful contractors habitually benefit from the favourable borrowing rates and tax breaks which would be available to the state itself; this is by way of the certificates of participation financing structure. Obviously, this is reflected in the total bid prices. However, both the UK and the Australian authorities have maintained an arm's-length posture, preferring to leave parties to sort out their own financial arrangements, whilst accepting that bid prices will thus reflect higher borrowing rates. Both positions are quite sensible and defensible. The matter is raised simply to exemplify the point that public authorities, for legitimate policy reasons, can reasonably decide to pay slightly more for a product or service, and that when this is done it is the policy itself that should be examined rather than the cost.

Management contracts

The price

Fortifying this last point, in no jurisdiction is there an absolute obligation for the public authorities to accept the cheapest bid. In the UK this is implicit from the notion of 'deliverability' built into the selection criteria. Indeed, the very first contract – that relating to The Wolds – was not awarded to the lowest qualified bidder. The eight bids were whittled down to three – Group 4, Wackenhut UK[2] and U.K. Detention Services.[3] The selection panel reported:

> [A]ll three companies presented good, high quality bids and the general consensus was that all three were probably capable of running Wolds. However, the panel concluded that the bid put forward by Group 4 offered the best value for money. Although not the cheapest of the three short-listed firms, Group 4's bid of £21.52 million over five years was

£3.66 million lower than the Prison Service benchmark, and offered assured quality.

(National Audit Office 1994: 2.15)

In fact, the costs subsequently escalated, because the contract had been written too loosely. 'The Home Office accept that there were gaps in the original contract and are sorting them out with Group 4 on a reasonable basis.' (National Audit Office 1994: 2.22; Tumim 1994a: 115–16.) This illustrates the point made earlier about the symbiotic relationship between contractual clarity and financial control. However, the immediate point is the desirability of leaving the public authorities with some room to make value judgements rather than subjugating them to the unyielding tyranny of the bottom line.

In this regard, the most formulaic of the US states still leaves some room for manoeuvre. Even Florida, which has 18 scoring zones subdivided into 107 different possible marks, allows for the possibility that the lowest-priced bid may not succeed. This is because in a standard DCFM contract only 20 per cent of the available marks are allocated to cost factors (15 per cent for operating *per diem* costs, 5 per cent for per-bed construction costs). Whilst this is the single largest scoring area, the theoretical possibility nevertheless remains open that a more costly bid may prevail – being, presumably, better value for money.

However, most US states require that, in order even to qualify for consideration, bidders must first surmount the hurdle of under-bidding the public system. After all, that is where it all began – the reduction of correctional expenditure. The reference in The Wolds discussion to a Prison Service benchmark price shows that, in practice, this is also a cogent factor in the UK.[4] But in the USA it has been promoted to a mandatory statutory requirement. The Florida formula exemplifies one of the two prevailing approaches to this issue:

The commission may not enter into a contract . . . unless the commission determines that the contract . . . will result in cost savings to the state of at least 7 percent over the public provision of a similar facility. Such cost savings as determined by the commission must be based upon the actual costs associated with the construction and operation of similar facilities or services as certified to the commission by the Auditor General.[5]

The section then sets out in minute detail how the auditor general is to make his calculations.

It must be said that this task has been carried out with great care and very informatively. Such an exercise compels very tight and precise attribution of expenses to activities. In relation to the first two proposed 750-bed private prisons, the auditor general conducted a close analysis of the bids of the two

successful bidders – Wackenhut and CCA. The benchmark was the
construction and operating costs of three state institutions of comparable
size. But care had to be taken to compare like with like. Accordingly, items
had to be added to the public sector costs to compensate for the fact that
neither education nor substance abuse programmes were being run in those
prisons. When this was done, both favoured bidders came out just over 10 per
cent ahead of the public system, so the contracts could go ahead (State of
Florida: Office of the Auditor General 1993).

Texas and Kentucky have a similar requirement, though with a saving of
10 per cent required. By contrast, states such as Arkansas, Virginia and
Tennessee have adopted more flexible formulae. The Tennessee provisions
exemplify this second main US approach. The applicable law states that the
initial contract

> shall be for three years to allow the contractor sufficient time to
> demonstrate its performance and to provide sufficient information to
> allow a comparison of the performance of the contractor to the
> performance of the state in operating similar facilities.

The key review thus takes place at renewal time:

> The contract may be renewed only if the contractor is providing at least
> the same quality of services as the state at a lower cost, or if the
> contractor is providing services superior to those provided by the state
> at essentially the same cost.[6]

A statutory body, the Select Oversight Committee on Corrections, is
mandated to undertake such reviews.

As with the Florida auditor general's evaluation, it must be said that the
first such review – of the CCA contract in relation to the South Central
Correctional Center – was thorough and informative (Tennessee Select
Oversight Committee 1995). Whilst many of the comparison points were
mechanical, nevertheless the review took in 'qualitative issues' such as
discipline, use of force, deaths in custody, programme activities and 'success'
rates. The contract was subsequently renewed, on the basis that services of
the same quality were being provided at a cost that the state could not match.

These two approaches – finite cost-saving and measurable value for money
– in essence capture the US position. The first approach seems to pose a
potential self-contradiction, however. If the public sector does indeed
improve its financial performance because of cross-fertilization and competition, its cost structures should eventually become comparable with those
of the private sector. A point will be reached where contractors simply cannot
under-cut by a further 7 per cent or 10 per cent or any other amount. Is
privatization to phase out at that stage? If so, the very foundation stone of
public sector improvement will have been removed. The Tennessee formula
seems preferable.

The Australian position (and also the New Zealand one) is akin to that in the UK. The enabling statutes make no reference to the financial criteria applicable to bids; these are to be settled in-house between the responsible ministers and bureaucrats. The invariable practice has been to leave open the possibility that the cheapest bid may not necessarily succeed. For example, the 1990 Request for Tenders in relation to Junee provided that 'the Principal reserves the right not to accept the best or lowest tender and may elect not to proceed or to accept any tender'.[7] More recently, the Tender Documentation relating to Woodford Correctional Centre in Queensland provided as follows:

> The aim of the evaluation criteria is to select a Contractor who can supply the best value for money service to the Commission. The Tender Evaluation Committee may recommend a Contractor who is NOT the lowest priced conforming tenderer. The Committee may recommend a Contractor who has proposed a higher quality service (than the lowest priced tenderer) which in the view of the Committee justifies payment of a higher fee.[8]

Of course, price sensitivity is bound to be a major factor. And as it happens, in contrast to the UK position, each of the Australian contracts so far awarded has gone to the lowest bidder. But that alone has not been the determinant factor.

In summary, initial pricing is interwoven with financial accountability. All of the jurisdictions which have embarked on privatization have, to a greater or lesser degree, recognized that there must be some room for the public authorities to manoeuvre, consistent with probity, when awarding or renewing the contracts. If they were ever in any doubt about this, the self-imposed angst of the INS in having accepted what possibly was a low-ball bid in relation to the Elizabeth, New Jersey, detention facility will have reinforced the point. But, equally, the public authorities are mindful of the fact that there is certainly some financial slack to be taken up, that they can expect to receive tenders that are substantially below their own previous costings, and that it is their responsibility to reduce public outlays if this can be done without compromising quality.

Occupancy rates and payment

The first Australian contract – Borallon – was based on the notion of 100 per cent occupancy of available places. The QCSC agreed to pay a set amount, averaging A\$34,670 per prisoner in the first year, A\$38,750 in the second year and A\$42,000 in the third year. It was thus incumbent upon it to fill up the places for which it was paying, and at such rates it was eager actually to do so. One advantage which seemed to flow from this way of structuring the costs was that the contractors had no incentive to keep pressing for a supply of inmates and thus, conceivably, to get involved in penal policy debates.

From the outset, the US public authorities have been more canny than this, recognizing that there is a point at which a critical economic mass of inmates is reached and that thereafter the marginal costs incurred by the contractor are considerably reduced. Most contracts accordingly provide for a *per diem* rate up to a given percentage and a lesser rate thereafter. A recent Florida contract epitomizes this approach, viz. US$47.30 per inmate *per diem* guaranteed up to 90 per cent notional occupancy and US$8.61 for each actual inmate above that percentage.[9] Variants of this are standard in the USA.

The initial UK contracts were not dissimilar to the Australian in the way the cost structure was agreed. During the first fully operational year at The Wolds, each bed cost the Prison Service approximately £350 per week or about £18,000 per annum, whether it was occupied or not. Subsequently, however, the contracts have become more subtle. For example, the 100 per cent occupancy costing is about to be modified. The contracts let in relation to Fazakerley and Bridgend focus upon the question of 'available beds'. Instead of assuming that 100 per cent occupancy will always be possible if sufficient prisoners are supplied, the contract now requires that the contractors establish positively on a daily basis the number of beds that are actually available. It is for these only that they will be paid. This is hardly, perhaps, the most radical tightening up of the previous arrangements, but certainly is indicative of a keener appreciation of the financial soft spots which previously have inured to the benefit of the contractors.

The other change is more fundamental. The most recent UK contracts – for example, Doncaster – specifically allow for overcrowding. This may be, and in the case of Doncaster actually is, up to 50 per cent, i.e. an extra 385 prisoners over and above the certified normal accommodation of 770. In the event that the public authority exercises its option to require overcrowding, the capital costs of tooling up to do so will be covered by negotiation. However, the operating costs will be increased by only 20 per cent or thereabouts – for 50 per cent more prisoners. Clearly, this is a 'cheap' option for the Prison Service but, if the comparative US figures are any guide, a profitable one for the contractor. This point will be explored further in Chapter 9.

Other standard clauses: escalation, insurance and indemnity

It is now normal for contractors in all jurisdictions to be required to carry building and plant insurance. With some recent history of riots and arson, this is not cheap – over £1.5 million per annum, for example, in relation to Doncaster. Contractors are not generally permitted to carry their own risk.

Public liability insurance is also required, as well as an indemnity from the contractor to the public authority for successful claims brought against it.

This is necessary because the prison remains in law ultimately the responsibility of the public authorities. A standard provision is that evidence that insurance cover is being maintained must be given to the public authority.

Price escalation is naturally allowed for in all contracts. Once more, authorities are getting cannier. The most commonly adopted formulae confine annual increases to inflation rates or less.

These areas, then, all demonstrate the kind of evolving contractual precision and hard-headedness which facilitate effective financial accountability.

Sanctions for breach

What public authorities require above all is an *administrative relationship* with their contractors. Running prisons is too volatile a business for litigation to be the primary means of dispute resolution. Apart from anything else, by the time litigation has got to court, the problem area would in all likelihood have blown up in the operator's – and thus the public authority's – face. That is why it is absolutely standard in all jurisdictions for there to be either a statutory provision or a contractual clause or both permitting termination of the whole arrangement at very short notice. Litigation can then take place, if necessary, retrospectively. Reference has already been made to the termination of the contract between the Immigration and Naturalization Service and Esmor Correctional Services Inc. This was done after a rapid internal inquiry carried out by INS – not a procedure required by the particular contract but certainly a prudent one if the ultimate sanction of termination is thought to be a possibility.

Short of this extreme recourse, if accountability is to be effective some kind of mid-level financial sanction may be required – something that treats the contract as of continuing validity but which nevertheless enables the public authority to assert some control. A few states require the contractor to lodge a performance bond, but this is unusual. No less effective is the fact that payment is always in arrears, normally by a month or so. As most contracts require that some appropriate person – the controller and/or the area manager in the UK, the contract monitor and/or a responsible head-office person in the Australian states and several of the US states, the executive director of the Correctional Privatization Commission in Florida, and so on – must certify due performance before payment, there is a strong control point and a ready mechanism to levy compensation for inadequate performance.

However, unilateral decisions to withhold fees are hardly conducive to constructive relationships between parties whose need to work together is ongoing and likely to be long-lasting. As one would expect, graduated responses are provided for either in the contracts themselves or as a matter of practice. The UK situation captures the essence of what is found in all jurisdictions. The practice which has evolved is as follows.

If the on-site controller sees a mismatch between required performance and actuality, the first stage will be informal negotiation with the prison director. Should the problem persist, the response is upgraded to formal notification, though still verbal. After that comes a warning letter, and if the matter is still unresolved a default notice is served. This identifies the rectification required and the scope of possible compensation. Experience so far suggests that the contractor will respond promptly at this point, but may be somewhat tardy otherwise. A four-stage process is certainly elaborate and possibly suggestive of capture – over-anxiousness to keep the working relationship intimate and friendly rather than formal and businesslike. Yet it is not so different from practices that have evolved in both the United States and Australia.

There has been one occasion in the UK where a contractor has been 'fined' for poor performance. On that occasion, the four-stage process was by-passed. The circumstances arose out of a major disturbance which occurred at Blakenhurst prison in February 1994, some nine months after it started taking in prisoners. In the words of the chief inspector of prisons (Tumim 1995: 42) the incident

> involved the loss for a short time of one set of security keys snatched from a . . . custody officer and subsequent damage to the main staff office in Houseblock 3 (costing £25,000 to £30,000 to repair). The causes . . . were . . . the absence of effective systems to control inmate behaviour within houseblocks, an excessively tolerant attitude to unacceptable behaviour and, crucially, inadequate training for prisoner custody officers in the detailed business of controlling prisoners and applying legitimate rules.

The disturbance lasted eight hours, but was resolved peacefully.

Each of these causes arguably involved to some degree a failure to attain or a positive breach of contract standards. Even so, the controller was apparently not initially minded to impose a penalty. It is possible he shared the chief inspector's view (Tumim 1995: 81) that 'errors were not confined to the Contractor. Too many prisoners had been transferred to Blakenhurst before a settled culture could be established and the prison's managers felt themselves unable to transfer troublemakers to other establishments.' However, head office saw the incident as providing an opportunity to demonstrate that the financial sanctions clauses were not included in the contract merely as a sham. A sum of £50,000 was withheld from the next due payment. No litigation was threatened or commenced, and the working relationship of the parties evidently recovered quickly from this incident.

External and internal accountability mechanisms

In a day-to-day sense, the people on the ground – monitors, controllers, internal auditors, and so on – inevitably and properly keep their eye on whether the services contracted for are being performed to the agreed standard. There can be no substitute for this. In the UK, however, it is considered that the adjudicatory or disciplinary function of the controller is so demanding of his time that the contract compliance aspect of the role needs boosting. It will be recalled that the chief inspector expressed some concern that, at both The Wolds and Blakenhurst, there seemed in this regard to have been some over-identification of the controller with the contractor. He went on to characterize as a 'serious weakness' the 'absence of systems for checking the financial aspects of the contract', which had led in his view to a surprising failure to impose monetary penalties upon Group 4 in default of their meeting some quite specific contract obligations at The Wolds (Tumim 1994a: 115–16).

The virtual inevitability of this kind of regulatory softness in the context where the controller is carrying out the crucial function of adjudications has been acknowledged within the Contracts and Competition Group. By the time Fazakerley and Bridgend are operational – with their greater emphasis as explained above on financial control – it is likely that the controller function will have been enhanced by the addition of a person whose main responsibility will be the nitty-gritty of contract compliance. It should be added that comparable stresses could be expected wherever the monitoring arrangement takes in a substantial range of tasks beyond that of contract compliance.

However, as already shown, the most searching reviews of the financial aspects of prison privatization have emanated from external bodies: the General Accounting Office of the United States at a system-wide level; the auditor general of the state of Florida within that state; the Select Oversight Committee on Corrections in Tennessee; the National Audit Office in the case of The Wolds in the UK. In Australia there are equivalent bodies – for example, in New South Wales the Public Accounts Committee of the parliament and in Queensland the Public Sector Management Commission. Each of these has already taken a searching look at privatization protocols, with unstinting approval in New South Wales that 'best practice' had been carried out with regard to Junee (New South Wales Public Accounts Committee 1993: 131) and with some minor adverse criticism in Queensland (Public Sector Management Commission 1993: 114–25).

Reviews of this type address the broader issues of costing, modes of writing contracts, benefits to the state, alternative approaches, value for money – not the minutiae of daily financial control. Effective financial accountability depends upon both limbs of control and scrutiny.

Market forces

There is one further aspect of accountability to which there is no public sector equivalent – market forces. The public sector simply does not go out of existence if it fails or see its market value decline if it does a bad job. When Strangeways was burned down, public funds rebuilt it; there were no Prison Service 'shares' to be savaged by disillusioned investors.

Contrast this with the fate of Esmor shares when the INS detention facility contract was terminated. During the second half of 1994 Esmor had become listed on the NASDAQ exchange. In trading over the next six or eight months, it had more than doubled its listing price. In June 1995, with the revelations about the troubles at the INS facility and the market anticipating the loss of the contract, the share price plunged from $20 to $8. The consequential loss to leading company personnel in the value of their stock options was in some cases of the order of $1 million. This has provided a powerful incentive for the company to get itself back on track, which it is now doing successfully.[10]

Similarly, consider the case of Pricor Inc. In early editions of Thomas's *Private Adult Correctional Facility Census*, Pricor appeared as a prominent player, operating or commissioned to manage no less than six facilities – at that time comparable with Wackenhut or CCA. However, its principal client – the Texas Department of Corrections – was not satisfied with its services. It announced that it was taking Pricor's operating institutions back under direct management at the expiry of the various contracts and not proceeding with the remainder. This was done. Subsequently, some of those institutions were reprivatized, with new operators. Pricor no longer exists as a corporate entity.

It would be naive to deceive oneself into thinking that stock market considerations can drive penal standards. Nor, indeed, should they do so. Nevertheless, the knowledge that one can fail so completely as to go out of business altogether or to lose major profits imposes a discipline to which the public sector has never been subject. These considerations of financial accountability keep operators on their toes in a way which has never been the case with the operators of Attica or Santa Fe or Strangeways or Bathurst or Mangaroa or Jika Jika. From the point of view of overall accountability and the public interest, that cannot be a bad thing.

Summary

Every indication is that the structure of financial accountability of the private prison sector is strong. Control points exist from the commencement of bidding right through to the letting of the contract and the continuation of its performance. At the level of financial scandal, it is inconceivable that some penological equivalent of the Savings and Loans débâcle or the plundering of the Maxwell group pension funds is in the wings waiting to make an appearance. With private prisons also there will be no equivalent of the construction contract scams or the transportation system extortion rackets which in the past have often bedevilled public sector contracts. Defalcations will, at worst, be comparatively minor; breaches will not involve the state in open-ended liabilities. On the incentive side, private operators will have every reason to comply with their obligations, to avoid penalties and to maintain corporate success. Whatever the philosophical, political or practical problems of prison privatization, financial accountability is not one of them.

Notes

1 In 1996 the General Accounting Office looked again at the issue of prison privatization. Once more its focus was predominantly that of comparative public/private sector costs, and the document examines five post-1990 studies on this topic carried out by various scholars and departments. Its rather lame conclusion was that 'we could not conclude . . . that privatization of correctional facilities will not save money. However, these studies do not offer substantial evidence that savings have occurred' (General Accounting Office 1996: 3). As in 1991, that in itself seems to be regarded as a sufficient basis upon which to procrastinate about privatization. However, in contrast to the earlier review, some attempt is also made to pursue the 'value for money'/regime quality question. In that regard also the findings of the report are ambivalent.

   Each aspect of the analysis is in several ways unconvincing, ignoring several other relevant studies, partially misconstruing those it does examine and making some rather pedantic arguments as to the validity of other work in the area. Despite its status as the most recent such study, it does not possess the cogency to displace the other meta-studies referred to at various points in the text.

2 Subsequently reincorporated as Premier Prisons Ltd.

3 The UK vehicle of Corrections Corporation of America.

4 The fear is that it has started to become an end in itself, providing the nominal justification for a cut of 13.3 per cent in the 1996/97 operating budget of the public prisons (see *The Guardian Weekly*, 21 January 1996; and *The Guardian*, 19 February 1996).

5 Florida Statutes, 957.07.

6 Tennessee Statutes, 41-24-105 (a) and (d).

7 NSW Department of Corrective Services, Request for Tenders for Junee Correctional Centre, 1990, clause 4.6.

8 Tender Documentation, §8.0.

9 Contract between the Florida Correctional Privatization Commission and Wackenhut Corrections Corporation for the operation of Glades County Correctional Facility, June 1994.

10 Of course, it could be said that this direct financial impact gives the operator an even stronger incentive to conceal malfeasance. That is certainly true. However, if the public accountability mechanisms which are the subject-matter of this book are working properly, along with media curiosity and ginger group activism, such a strategy would have an extremely limited likelihood of success for more than a very short time. Once exposed, the damage to the operating company would be even greater.

8

Comparing public and private prisons

Empirical data will never refute ideological objections to privatization, of the sort identified and discussed in Chapter 2. The proponents are arguing from a different premise. However, there are other critics of privatization who are at the same time profoundly uncomfortable at the waste, squalor, brutality and demoralization of much of the public system. Sensible and rigorous evaluations of the comparative performance of the two systems could sway their judgement. By the same token, there are some protagonists of privatization who could never be dissuaded by data, whilst the continuing support of others may be influenced by the cogency of the research evidence.

During the last decade or so, as privatization has spread, evaluation studies have become more numerous. One of the first (Levinson 1985) related to the operation in Florida by a private, not-for-profit organization of a secure facility for adjudicated delinquents. This book, as was emphasized earlier, is not directly concerned with either the juvenile private sector or non-governmental organization/volunteer/not-for-profit participation in any level of corrections. However, the methodological problems of evaluation in these areas are common to those relevant to adult imprisonment. The studies themselves in fact overlap, for one part of the literature feeds off the other parts. Accordingly reference will be made, where appropriate, to the whole gamut of such studies. In fact, several more years went by before evaluations relating principally to adult private prisons began to appear (Brakel 1988; Hatry *et al.* 1989; 1993; Logan and McGriff 1989; Logan 1992; Ethridge and Marquart 1993; Sechrest and Shichor 1993; Brown 1994; Moyle 1994; Bottomley *et al.* 1996a).

It is not proposed to set out here the findings of these studies. At least three conscientious and comprehensive meta-studies are now available (Thomas and Logan 1993; Shichor 1995; Bottomley *et al.* 1996a). However, the point for present purposes is that, valuable as such evaluations can be, they may proceed on a shaky premise – namely, that the issue of whether or not privatization should go ahead can be decided by lining up examples of the two systems side by side and somehow measuring their respective perform-ances. The hypothesis of this book is that public and private prisons are merely two (and not necessarily the only two) alternative forms of service delivery within a single system, two components of a total system; and that it is the performance of that total system which, if at all, will justify the adoption and retention of the private sector component.

It is important to pursue the logic of this position. It follows that if the performance of the public sector component comes to exceed that of the private sector component either across the board or in particular ways, the justification for the private sector component does not automatically fall away. The key question would remain whether the performance of the total system continues to be enhanced by the involvement of the private sector: the notion of cross-fertilization. Ways of identifying, if not precisely measuring, these enhancements will be discussed later. In the previous chapter, it was warned that a cost formula which eventually squeezes out the private sector would almost certainly be counter-productive; the costs of the public sector would inexorably drift upwards once the competitive discipline was re-moved. The same is likely to be true of qualitative factors, such as programme delivery, health regimes and general penal environment.

To pursue this point even further, neither would it follow that the public sector component should be phased out if it could be demonstrated that it was uniformly inferior to the private sector component. Service monopoly, who-ever the monopolizer, begets slovenliness and self-interest. Systems require balance. Learmont's (1995: 106) report grasped this point when it stated:

> The Inquiry concluded that the continued existence of a substantial public sector is vital for the stability of the [Prison] Service as a whole . . . However, there were lessons to be learned from private prisons which should be applied across the Service.

Coming back, then, to evaluative studies, their value does not reside primarily in their ability to resolve the question whether or not to privatize. Rather, they should enable strong and weak aspects of the two components to emerge and areas for productive cross-fertilization to be identified. This is so whether the studies relate to cost, programmes, environment or attitudes, and whether they are processual, quantitative or qualitative in their approach.

Official attitudes towards research: control or co-operation?

One of the tenets of accountability highlighted in Chapter 2 was that in-dependent research and evaluation must be built into private sector arrange-ments.

In the USA, neither the enabling statutes nor standard contracts make explicit reference to this issue. However, American Correctional Association (ACA) standards – invariably built into the contract by cross-reference – are drafted in terms which apparently regard independent research as a normal, rather than an abnormal, aspect of prison management:

> Written policy and procedure govern the conduct of research in the institution, including compliance with professional and scientific ethics and with state and federal guidelines for the use and dissemination of research findings.
>
> The warden/superintendent reviews and approves all institutional research projects prior to implementation to ensure they conform with the policies of the parent agency.[1]

Whether on account of these formal provisions or because there in any case exists a strong research tradition in US penology, it is worth noting that the earliest and most numerous independent research projects relating to private prisons have in fact emanated from there. Researchers have evidently not encountered too many stumbling blocks.

The contrast with the UK could hardly be greater. The experience of Bottomley and his colleagues, investigating the operation of The Wolds and a comparable public sector prison, encapsulates the profound ambivalence of the public authorities towards research into private prisons. The first point to note (Bottomley *et al.* 1996a: 2) is that the Prison Service, about to embark upon a major innovation in service delivery, had given no thought at all to the possibility of either undertaking directly or commissioning any evaluation of this project. The pressure came from various researchers and also from Group 4, the successful bidder. Eventually, research was commissioned and funds made available by the Home Office. One could be forgiven for imagining that the authorities would, at this stage, want to ensure the best value for their own money. However, as already mentioned, the astonishing corollary was that the researchers were not permitted access either to the tender documents or even to the operating contract itself (Bottomley *et al.* 1996a: 3). Group 4 itself had no objection; it was the Contracts and Competition Group within the Home Office which prevaricated and eventually refused. This tasteless saga continued with a long delay in publication of the work, completed in December 1994 but not available until mid-1996.

The present point is not to try to make sense of all this by ascertaining the minutiae of how it came about. It is enough to recognize the culture of control which this epitomizes and which is also to be found in relation to *all* prison research in the UK. This culture is the very antithesis of an approach to prison privatization which would work so as to benefit the total system. What is needed is a research–evaluation–modification loop, not a cul-de-sac.

The Australian position lies somewhere in between. The niggling issue which has not quite been resolved is whether the decision to approve an independent research project should lie with the public authority or the private operator. And if initially with the one, should the other have a power of veto? This is the problem which Moyle (1994) encountered with regard to Borallon, though in the end neither party would permit the project to move to the second stage. The latest version (1 April 1995) of the Borallon contract is silent on this issue. The other states have also left the matter up in the air.

New Zealand, teeing up for privatization, has taken a clear position. Contracts will contain a clause providing that the secretary of the Department of Corrections will have access to the institution for the purposes of research, either directly or through persons authorized by him, but that no one else shall access for that purpose. In other words, the contractors will not have a power to veto approved researchers, nor will they be permitted to by-pass the public authorities and make direct deals with outsiders (personal communication, 9 June 1995). Of course, their freedom to carry out their own corporate research will not be constrained.

Whether the Australian and New Zealand positions will conform with the suggested tenet of accountability will very much depend upon how administrators choose to apply their powers. The issue will certainly be tested quite soon, for interest in this kind of research is building up. Although the present author's own experience stands in marked contrast to that of Bottomley and his colleagues,[2] nevertheless it does seem that in the UK a change of culture is needed. So far the US approach is the preferable one.

The aims of imprisonment and Logan's 'confinement quality index'

It has been suggested that it is 'not entirely without significance that the era of the development of private prisons has coincided with the decline of the "rehabilitative ideal" within prisons' (Bottomley et al. 1996a: 6). This view seems to presuppose that the public system somehow could boast some previous achievements in this regard and that, by contrast, it is endemic to private imprisonment that such achievements could never be matched. Whatever one's view as to these matters, it can confidently be said that it would be wellnigh impossible methodologically to evaluate the comparative performance of the private and the public sectors of the prison system in this regard. Apart from the usual difficulties of isolating the factors which drive criminal careers, there is also the fact that most prisoners who serve some part of their sentence in a private prison will also serve some part of it in a public prison. The researcher would be chasing a shadow.[3]

It is in this context that Logan (1992) developed his 'confinement quality index'. This represents one of the most viable ways of approaching comparative studies. He states:

> The criteria proposed here for comparative evaluation of prisons are normative, rather than consequentialist or utilitarian. They are based on a belief that individual prisons ought to be judged primarily according to the propriety and quality of what goes on inside their walls – factors over which prison officials may have considerable control.
>
> (Logan 1992: 579)

He goes on to identify eight distinct dimensions of prison regime quality: security, safety, order, care, activity, justice, conditions and management. These notions are further operationalized by identification of sub-themes. A confinement quality index can then be constructed drawing on formal protocols, staff perceptions and prisoner perceptions, and comparative ratings made using statistical methods.

It is all too easy to be derogatory about this sort of approach. Sparks (1994: 23), for example, complains that, however well private prisons come out in such comparisons, this settles none of the prior questions about the legitimacy of the penalty of imprisonment in any given case. Quite so. Sparks's observation simply takes one back to the point that ideologically derived positions can seldom be influenced by empirical data.

However, Logan's approach does not lack a theoretical basis. Rupert Cross (1971: 84) argued that 'the chances of deterioration in prison are at least as great as those of reform'. He continued:

> [N]o one should be disposed to doubt the existence of deformative risks ... There is a real danger that someone who is already a bad man when he goes into prison will come out worse; hence the crucial importance of what can best be described as 'anti-deformative action' in our prisons ... [T]he main aim of prison reform should be the prevention of prisoners' deterioration.
>
> (Cross 1971: 85–6)

This also ties in perfectly with the philosophy running through the Woolf Report (Woolf and Tumim 1991). Above all Woolf emphasized 'the importance of security, control and justice to a stable prison system' (Woolf and Tumim 1991: 9.1–9.99), as well as the impact of overcrowding upon conditions (particularly hygiene), the paucity of programmes and other out-of-cell activities, and the frustration of the managers and officers on the ground in not being able truly to manage their prisons according to local needs because of the stifling effect of centralized control.[4] His report thus focuses upon all of those matters which can and do lead to deterioration. An alternative way of viewing the report is that, without ever using that phrase, Woolf is in fact echoing and endorsing Logan's 'confinement quality index'. Clearly, a prison which erupts in riots, arson and sodomy, as did Strangeways, can hardly rate well in terms of confinement quality.

Since Woolf, several inspections by the chief inspector of prisons have cast doubt upon the capacity of the public system to improve itself from within. For example, the Cardiff inspection (Tumim 1993: 1) concluded:

> The treatment of prisoners at Cardiff was, in some important respects, a disgrace. Very low standards of hygiene, inadequate clothing arrangements and failure to provide basic programmes for prisoners had gone unchecked for several years. Lethargy had overtaken the Establishment, and Management was paralysed from bringing about improvements . . . [T]reatment and conditions were as bad as we have found in any prison inspected by us.

The Leeds inspection (Tumim 1994b: 104) was equally dismal:

> Conditions for inmates and staff at Leeds were deeply unsatisfactory and well below the standards expressed in the Prison Service's vision and values statement. It was depressing that, in spite of improvements to some buildings, little had changed in conditions since the last inspection in 1989 [i.e. pre-Woolf].

In this context the value of some viable measure of the quality of confinement, as opposed to grandiose abstractions about the socio-political legitimacy of the penalty of imprisonment, can hardly be doubted. It is, as Cross pointed out, commonly observed that many offenders come out of prison 'worse' than when they went in – worse not only in the sense that they have now 'graduated', as the popular press would have it, from 'a university of crime', but also because their exposure to the contempt, indifference and moral brutality of prison leaves them angrier, more bitter and even less well equipped emotionally and attitudinally to seize the decreasing number of positive choices that may still exist for them upon release. Indices such as Logan's enable some attempt to be made to keep track of a prison's 'anti-deformative' ethos. Applied equally across the two components of the total prison system, they facilitate identification of strengths and weaknesses, achievements and failures; and they enable the process of positive cross-fertilization to commence by highlighting managerial, processual and other differences between those components. But, to reiterate, they do not provide a sole platform from which to answer the question whether or not to privatize.

The perceptions of the players: prisoners, managers and staff

The prisoners

Reference has already been made to the fact that, in the early days of Borallon, experienced inmates tried to vote with their feet, and a stand-by list of applicants for transfer came into existence. The formal review (Kennedy

1988) preceding the decision to go ahead with privatization in Queensland had likewise heard evidence from prisoners that this was likely to be their response. In the same vein, the UK chief inspector of prisons, reviewing The Wolds, recorded that 'several inmates claimed that, anticipating conviction and sentence, they had repeatedly pleaded not guilty in order to extend their time at The Wolds to take advantage of the excellent conditions' (Tumim 1994a: 50). Of course, evidence of this kind should be treated with a degree of scepticism because of the structural inequality of the parties and the circumstances in which it is given. And naturally what prisoners desire may not necessarily be what is optimal for penal policy as a whole. Nevertheless, it would be perverse and intellectually arrogant to disregard completely the views of 'consumers'. It should be noted in this regard that Woolf (Woolf and Tumim 1991: Appendix 1, Chapters 1 and 2) regarded prisoner views and feedback as methodologically a crucial aspect of his own report, giving ballast and illustrative detail to his committee's own observations.

Some evidence of prisoner perceptions is anecdotal or journalistic; other evidence is survey-based. An interesting example of the former arises out of the publication of the Tennessee Select Oversight Committee evaluation of the South Central Correctional Center in that state, operated by CCA, as compared with two state prisons. A press story (*New York Times*, 19 August 1995) found one inmate who regarded South Central as the best of half a dozen he had sampled over the years – 'It's cleaner, you get more choice of food and the staff is more patient and willing to make time' – and another who was ruing the day he had sought transfer to a state facility to be with his brother. The present author's conversations with private prison inmates in Australia, the UK and the USA revealed similar sentiments – and not once the contrary. Similarly, the chief inspector of prisons encountered enthusiastic reactions from prisoners at The Wolds (Tumim 1994a: 49–50), although he found less enthusiasm at Blakenhurst (Tumim 1995: 34–5).

Obviously, survey-based evidence, where available, is preferable to anecdotal. The earliest example in the literature is that of Brakel (1988), who reported positive inmate attitudes towards a private prison in Hamilton County, Tennessee. A small number of prisoners were able to offer direct and recent comparisons with a nearby public system facility, mostly to the advantage of the private prison. But, as Shichor (1995: 212–13) points out, the sample was not truly random but selected by the chaplain on the basis of the respondents' being reasonably articulate.

However, that part of the work of Hatry *et al.* (1989; 1993) relating to secure juvenile institutions was methodologically not problematical, and indicated that 'for a substantial majority of the performance indicators the privately operated facilities had at least a small advantage'. This view was based on survey data, and was shared by staff and inmates.

Logan's own findings in his confinement quality index study ironically point in the opposite direction. In terms of both the formal protocols and staff perceptions, the private facility scored best, often by very large margins. But in relation to inmate perceptions the state prison outscored the private one, by more modest margins.

In the UK, the work at The Wolds by Bottomley and his colleagues is the first independent attempt to ascertain inmates' views in a formal way. Despite the early operational problems identified by the chief inspector (Tumim 1994a) and the subsequent alteration to the inmate mix, a very high degree of satisfaction was expressed. As many as 80 per cent of prisoners regarded The Wolds as better than other (public sector) prisons they had experienced, and the quality of staff–inmate relationships was highlighted as a particularly strong feature (Bottomley *et al*. 1996b). The private operators at The Wolds also conduct regular inmate surveys for their own management purposes – something that is anathema to public sector traditions.

In Australia, this line of research has not yet come to maturity. As mentioned, Moyle's (1994) Borallon work was not able to be completed; part of it was based on semi-structured interviews with inmates. Conducting their own audits and research in New South Wales (Bowery 1994), the public authorities have not yet come to see inmate perceptions as a valuable or even a valid data source.

The very fact that prisoner survey information does not at this stage all point in a single direction makes it particularly valuable as a marker for identifying areas of interest and concern. It should become a standard part of the research–evaluation–modification loop which is necessary for all prison management, including management of private prisons.

The managers

Again, anecdotal evidence, as long as one is not uncritically swept along by it, is worth mentioning. My own observations in the UK, the USA and Australia, based on long off-the-record conversations, are uniformly that the managers are committed and enthusiastic about what they see as an opportunity to improve a penal regime. Virtually all of these managers have come out of their respective public systems; and each of them expressed frustration at the red tape and rigidity of the highly bureaucratic public prison regimes.[5] As mentioned above, the Woolf Inquiry (Woolf and Tumim 1991: 12.69; 12.71) had picked up on this feeling:

> What is heard in establishments is that Headquarters, who are regarded overwhelmingly as being administrators without practical experience, [are] telling very experienced governors and staff how to do the jobs which they have been doing for most of their working lives ... Headquarters must, of course, know what is going on in prisons ... Headquarters must also be able to create and establish consistent policies and practices between prisons ... But these policies and

practices need to take account of the practical requirements of running a prison. They need to help the ultimate aim of the Service, not shackle the establishments into uniformity and inappropriate procedures.

What privatization has undoubtedly been able to achieve to this point is a feeling amongst managers that they can actually *manage* their prisons. That is certainly to the good. Of course, it is possible that a counter-pressure will build up – to run a CCA prison the CCA way or a Wackenhut prison the Wackenhut way, and so on. In fact, one of the managers interviewed in the course of this research did confess to feeling 'over-audited', not only by the panoply of general monitors, inspectors and controllers but also by his own corporate head office. This was a perspective shared by the chief inspector of prisons (Tumim 1995: 18–19). Nevertheless, on the basis of the available evidence, the private sector as a whole remains, in comparison to public sector systems, loose and flexible and encouraging of initiative.

Survey evidence is less common in relation to managers than either prisoners or general staff. The most interesting to date is a study by Kinkade and Leone (1992). The researchers carried out a national census of public prison warden attitudes towards three types of private sector involvement: prison industries; private financing of public system facilities; and prison privatization as such. The survey was carried out at a time (1990) when there were still relatively few (38) private prisons in the USA so that direct familiarity with or knowledge of them amongst the survey population was necessarily rather limited.

In this context, the researchers expected to observe 'domain consensus/ dissensus' (Aldrich 1979), that is, reluctance to accept encroachment on a domain long held by public sector correctional officials. As Kinkade and Leone (1992: 64) state:

> Acknowledging that privateers may be able to successfully manage general populations of offenders threatens the domain of traditional public sector corrections; suggesting that such arrangements could work in unique circumstances differentiates between public and private sector corrections, while maintaining the autonomy of the former.

Consistent with this theory, the survey revealed a diminishing level of support as the private sector activities came closer to core custodial responsibilities. Private involvement in prison industries was one thing; private sector operation of a maximum-security prison quite another. Likewise, private prisons for drunk drivers or illegal immigrants or juveniles were more acceptable than for ordinary criminal offenders.

Since that time, the penal context has changed. The private sector now operates more prisons; their security rating ranges from minimum to maximum; managers of private prisons are increasingly involved in system-wide conferences and briefings. Kinkade and Leone's survey had shown much higher acceptance for activities which had already occurred, particularly with regard to juveniles and illegal immigrants. In this context, as private prisons demonstrably become more integral to the prison system generally, it is likely that public sector managers may be slightly less protective of their domain and somewhat more willing to concede that the private sector may be able to contribute positively to the total system.

The staff

Public sector staff must have been expected to look upon privatization moves with hostility. After all, in many states a significant factor driving this development was the intention of the public authorities to break, or at least tame, strong prison officers' unions. Trust was hardly enhanced by the fact that most of the operators in the USA, the UK and Australia initially had a policy of not hiring uniformed staff from the public sector. This policy now seems to be somewhat less rigid. Although adopted primarily for industrial reasons, there was also a desire to bring in 'clean skins' – officers not yet tainted with the cynical occupational culture endemic to the public sector (Williams 1983). It follows from this that surveys could be expected to throw up differences of perception between the two groups. This has, in fact, been the case.

Hatry *et al.* (1989; 1993) found greater staff belief in the value of their work in the private sector institution. Logan (1992) found much higher appreciation of the quality of their institution amongst private than amongst public prison staff. In Australia and the UK this line of research is not yet adequately developed, though Bottomley *et al.* (1996b) lend some support to the view that staff morale is high in the private sector. The basis for this, and the factor that possibly makes the finding an ephemeral one, is that the staff in private prisons are younger in years and also in experience. Once more, the area is one for further research.

Summary

If the justification for privatization lies in the possibilities for cross-fertilization between the public and private components, with consequential improvement of the prison system as a whole, then a research–evaluation–modification loop is necessary. The most fundamental penological issues, particularly recidivism, cannot be isolated out methodologically or practically so as to compare the two components by this measure. But short of that, valuable research can be done – the quality of confinement, managerial performance, prisoner morale, staff attitudes, programme outcomes, post-release employment rates, and so on.

A research culture is slowly developing, particularly in the USA. So far studies have tended to be 'one-off' rather than fitting within a clear research tradition or reflecting the overarching theoretical position – cross-fertilization – which has been suggested.

Notes

1 American Correctional Association (1990: 3-4108, 3-4109).
2 In the course of carrying out research for this book, I have visited the Contracts and Competition Group on several occasions over a period of four years. These visits span the directorships of all three incumbents to date. Documentation I have requested has been made available to me, and other material of which I was previously unaware has been brought to my attention and likewise made available. I have been permitted access to each of the private prisons upon request, as well as to Manchester which has been market-tested: see Chapter 10.
3 The only way in which regime impact could be isolated would be by way of allocation of matched groups of prisoners to private and public prisons and their continuance in those institutions for the duration of their confinement. Such a course poses profound ethical problems.
4 For more detail, see Woolf and Tumim (1991: 2.1–2.59; 11.133–11.159; 12.66–12.97, Appendix 1, Chapter 1; Appendix 1, Chapter 3, 1.14–1. 17).
5 Shichor (1993: 125) takes a rather more jaundiced view of this matter. Accepting that most private prison managers have come out of the public system, he refers to some earlier work which had purportedly demonstrated that some of them had 'had legal and disciplinary problems during their tenure in public institutions'. He then asks: 'How [is it that] these administrators, some of whom did not show much creativity and efficiency in the public sector, will be able to run a new, more effective private correctional institution?' Shichor's experience seems to be vicarious. My own direct experience is in sharp contrast.

9

Special custodial issues and privatization

Prison management is a hard enough business at the best of times, even with an established workforce. Understandably, there is some concern that private operators, necessarily cost-conscious and initially dependent upon inexperienced staff, may not handle the most sensitive difficulties confidently or well. This concern is sometimes expressed by open-minded and pragmatic observers of privatization, not merely by those who are ideologically opposed.

What, then, are these special custodial issues? They seem to fall into four main categories. First, there is the overarching problem of overcrowding. This is the bane of the public sector system, and its existence invariably exacerbates or triggers other problems (Woolf and Tumim 1991). Second, there is the question of how to deal with riots and disturbances. Next, there is a group of other security issues, such as the imposition of discipline, drug use by prisoners and the control of escapes. Finally comes the question of the prison regime as it affects inmates – such matters as suicide prevention; health services; the management of vulnerable, HIV-positive and protection prisoners; race relations; intimidation and bullying by prisoners; food; and visits.

Overcrowding

At the outset, the hope was that private prisons would not just help relieve overcrowding across the total prison system but would themselves be insulated from overcrowding. This belief manifested itself in the fact, explained previously, that the standard contracts in the USA, the UK and Australia were predicated upon a fixed payment per prisoner up to a specified maximum number. In the USA in particular, since lack of accommodation was one of the main catalysts for privatization and since federal courts had become so active in putting overcrowded prisons under court order, it seemed natural enough to expect that private prisons would continue to operate to their certified normal capacity.

At this early stage also, it was probably true to say that there was a continuing expectation of what one might call 'normal' overcrowding in relation to 'normally' increasing prison populations. Against that background, it was anticipated that private prisons could remain quarantined from overcrowding pressure, whilst nevertheless doing something towards relieving or at least stabilizing system-wide overcrowding. Of course, this invited the criticism that a dual system was being created – an up-market private one and a run-down public one. However, the last few years have seen not 'normal' but exponential increases in all three countries – far outstripping population increases or jumps in crime rates or improvements in clear-up rates. Reference has already been made in general terms to these increases. Three specific examples will highlight this crucial point.

First, in California – already having more prisoners than any other state but still only a second-tier private prison state[1] – it is estimated that the impact of the 'three strikes' legislation will be a 70 per cent increase in the state's prison population by the end of 1999, to 211,000! This will necessitate building at least 15 extra mega-prisons or their equivalent. In the meantime, with much of the system under court order for overcrowding, many offenders are being released early to make way for remanded or convicted three-strikes offenders (Criminal Justice Newsletter 1995). Next, in the UK the increase in the prisoner population between December 1992 – seven months after the first private prison became operational – and March 1996 was of the order of 27 per cent, from 42,255 to about 54,000. This brought the system to the point where, in March 1996, a state of emergency was declared in relation to 46 prisons – one-third of the establishment. The effect of such a declaration is to require governors to provide 'additional space over and above their normal operational capacity' (for example, by using corridors or day-rooms or prison hospital beds for accommodation) and to suspend industrial agreements restricting overcrowding (*The Guardian*, 29 February 1996). Third, in Australia, the Queensland prison population increased by 47 per cent, from 2088 to 3070, in the period from 1 July 1993 to 31 December 1995. This occurred without any change to sentencing legislation, but seems to have reflected a shift in judicial attitudes as to appropriate tariffs across the whole range of offences.

Against this sort of background, the quarantined status of private prisons could not be expected to remain intact. The criticism that a dual system was being allowed to develop would disappear by default. In Florida, when in late 1995 by the stroke of an administrative pen the total prison system was authorized to run at 50 per cent above certified normal capacity, the private sector was not exempted. The 3900 private sector spaces could thus be expanded to 5850 – albeit subject to satisfactory contractual negotiations, for the original contracts in this first phase of privatization did not allow for this eventuality.[2] In the UK, as already described, the third private prison contract relating to Doncaster, signed at a time when the exponential increase was starting to make its run, contains a 50 per cent overcrowding clause. It is intended that all future contracts will contain some comparable clause.

In Australia, the Junee contract put out to tender in December 1990, at a time when the exponential increase in the New South Wales prison population had been under way for almost two years, contains a requirement that 'for future management flexibility, the utility services should be designed with spare capacity of 80 per cent of that required for 600 prisoners'. If this seems to contemplate overcrowding by a single grandiloquent gesture, Queensland, by contrast, has brought it about by steady accretion. Borallon's 1990 built capacity was 240. In March 1995 new construction work was completed, taking the built capacity to 335. The new contract with CCA, signed a week or so later, provided for double-bunking in 54 cells, and in late 1995 a further agreement was reached for double-bunking in an extra 36 cells. So with a built capacity of 335, Borallon now houses 425 prisoners – 25 per cent overcrowding. Similarly, at the Arthur Gorrie Correctional Centre, where the initial built capacity of 380 was extended by construction work to 458 in November 1994, three subsequent double-bunking contract variations have increased prisoner numbers to 578, 596 and 632 respectively – overcrowding of 38 per cent.

So it can be seen that the brief halcyon period when private sector prisons were in effect quarantined from overcrowding has already come to an end. Perhaps this is not altogether a bad thing; perhaps if there is to be effective cross-fertilization each part of the total prison system should face comparable dilemmas. On the other hand, the idea of permitting some part of the total prison system to develop and improve its regimes against a stable background has much to be said for it. That way, it is easier to begin to assess whether the whole task can be carried out better than hitherto.

The real lesson from all this, however, is that penological practice is always subject to penal policy. In the last decade of the millennium, western politicians, by distorting the penal agenda, have undermined penological advance. Overcrowding is the bane of correctional managers. Even the modest 'anti-deformative' objective discussed in Chapter 8 becomes virtually unattainable against the backdrop of serious overcrowding. It remains to be seen whether the private sector will be any more successful than the public sector, once the nature and extent of its overcrowding are comparable.

Disturbances and riots

New prisons are potentially volatile environments. Routines and relationships among uniformed staff have yet to be established; prisoners do not know exactly what to expect from officers, which other prisoners may turn up there, what their own coping mechanisms accordingly will be. In a total institution, the less scope there is for the unexpected, the better the prospects for good order. Knowing all these things, experienced prison administrators prefer to fill up a new prison slowly, so that arriving inmates encounter a consolidating culture rather than a behavioural vacuum or melting-pot. However, in the context of acute shortage of accommodation, described above, new prisons are usually brought up to full operational capacity far too quickly. Not infrequently, therefore, the early months are beset with problems, tensions and sometimes disturbances.

This is so with public prisons. In the UK both Moorland and Full Sutton had major disturbances shortly after opening, in the course of which a wing was destroyed in each institution. It has likewise been the case with private prisons. For example, the chief inspector commented with regard to a disturbance at Blakenhurst that:

> the [prison] had been unstable for several months before the incident, not least because it had filled up too quickly as a response to the general prisoner population. In one month (September 1993) over 200 prisoners had been received. This is far too many for a new prison to assimilate. This is a recurring mistake on the part of the Prison Service's tactical management.
>
> (Tumim 1995: 43)

Doncaster also had a very difficult opening period (Prison Reform Trust 1995). The climax was a major disturbance in November 1994, some six months after it became operational. In the view of the director, the various disruptions were in no small way due to the fact that it was brought on stream much too quickly – from 0 to 770 prisoners in less than six weeks (personal communication, 21 February 1995). Subsequently, things seem to have settled down somewhat. By contrast The Wolds, which had only taken up half of its certified normal accommodation of 320 a full five months after its opening (personal inspection, 3 September 1992), encountered no serious disorder in the first year.[3]

Given that these disturbances occurred, the private contractors seem to have dealt with them quite adequately. With regard to Blakenhurst, the chief inspector reported as follows:

> [O]ther aspects of the incident demonstrated the strengths of the civilised approach [to staff–inmate relations], in that there had been no serious injuries to staff or inmates. The report of the inquiry concluded that staff were not at any time at personal risk except when in the office which was the focus of prisoner aggression. Furthermore, the security keys were very quickly returned to staff, while prisoners themselves ultimately helped to regain order; testimony to the fact that many felt

the incident unwarranted whilst others feared that they would be transferred to prisons where conditions were less comfortable.

(Tumim, 1995: 42–3)

The Doncaster incident was also resolved quickly and peaceably, the official inquiry finding that 'staff acted properly throughout'. However, the atmosphere there was sufficiently unstable for the company to employ on short-term contracts some very experienced officers who had recently retired from the Prison Service (personal communication, 21 February 1995). Doing this was tantamount to an admission that the initial training of the new staff – carried out largely under the direction of imported American training staff – had fallen short. The recurrent theme of prisons being cultural organisms which require culturally appropriate protocols thus reveals itself once more.

In Australia, two of the first three private prisons encountered major difficulties during the early stages. It is perhaps worth noting that each had depended on imported American managers during its opening period, apparently thus fortifying yet again the cultural organism point. However, it should also be said that in at least one of these instances the private contractor was obliged to function against the background of questionable decisions made by the public authorities.

This was the case with Junee. It will be recalled that Junee prison is situated at a location where there is no natural catchment area for prisoners, and that most inmates are sent there from the greater Sydney metropolitan area some 600 kilometres away. It will also be recalled that the town is in a transportation limbo. Visits were always going to be problematical – a predictable source of stress and tension (Harding 1993). In this context, it was no surprise that the first year's operation involved five 'significant incidents' (Bowery 1994), the most serious of which, occurring in May 1993, only two months after the first prisoners were received, led to the use of gas against 100 prisoners to restore order.

But the prison did not really settle down after this. In the first half of 1994 there was an upsurge in the number of custodial offences, including assaults on officers (Bowery 1994: 26–30). Against this still unstable background, in November 1994 the Department of Corrective Services sought to change radically the prisoner profile by transferring there 300 protection prisoners (informers, child molesters and the like) from around the state. This is a classic case of ignoring the adage that the more settled a regime and the less scope for the unexpected, the better the prospects for good order. Predictably enough, a small incident triggered a major disturbance; a Corrective Services Emergency Response Team was called in, and it took four hours for it to quell the riot using gas.

Parenthetically, it is worth mentioning that the Junee monitor's report for the period within which this riot fell makes no mention of it at all (Sneddon 1995). The monitoring exercise in that state has now, it seems, become irretrievably processual. The report's focus was on whether the 'serious incident reporting procedures had been followed'. They had; so that was evidently the end of it. Whatever the formal responsibilities of the monitor – and clearly in the Department's terms they had been properly discharged – the reality seems to be that there has been accountability slippage within the public authority responsible for the contract. Judge Tumim, when UK chief inspector of prisons, would certainly not have passed through a recently rioting prison without mentioning that fact and analysing its problems.

In November 1992 a small-scale riot occurred at the Arthur Gorrie Correctional Centre, Queensland. The immediate cause was the suicide of a young prisoner and the belief of fellow prisoners that the officers had been callous or indifferent towards him. Evidence was given at the inquest that the rioting prisoners were stripped naked and left overnight, all bedding and clothing removed from their cells. When they attempted to keep warm by turning on a hot shower, the water supply was cut off.

By any civilized standard, this sort of conduct is unacceptable. The responsible public authority, the Queensland Corrective Services Commission (QCSC), conducted an inquiry which ascertained the above facts. Referring to the prisoners' 'indignity and acute physical discomfort', the internal Commission report concluded that official (that is, contracted) confinement standards had been breached. Yet, as far as is known, no contractual penalty was imposed. Queensland has already been characterized as having been, at least in the first few years of privatization, captured; and this evidence certainly supports such a characterization.

The Australian position, in summary, seems to indicate a somewhat cruder approach to riot control in private prisons than found in the UK, and must leave some real sense of concern. However, the private contractors would certainly lift their performance if they were put under suitable pressure to do so by those to whom they are formally accountable. Moreover, it must be said that public prison riots have not been handled with much finesse in recent years (Nagle 1978; McGivern 1988; Hallenstein 1989).

In the USA evidence of riots at private prisons is not readily discoverable. The most notorious recent one, already mentioned in several other contexts, was that at the Esmor facility at Elizabeth, New Jersey. There can be little doubt that the alleged custodial practices leading to the uprising (for example, shackling, hassling during sleeping hours, verbal and physical abuse) were absolutely unacceptable. In its early privatization contracts, the Immigration and Naturalization Service (INS) had apparently provided for the presence on-site of a 'Contracting Officer Technical Representative' or monitor (McConville 1990: 85–6). It is not clear whether such an arrangement was in place for the Esmor facility. If it were, one is entitled to wonder what that person was doing as the preconditions to riot were building up. The likelihood must be that some form of capture, or more probably surrender, had occurred. Certainly one can say that the INS, as principals, having initially written the contract in such imprecise terms, had been unwilling or unable to make the company accountable in an ongoing way, and also that it had undermined the contractual foundation by assigning inmates for medium-term stays. To this point, however, there is no basis for thinking that this saga is representative of privatization in the USA as a whole.[4]

Finally, it should be emphasized that in all jurisdictions the state authorities, by dint of statute and/or contract, may in an emergency reclaim direct management of a private prison. Short of this, the policy is progressively being clarified in many states whereby public prison emergency response teams will assist private prison operators if invited to do so. This is an area of interaction which as yet has not been formulated in practice and which should certainly be kept under scrutiny as actual cases begin to occur.

Other security issues

It is not proposed to discuss further the question of discipline and punishment; this has been dealt with in Chapter 6.

Drug use by prisoners

Drug use seems to be an endemic problem in prisons throughout the world. Very few regimes seem to have eliminated it. Those that have done so have used methods which are not generally acceptable in the western world – namely, very strict control or even prohibition of contact visits and unannounced and frequent random searches of staff. Even so, generally their success is only temporary.

In that context, it is unrealistic to expect to find drug-free prisons, public or private, in the USA, the UK or Australia. It is not in itself a measure of private sector failure, therefore, that drug use is discovered in private prisons. Only some sustained and very unusual departure from the norm could sensibly be regarded as failure in this regard.

The Wolds initially caused some concern. The chief inspector's report (Tumim 1994a: 109) noted:

> We believe there to be an unacceptably high level of drugs at The Wolds, not perhaps surprising in view of the time out of cell, the nature of the visits, the money available to inmates, and the culture of lack of occupation.

The factors highlighted in this statement are shorthand for saying that the prison was occupied at that time entirely by remand prisoners possessing privileges, in terms of numbers of visits and purchasing power, which have no parallel in an ordinary prison with a standard inmate mix. Subsequently, the prison's muster was altered to take in convicted prisoners, with consequential regime changes. The expectation must be that drug-use patterns will be modified as a result. Some encouragement of this view is provided by the fact that Blakenhurst, possessing a standard inmate mix, seems to have a standard drug problem. As Tumim (1995: 44) stated: 'We judged the prevalence of illicit drugs to be no better or worse than in any local prison.'

Experience at Junee is similar. During its first year of operation urine analysis sampling was carried out at a comparable rate within all New South Wales prisons, including Junee. Positive findings across the board were 7.9 per cent; for Junee 7.4 per cent (Bowery 1994: 16).

In the USA, private prison contracts, by incorporating American Correctional Association (ACA) accreditation standards, ensure that written rules must provide for various levels of inmate misconduct and disciplinary hearings. These include illicit drug use. There is no evidence to suggest that it is any better or worse in private than in public prisons.

In summary, drug use in prisons is a significant issue of correctional management. Attempts to control it must be system-wide, with the private sector brought within any overall strategy which is attempted. In the meantime, private prisons do not pose any distinctive problems.

Escapes

Opponents of private prisons take understandable delight in summoning up the image of imprisonment being 'optional' when left to the private sector. In the UK, Group 4, the operators of The Wolds, had a horror run when it commenced court escort services for prisons in that area, including The Wolds itself. Within the first week there had been three quite simple escapes from the vans, and one prisoner who had been remanded in custody had been allowed to walk free. A Prison Officers' Association representative claimed that 'public safety is being put at risk' by government policy (*The Independent*, 10 April 1993), whilst a police spokesman lugubriously remarked: 'To have a person remanded in custody is difficult enough these days . . . To have him then released in this way is to say the least disappointing' (*Daily Telegraph*, 12 April 1993). Has privatization made imprisonment somewhat 'optional', then?

Not surprisingly, the answer is 'no'. Escape rates from private prisons are congruent with those from similarly rated public prisons. As with the control of illicit drug use, there have been teething problems – for example, at The Wolds. However, the particular circumstances there were such that Tumim (1994a: 66) 'did not draw . . . any adverse conclusions about the standard of vigilance maintained by staff'.

It would be most surprising, in fact, if there were any substantial disparity between private and public prisons in this regard. A key aspect of all Requests for Proposals (USA) and Invitations to Tender (Australia and UK) is the proposed security regime, as evidenced (for example, in the Florida

Guidelines) by previous experience in operating an institution of similar security level. Interestingly, contract performance criteria (for example, in relation to Doncaster) are now beginning to specify a number of permissible escapes, beyond which there is a breach of contract – something to which no equivalent is found in even the most permeable parts of the public system.

The prison regime

The thrust of Chapter 4 was that the general accountability mechanisms applicable to public prisons were no less, and in some respects significantly more, applicable to private prison regimes. Moreover, the standards required were similar. For example, the provisions of the Prison Rules: Contracted Out Prisons 1992 were in substance identical to those contained in the Prison Rules applicable to public prisons; and the ACA accreditation standards which were invariably to be applied to private prisons in the USA were the same standards as would apply to those public systems that had sought and obtained accreditation.

Of course, the abstract standards are one thing and the standards on the ground may be another. As already discussed in Chapter 8 and to be further highlighted in Chapter 10, the private prison standards in the actual institutions have on the whole initially been superior to those in public prisons. This is in no small part due to the fact that they have been formulated with more precision than is always the case with the public sector, as emerged in Chapter 5. Nevertheless, there are some particularly sensitive areas of the prison regime which merit more detailed attention.

Suicide and self-harm

Over the last decade suicide and self-harm, and related matters such as death through drug overdose, have emerged as volatile areas of correctional management (Biles and McDonald 1992; Hayes 1994; Liebling 1994; Rowan 1994). The ability of prison managers to run suicide-free institutions has come to be seen by inmates and outside critics as a touchstone of whether the regime is acceptable at all. This may be an over-simplistic view; but the fact is that it is a commonly held one, particularly amongst indigenous groups and minorities.

Reference has already been made above to the riot at the Arthur Gorrie Correctional Centre following a suicide which other prisoners considered should never have been allowed to occur. In fact, this was one of five suicides which occurred at that prison during its first 18 months of operation. There were only four other prison deaths in the remainder of the Queensland system during that period. A reasonable inference seemed to be that management protocols were defective in some way: whether as to initial recognition of at-risk prisoners or as to bullying amongst the prisoner population or as to staff abuse or indifference. As already mentioned, the QCSC, being insufficiently hands-on in its monitoring role, did not pick up or act upon this issue at once. Eventually, the operating company of its own volition brought in American consultants to advise it on suicide prevention, and the problem seemed to settle down.

Of course, the public system is no less capable of inadequate diagnosis and slow response. In the UK it needed five deaths at Leeds prison during 1987–88 to get the Prison Service belatedly moving; the bureaucratic complacency preceding its eventual response exceeded any conduct which might be construed as commercial arrogance (Harding 1994b: 204–7).

Doncaster prison also left something to be desired with regard to suicides and self-harm. During the period from June 1994 to November 1995 the number of 'attempted suicides' – an imprecise term which in UK Prison Service parlance takes in self-harming incidents falling well short of trying to kill oneself – was higher than in any other prison in the UK (Prison Reform Trust 1995: 20–1). Rather as with Arthur Gorrie, the public authorities seemed slow and diffident about asserting their own legitimate interest in these events. Here is another area of capture, or at the very least inadequate audit. On the other hand, the chief inspector found suicide awareness and prevention programmes up to an acceptable standard at both The Wolds (Tumim 1994a: 103–5) and Blakenhurst (Tumim 1995: 77–8).

It does seem, in summary, that there has been and continues to be some cause for concern as to the capacity of some private prisons to deal with this absolutely key custodial issue. Wherever there have been shortcomings by the operator, however, there seems also to have been some failure or apathy by the public authority whose duty it is to ensure accountability.

Bullying and intimidation by prisoners

Power vacuums can occur in the management of prisons. Such situations enable the strongest and potentially most violent prisoners in effect to take control of the daily regime. For other inmates the prison experience becomes a question of survival, nothing more. This is well understood and docu-mented (Jacobs 1977). When these extreme situations occur, the associated factors often are: huge prisons; the transplanting of gang cultures and rivalries from the streets to the prison; related racial tensions; and acute overcrowding.

Mostly, these associated factors have been found in the USA. In many states mega-prisons, with accommodation for several thousand inmates, are still not uncommon; gang cultures are stronger; and race issues are seldom far beneath the surface of American life, whether inside or outside prison (Wicker 1976; Weiss 1991). Of these factors the only one – and most commentators would regard it as the single most important one – which is within the direct influence of the correctional authorities is the size of the institution.

As at the end of 1994 the largest operational private prison in the USA had a rated capacity of 1336. This was the South Central Correctional Center in Tennessee, whose performance, both financial and qualitative, has been the subject of intense scrutiny by the Select Oversight Committee of that state. Most correctional administrators would regard this figure as being at the outer limit of the size where they can maintain control of what is going on within the institution. Another CCA institution in Tennessee is the Metro-Davidson County Detention Center, with a rated capacity of 1092. In 1995 a contract was signed to add capacity for a further 956 prisoners. However, it was agreed that this should be done by construction of a stand-alone and separate facility, located on the same green-fields site and sharing many of the infrastructure services, rather than by direct accretion to the existing prison. In management terms and from the point of view of permitting possible power vacuums to develop, there is a world of difference between two prisons with a thousand prisoners each and one prison with two thousand.

However, some of the more recent contracts have been for larger prisons. Indeed, seven relate to prisons with rated capacities in the 1500–2000 range – not the mega-prisons which still characterize parts of the USA's public prison system, but quite large enough. This may be indicative of a shift away from the apparent early recognition by the authorities that the private sector should if possible operate without the potentially crippling management difficulties evident from public sector experience.[5] On the other hand, it is still true to say that the great majority of private prisons are of manageable size, with 49 out of 92 having rated capacities of less than 500 and a further 29 of 501–1000 (Thomas 1996).

Short of surrender of control, there can of course be incidents of bullying, assault, drug-related extortion and homosexual rape. Such matters are all too familiar to public prison staff, and there is no reason to suppose that they will not occur within private prisons. The Prison Reform Trust (1995) has produced evidence – mostly anecdotal, but some of it documented through Parliamentary questions and answers – that in its early days Doncaster has fallen into this mould.[6] On the other hand, the chief inspector of prisons, following his invariable practice of obtaining confidential inmate reactions as to conditions and the prison regime, turned up no comparable allegations at The Wolds or Blakenhurst.

In Australia, just as the Arthur Gorrie Correctional Centre seemed initially to be the least effective private prison with regard to suicides, so also was it the subject of the greatest number of anecdotal and media allegations about these other undesirable aspects of the regime. It is not possible from the available evidence to determine the validity of these complaints. However, an effective monitoring or inspection system would take one some of the way. To the extent that these matters surface in official records (and there exists in relation to formal prisoner complaints and reports exactly the same filtering effect as with ordinary crime), the experience at Junee offers some support for the view that in New South Wales the private prison is much the same as the public ones (Bowery 1994: 25–30).

Vulnerable and protection prisoners

When prisons explode, inmates usually head straight for the wing where informers, child molesters and so on are held on protection. The first killings or acts of sodomy occur there (Wicker 1976; Dinitz 1981; Weiss 1991; Woolf and Tumim 1991). Even in an apparently orderly situation, such prisoners are vulnerable. That being so, the ability of private prison operators to manage these people is important. In this context, it should be recalled that the private sector now deals with the full gamut of prisoner classifications; this is a real, not merely a hypothetical, issue.

As with all of the issues discussed, the evidence of private sector performance is not yet definitive. In the USA the ACA standards seem to contemplate that there should be a 'segregation unit' in a prison, though this appears not necessarily to mean a separate unit secure from the remainder of the prison.[7] With private prisons this arrangement will be settled by contract – depending on such factors as the capacity, security rating and location of the prison.

In the UK, all three currently operational private prisons have protection units. At The Wolds the chief inspector, whilst not over-enthusiastic, particularly with regard to staff training, considered it adequate (Tumim 1994a: 64–6). He was somewhat more impressed at Blakenhurst:

> To safeguard vulnerable prisoners a separate suite of keys had been fitted to the gates of the unit . . . Given the limited facilities available, the regime for vulnerable prisoners was good . . . Overall, the regime on offer to vulnerable prisoners was impressive.
>
> (Tumim 1995: 79–80)

In Australia, the Arthur Gorrie Correctional Centre was set up as the principal location in Queensland for protection prisoners. The difficulties which that prison has experienced in its early years did not occur for the most part in that unit or because of that unit's being situated at that prison. In Junee, as has been seen, a decision to move protection prisoners *en masse* to that prison, which was not specifically designed for this purpose, sparked a major disturbance. There were sensitivities which did not seem to have been fully appreciated.

These examples of the impact of the prison regime on inmates will suffice. Other issues – such as race relations, visiting arrangements, the handling of HIV-positive prisoners, and so on – will show comparable patterns – namely, of evolving practices against a backdrop of general prison management policies.

Summary

Some of the most difficult issues of custodial management have been touched on in this chapter. The aim has been to try to ascertain whether the private sector is capable of dealing with them effectively or whether the prison regime, or possibly even the whole system itself, will be put at risk. A few areas of concern – in particular, riot control and suicide prevention – were identified. Naturally, there was some variation between countries. At this early stage, custodial practices are still evolving and standards being refined. It is premature to reach firm conclusions. However, public authorities responsible for the accountability of private prison operators should keep a close watch on these areas, which lie at the heart of just and sustainable imprisonment regimes.

Notes

1 Thomas (1995a) shows California as having the second highest number of prisons, but as being well down the list in terms of numbers of prisoners.
2 The actual numbers incarcerated are already approaching this administratively created upper limit. It is not entirely clear how Florida, which has previously been subject to a federal court order, will escape future supervision.
3 There were, however, inspired rumours of major disturbances, including a story that it had been partly burned down by prisoners. These false stories coincided with the period of most vehement opposition by interested parties to the then novel concept of privatization. See also Tumim (1994a: 28).
4 However, it has subsequently been reported that a 'major disturbance' occurred at Eden Detention Center, Texas – a CCA facility – on 22 August 1996 (Prison Reform Trust 1996: 4). The same source also refers to two other minor disturbances which have allegedly occurred in CCA facilities (one of them a juvenile detention centre). At the time of writing no other independent information is available about these matters.
5 An example of this was the Texas provision (Texas Statutes, Government Code 495.001(b)(1)) whereby private prisons constructed and managed for county authorities should not exceed 1000 capacity. This provision is still in effect.
6 Subsequently, in mid 1996, the chief inspector of prisons formally inspected Doncaster. He pronounced it to be 'the most progressive in the country' in terms of its anti-bullying strategies, its management of young offenders and its care of suicidal prisoners (*The Guardian*, 12 October 1996).
7 American Correctional Association (1990: 3-4237–3-4239).

Enhancing the prison system: cross-fertilization and market testing

Will private prisons improve the total prison system? Overarching the answer to this question is, as always in areas of penal policy, the attitude of governments. It has been seen that there is already some distinct ambivalence as to whether, for example, the UK government is prepared to let this happen. But subject to that caveat, the answer to this crucial question will be found first in the performance of private prisons and second in their impact upon the public sector component of the prison system. The quality of their own performance will in turn be affected by the efficacy of accountability mechanisms, the discussion of which will be drawn together in the final chapter. As to cross-sector impact, the threshold question is how receptive the public component will be to the changes and challenges posed by the private sector. The first issue, then, is to identify the barriers to change and thus to cross-fertilization that exist within the public prison system.

Barriers against change and cross-fertilization

Uniformed staff

In public prisons uniformed officers have traditionally provided the greatest resistance to change. Privatization has put the spotlight on the fact that many public prison systems had come to be run very much for the convenience of officers and in conformity with their own penal values. In public prisons if programme delivery or penal objectives cut across either of these and a compromise could not be negotiated, then the officer viewpoint would usually win out. The point is of such importance that several examples will be given to capture something of the tone and depth of this culture. The broader context is, as mentioned earlier, that senior management also bore responsibility for this state of affairs through permitting it to become embedded in the prison system.

Let us start with a New Zealand example. A new prison, Mangaroa, was opened in 1989. Its penal objectives revolved around the notion of prisoner self-development in a unit management setting. An aspect of this is free communication between staff and inmates, promoting productive inter-relationships; social distance is reduced as the officers take on case management responsibilities. Reliance on physical barriers and control is also minimized. That, at any rate, was the theory. However, by 1992 allegations of brutality by officers were starting to surface too frequently to be ignored. A ministerial inquiry was set up. Its observations on the unit management approach were as follows:

> Support for the new regime has not been universal. The abolition of ranking structure inherent in unit management is opposed by many staff. Non compliance has resulted in an untenable dual structure which sees many continuing to wear ranking insignia and expressing concern and surprise when this is not respected.
>
> The PSA [prison officers' union] sees unit and case management introducing a 'horrendous conflict of roles' . . . There is conflict too on the programmes front. The retributive beliefs and values of some staff are incompatible with the habilitative, reintegrative thrust under-pinning programmes. This creates tension, conflict and dysfunction.
>
> (Logan 1993: 49)

The report goes on to document the failures of senior management which had exacerbated officer resistance.

In the UK, the chief inspector of prisons has regularly uncovered officer resistance to new programmes. At Leeds, for example, he observed:

> Some inmates alleged that they were prevented from attending classes by a few officers who were not unlocking them for the activity. We were not able to verify this allegation but it was given credence by information from different staff sources . . . Outside the education department there was an evident lack of respect for education amongst prison staff . . . The [education staff] seemed to be regarded as outsiders, almost intruders.
>
> (Tumim 1994b: 59)

This echoed his 1992 finding that, at Wandsworth, the Prison Officers' Association was resisting the introduction of increased association amongst prisoners as well as blocking the use of nurses in the health centre.

Of course, resistance to change is nothing new. Vinson (1982) continually encountered this throughout the New South Wales prison system during his period as commissioner. Similarly, the inquiry into the 1986 riots at several UK prisons found that at least one disturbance had been actively provoked by officers intent on forestalling reform (HM Chief Inspector of Prisons 1987). A comparable incident may also have occurred in the Queensland prison system during 1991 (Harding 1992). This radical diagnosis, if correct, certainly highlights the extent of the problem and is consistent with the thrust of the literature about the strength of subcultural values in hierarchical organiz- ations whose members feel socially beleaguered (Westley 1966; Williams 1983; Kauffmann 1988; Carter 1995).

Managers

Uniformed staff may not be alone in finding change threatening. This attitude is certainly shared by some line managers. At Mangaroa, for example, 'opposition by some management . . . has undermined the reforms' (Logan 1993: 9). It is a matter of common observation also that some managers are not all that unhappy with union resistance to proposed changes, for this provides a ready-made 'industrial' justification for not pressing ahead with changes they themselves feel uneasy about. Thus Tumim (1994b: 20) observed at Leeds prison that 'management was not leading the culture'. The US study of the attitudes of wardens to privatization (Kinkade and Leone 1992) ties in with this; good ideas coming out of the private sector may seem simply to be encroachment upon the public sector domain.

Of course, the converse of this is the enthusiasm felt by former wardens coming into the private sector for the changes which privatization may facilitate, and the sense they have that they are actually expected and encouraged to *manage* institutions. Clearly, the picture is a mixed one.

Head offices

Reference has already been made to the ways in which head offices often frustrate managerial initiative in the workplace. For the UK, Woolf identified the fact that management has become over-centralized and head office 'has shackled the establishments into uniformity and inappropriate procedures' (Woolf and Tumim 1991: 12.71). This observation finds its equivalent in most of the prison systems under consideration here.

With regard to privatization, it is of course head offices – chief executive officers along with their policy-level staff – that are generally empowered to commence the process; and not infrequently it is also head offices that tie the process up. The most notable example to date was the dragging reluctance of the Florida Department of Corrections over a period of eight years to utilize its newly created statutory power to commission private contractors (Thomas 1995b: 3). However, this is an extreme case.

More typical is the UK situation. There, it will be recalled that the Contracts and Competition Group is a quasi-autonomous unit within the Prison Service charged with the task of overseeing a governmental decision to establish a private prison right through the numerous processes up to the point where a contract is ready for the minister to sign. For public prisons a system of area managers exists – people in overall charge of a geographical grouping of prisons who work very closely with head office to ensure that the rules and protocols developed centrally are followed exactly. At first private prisons stood completely outside the area manager structure. Controllers were appointed by and reported to the Contracts and Competition Group; and it was the director of that Group who, on the advice of the controller, certified that contractual instalments were due and payable. But in 1995, quietly and unannounced, head office altered that arrangement. Controllers are now appointed by and report to the area manager, and it is the latter who authorizes contractual payments. The purpose of this, it is informally conceded, was to draw private prisons into the general UK prison management culture. This is, of course, the very antithesis of cross-fertilization – a notion which applauds difference rather than uniformity. And yet the very same people who are responsible for this genuinely believe that a vibrant and contrasting private sector is desirable and necessary. Bureaucratic conscience and entrepreneurial confidence sit ill at the same desk, it seems.

Overview

In summary, then, barriers to change are found at all levels of public prison personnel. They range from sabotage through dumb insolence to apathy or apprehension. The scope and depth of these barriers vary between systems and across time. Prison managements have generally not invested enough organizational commitment to change – by way of in-service training, lateral recruitment, employee participation in planning, and so on. Nevertheless, the barriers are not insuperable. If private prison experience has enough to offer, there is already evidence to suggest that it may be transmitted to and adapted by the public sector component of the prison system.

Cross-fertilization in practice

There are three issues to consider here. First, where might it be expected that differences will emerge, beckoning change? Second, where has change through cross-fertilization already tangibly occurred? Finally, by what mechanism is cross-fertilization brought about? Distinct as these issues are conceptually, they inexorably merge in discussion and illustration.

Take, for example, the question of running costs, particularly in relation to uniformed staff. Presumed cost reduction has always been a primary motivation for governments. Some work practices, driving costs, were impossible to defend. Woolf put his finger on something well known to any Australian or UK prison administrator, though less true of the USA because there is weaker trade unionism in that country: 'The need to maintain earnings by working overtime led to the widespread adoption of what were known as "Old Spanish Customs". They were of labyrinthine complexity. They were used to justify a massive quantity of overtime working' (Woolf and Tumim 1991: 13.20). This featherbedding is a matter of concern not because one is opposed to prison officers receiving a decent and deserved wage but because such expenditure simply limits outlays on other items. The budgetary size of the correctional pie is rather inelastic; the first bite is always going to be taken by security expenditure; the larger that bite, the less will be left over for programmes, welfare, maintenance of a reasonable quality of confinement and so on.

In Australia the Borallon contract immediately highlighted this fact. The number of uniformed staff, at 100 or so, was about half the number which would have been required according to public prison manning levels. The corollary was that the contractors reserved a far bigger slice of the cake for education and industrial training programmes as well as health services.[1] This example was not lost on correctional managers throughout Australia. In the Northern Territory, where officers at the substandard Alice Springs prison had been reluctant to trial a unit management approach, the preparedness of senior management to put the scheduled replacement prison out to private tender worked marvels in changing the union stance (Harding 1992). In Western Australia, much the same scenario was enacted in 1994, though in that state it was not felt necessary to emulate the Northern Territory ploy of actually seeking expressions of interest from the private sector. In New South Wales, a new 900-bed public prison under construction at Silverwater will have only 300 uniformed staff – markedly fewer than would have been the case before the Junee contract was let. Once more, it is intended that flexible prisoner management practices and enhanced programmes will be put in place.

It is a matter of taste whether one describes these examples as 'cross-fertilization' or 'industrial blackmail'. Undeniably, the mechanism of change in this area has been recognition, forced upon a powerful group, that their strength could successfully be confronted. In the light of Woolf's comments, it would be perverse to try to justify completely the pre-existing situation. The important matter which must be monitored, the one for which the public prison sector must be made accountable, is that the consequential savings are at least partly spent on programmes and other matters which tend to improve the quality, humanity and effectiveness of confinement.

A less controversial mechanism is statutory – where the state, under whatever motivation, decides to set a statutory standard. The best example relates to American Correctional Association (ACA) accreditation in the USA. As already mentioned, many states embarking upon privatization have included a provision that the contract shall require the private operator to seek and obtain accreditation. Yet frequently this very same requirement has not been imposed upon the state department of corrections. An example has already been given of how the fact that a Louisiana private prison had to obtain accreditation worked its way into the organizational fabric of public prisons. A new chief executive officer of the Louisiana Department of Corrections apparently found it unconscionable and somewhat embarrassing that a higher standard should be expected of the fledgeling private sector. This, incidentally, serves to highlight another important mechanism of change – individual initiative or inspiration.

Accreditation takes one to the issue of confinement quality, and the menu of regime conditions identified by Logan (1992) in constructing his index. Experience at The Wolds has been very informative in showing cross-fertilization at work. Morgan (1994: 150–1) has commented on the significance of the fact that

> five of the six most serious disturbances on which the Woolf inquiry concentrated its attention were remand establishments and that remand prisoners played a leading or a contributory part in what happened. Woolf found that these remand prisoners had good reason to feel aggrieved.

Whilst Woolf's inquiry was in progress, the Wolds regime was being negotiated. Table 10.1 (pages 140–1) contrasts the contractual requirements and the actual provision (columns 2 and 3) with the minimum facilities required in a public sector remand prison (column 4).

Shortly thereafter the Prison Service began to develop a draft Model Regime document. As it was circulating Morgan (1994: 159) commented: 'It is clear that the Prison Service's aspirations are not being pitched at a lower level than that required for The Wolds.' This observation is borne out by the regime conditions listed in column 5 of Table 10.1. Although these relate to a juvenile, not an adult, remand centre, the subsequent history of the 1992 Model Regime document suggests cross-fertilization at work:

> Group 4 was required to provide 15 hours 'out-of-cell' activities for all prisoners at The Wolds . . . [T]he provision of 'out-of-cell' activities for remand prisoners in the public sector was probably lower than for any other type of prisoner. However, the other new prisons in the study were increasingly expected to reach similar 'out-of-cell' provisions for prisoners as laid down in the Model Regime for Local Prisons and Remand Centres (1992). The threat of market testing also acted as a powerful spur to innovation.
>
> (Bottomley *et al.* 1996a: 3)

The impact of The Wolds, and later Blakenhurst, went further than out-of-cell hours. The details of Table 10.1 suggest this. Also repeated anecdotal evidence from directors of private prisons and governors of public prisons fortified this perception. Association rules for prisoners started to be

Table 10.1 Comparison between The Wolds and public sector regimes for remand prisoners

	Wolds		Public sector remand prisons	
	Contractual requirement	*Actual provision*	*Minimum facilities*[b]	*Actual provision in new remand centre*[c]
Hours out of cell	14 hours, 7 days a week	14 hours, 7 days a week	1½–2 hours each day	12¼ hours, 7 days a week
Showers	At least daily	Prisoners can shower whenever unlocked (unless undertaking activities)	Once a week	Prisoners can shower daily in residential units and each time they use the gym
Hours out of doors	At least two hours a day	At least two hours a day	At least one hour a day	One hour a day, 5 days a week, and a range of structured PE and spectator hours out of doors
Clothes (Remand prisoners may wear own clothes) Change: Socks/underpants[a] Shirts/T-shirts Other clothing Sheets etc.	Daily Alternate days Weekly Weekly	Daily Alternate days Weekly Weekly	Weekly Weekly Weekly Weekly	Own clothes worn. See laundry Weekly
Education	Minimum 6 hours a week	Minimum 6 hours a week	No guaranteed access	5½ hours a day weekdays[d] plus mid-week evenings: total 35 hours
Visits	1 hour, 7 days a week	1 hour, 7 days a week	15 minutes, 6 days a week	1 hour 5 minutes, 6 days a week

Physical education	Minimum 6 hours a week	Minimum 6 hours a week	Virtually no access	Minimum of 7 hours a week
Visits from legal representatives	0800–2200 [each day], without booking and guaranteed	0800–2200 [each day], without booking and guaranteed	0900–1530, 5 days a week but only by appointment and not guaranteed	0930–1130, 1330–1600 each day by appointment and guaranteed
Send/receive letters	Unlimited number	Unlimited number	Limits imposed	Unlimited number
Access to telephones	Available	Available in all houseblocks	Not available	Available in all residential areas
Change library books	At least twice a week	At least twice a week	At least once a week	Once a week in main library; access to unit libraries
Shop/canteen	At least twice a week	At least twice a week	Once a week	Twice a week
Laundry	3½ hours a week	Available while unlocked	Access in some establishments	Access to laundry facilities while unlocked
Meals	3 meals a day, at least one hot	3 meals a day with one hot option at each meal	3 meals a day, at least one hot	3 hot meals a day, cold cereal and salads at appropriate times of year

a   For those who choose not to wear their own clothes.
b   These are the minimum facilities; in practice many local remand prisons achieve much higher levels of delivery.
c   Actual provision at a new young prisoner remand centre.
d   Higher educational requirement for young prisoners. This would not be typical for a new adult remand centre.
Source: National Audit Office (1994).

relaxed; in some prisons privacy keys to cells were being issued; prisoner ID bar-coded cards to facilitate movement were being trialled; reception processes, particularly praised by Tumim (1995: 83) at Blakenhurst, had changed; and visits were being permitted in the evenings, a time which was often more convenient for visitors.

It should be emphasized that not all of these changes were occurring in all prisons. Far from it. But these were examples of innovations in the contracted private prison regimes which had been picked up and, where feasible, implemented in some public prisons. These changes pre-dated the exponential increase in the UK prison population which was so marked in 1995, and there are unfortunately distinct signs that the Prison Service, under the pressure of population growth and overcrowding, is now retreating from the Model Regime and the derived changes for public prisons (*The Independent*, 28 November 1995; *The Guardian Weekly*, 21 January 1996). But the point for present purposes is to demonstrate that cross-sectoral change, or cross-fertilization, is a highly practical notion, not a fanciful one.

Another level in the UK where cross-fertilization made a halting start, temporarily stalled now under pressure of central budgetary cuts, was devolution of financial control. The Woolf Report (Woolf and Tumim 1991: 12.75–12.77) gave a striking example of how stifling centralized financial control can be on imaginative and enthusiastic managers:

> A vivid example of the need [for determining at prison level how budgets should be spent] was provided when the Inquiry visited Birmingham (Winson Green) Prison in April 1990. [This] is one of the local prisons which is struggling with the problems of overcrowding. Nonetheless, the governors and staff are seeking to improve the regime for prisoners and are committed to doing so. One problem which they have is in relation to association areas for unconvicted prisoners.
>
> At present . . . there is no opportunity to offer association to unconvicted prisoners. We were told, however, that there were some rooms which could be converted to association areas at a cost of £400 or £500. If three officers were available, it would be possible to supervise association for two hours each forenoon and afternoon for about 80–100 prisoners per day in those rooms. Furthermore, if the unconvicted exercise yard were to be fenced off . . . (at a cost of £11,000) staff who were used to supervise exercise could also supervise the association. The necessary supervision could therefore be met without extra staffing costs . . .
>
> Expenditure on this scale which would have been good for the morale of both staff and inmates should have been within the discretion of management at Establishment level.

Anyone conversant with centralist bureaucratic systems generally, but particularly with prison bureaucracies, will be familiar with the almost daily frustrations pointlessly imposed on local managers. The private sector in the UK, the USA and Australia is getting away from this – not always entirely successfully perhaps, but it is on its way. In the UK so-called service-level agreements between the Prison Service and prison governors were intended to provide a structure for a degree of financial devolution. However, financial pressures if not crisis have stopped this process in its tracks, with devolution in practice now going down only as far as the area manager.

The last two examples show how cross-fertilization will only take root if the public prison authorities either will let it occur or are themselves permitted by governments to operate in a financial or political context where it is achievable. But the opportunity is there, and tangible examples can already be seen. As the private sector grows, more comparison points and contrasts will show up. And if governments allow or enable the public sector to respond, there will in turn be changes and improvements which the private sector will want to pick up. That should be emphasized; to this point the assumption has mostly been that the public sector can learn from the private sector, but as a competitive situation matures cross-fertilization will increasingly be seen as a two-way process.

Scepticism is sometimes expressed (Bottomley *et al.* 1996b: 3) as to whether it is possible to isolate those achievements of private prisons which are attributable to their status within the private sector rather than to penal developments generally. On the basis of the material set out in this chapter, it seems relatively easy to isolate some of the more prominent matters. However, that is not quite the right question to ask. The right question is the extent to which one cross-fertilizes with the other, to the mutual benefit of each and the advantage of the system as a whole. This too arouses some scepticism, mainly because of doubts about the mechanics of any such process (Bottomley *et al.* 1996a: 9).

For sure, this does not take place through some kind of organizational osmosis. However, several mechanisms have been identified so far. The crudest is industrial muscle. Examples have been shown of major changes to workplace practices, with consequential benefits to the correctional regime, being brought about by the mere threat of privatization. There is a limit to how far one can progress by such means; and in any case top-down, enforced changes are not the most desirable means of pursuing organizational development.

Other than this, the mechanisms of change all involve recognition at some point within the organization that the public sector, which still has a strong culture of believing that it is the primary trustee of the use of imprisonment against citizens, has come to fall short of the private sector. This may be because statutory standards are imposed upon the private sector, or because it is expected to meet demanding contractual standards, or because it finds more flexible methods of prisoner management or more sensible methods of financial control for itself. Whatever it is, at some point it becomes within the public sector a standing reproach or a source of embarrassment or even a political albatross, until some individual or group somewhere signals that the time has come for change. Without that context, however, the signal might well pass unnoticed or, if it is seen, the ability of the leaders in the public sector culture to bring about change may be circumscribed. The seemingly endless catalogue of low standards within the public system suggests that the processes of internal change have indeed clogged up. Competition – a notion that it is sometimes forgotten covers standards in public life, not merely economic or financial rivalry – will facilitate change.

An excellent example of prisons, both public and private, striving to improve their standards in a competitive setting, one where they were each being audited, relates to the Tennessee Select Oversight Committee (1995). It will be recalled that a private prison contract in that state may only be renewed 'if the contractor is providing the same quality of services as the state at a lower cost, or if the contractor is providing services superior to those provided by the state at essentially the same cost'. The first renewal exercise related to CCA's South Central Correctional Center. Feeling its way with this first such review, the Committee lined South Central up against two comparable state prisons. Moreover, it carried out two inspections of all three prisons at a year's interval. Between the first and the second inspection all three prisons raised their standards. The standards in question were qualitative, not merely financial. The percentage improvements which occurred during this inspection period were 5 per cent and 8 per cent for the two public sector prisons and 15 per cent for South Central. Evidently, competitive monitoring by an independent auditor was a mechanism for bringing about mutual improvement.

Other mechanisms could be explored. For example, joint in-service training conferences might be productive. The aim of such conferences would not be for one sector to impose its approaches and perspectives on the other, or for one private operator to lord it over another. Rather, shared dilemmas such as those highlighted in Chapter 9 could be discussed, and alternative approaches to their solution and thus to the training of staff who might have to participate in their solution could be explored. Which participant would learn what from whom could safely be left to them to sort out. Generally, the prison industry as a whole would find ways of profiting from each component's experience if that were the culture within which it operated.

Market testing

'Market testing' is a rather imprecise phrase which has become part of the jargon of privatization generally and prison privatization in particular. Broadly, it describes the process by which the public authority seeks to ascertain the true price at which its own agents can deliver given services, so that this may be compared with the price offered by the private sector. This may be simply for the sake of having a benchmark against which to determine whether the private sector bids are realistic, as was the case at The Wolds and the Arthur Gorrie Correctional Centre. Or it may be more focused and rigorous, as with the bidding process in Florida which requires a 7 per cent private sector saving or the renewal process in Tennessee which looks to value for money. In each of these cases, market testing is really a way of monitoring the good faith of the bidders and exercising some financial leverage over them, in a context where a decision has already been made that the prison in question will be operated by someone from the private sector.

However, the most radical and interesting form of market testing occurs where the public agency is permitted to bid against the private sector *in a real contest*. The decision as to whether the prison is to be run by the private or the public sector will only be made after the bids are received. Clearly, the public sector should not be judge in its own cause, which is why 'Chinese wall' arrangements have had to be made to handle bids. Assuming that problem can be sorted out, this kind of market testing is at the cutting edge of the privatization debate.

Its explicit premise is that the public sector, goaded by the presence of the private sector, can and will improve its performance. This means formulating its outputs more carefully, rethinking its staffing inputs, meeting regime standards, being monitored in the same way as the private sector, putting a price on the package, sticking to that price in the knowledge that the contracting authority must also do so, devolving control, and so on. In principle, market testing – both winning a contract and then performing it satisfactorily – is the acid test of the efficacy of privatization. If the public sector can outperform the private sector, cross-fertilization must surely have taken place.

Three cases of market testing will be discussed here: those at Manchester (Strangeways) and Buckley Hall in the UK and at Woodford in Queensland. This kind of market testing does not yet appear to be a feature of prison privatization moves in the USA. The first two cases related to already existing prisons, so that in effect management contracts were being sought; whereas Woodford was a design, construct and manage (DCM) project in relation to a green-fields site prison.

A preliminary point is that there are normally going to be great industrial difficulties in market-testing a prison which is currently being run by the public sector. A successful private sector bidder would not willingly inherit the work practices which had been accepted by his predecessor. Yet a wholesale changeover of staff – apart from the system-wide industrial disruption it might well provoke – would not be feasible in relation to a functioning prison with current inmates. For a private contractor, the ideal is: a green-fields site, a prison constructed to its own design; no existing staff; no prisoners; no established subculture. Taking over an operational prison is the very antithesis of this.

So how did Manchester and Buckley Hall come to attract strong private sector bids when market-tested? The answer is, because they were each in effect mothballed at the relevant time – Buckley Hall because it had been closed down and was being converted from juvenile to adult use, and Manchester because it was closed for reconstruction following the 1990 riots which had led to the establishment of the Woolf inquiry. But apart from exceptional circumstances such as these, it is likely that market testing will only occur in relation to planned rather than existing prisons.[2]

Manchester (Strangeways) prison

Bidding to run this 1100-bed prison closed in April 1993. The Prison Service itself had been invited to make a bid; the other three short-listed bidders were Group 4, Securicor and UK Detention Services. The Contracts and Competition Group was to evaluate bids and make a recommendation to the minister. As previously explained, the Group is sufficiently at arm's length from the Prison Service mainstream for this to be an acceptable procedure.

The evaluation process lasted about nine months; quite soon it was known that the short-list had been reduced to two – the Prison Service and Securicor. Although there was apparently widespread cynicism as to whether this was ever a genuine exercise, whether the Prison Service would in fact ever be permitted to lose, information strongly suggests that it was a very closely run thing and that the Contracts and Competition Group would have felt no qualms about awarding the contract to Securicor if that company's bid had been the best. Perhaps the notion of 'deliverability', explained in Chapter 5, assisted the Prison Service's case. In any event, it was successful, and in February 1994 a service-level agreement (SLA) was signed. This was intended to be the equivalent of a contract which the Prison Service would have signed with a private operator.

The SLA contained four schedules: the terms and conditions; the performance requirements and indicators; the financial arrangements; and plant and equipment matters. However, the SLA contained one of those classic barriers to change and cross-fertilization referred to above – namely, head-office dominance. This was to be exercised through the area manager, as indeed was everything to do with contract compliance. The Contracts and Competition Group was now sidelined.

It was no great surprise, therefore, that within a year the prison's status had become almost indistinguishable from that of every other prison within the area. The confirmation of this came with Prison Service funding cutbacks. Manchester was treated as being just like every other prison in the region, having to accept a cut of 8 per cent (from £19 million as 'contracted' to £17.5 million). To add to this indignity, the Manchester governors were instructed as to how and in what programme areas they should make these savings. This completely undermined, and probably destroyed, the point of market testing.

Long-term plans were subjugated to financial exigencies; this new attempt at management was caught up in the maelstrom of head-office machinations. It would never be discovered whether the public sector could do things more imaginatively or efficiently or humanely or cost-effectively than the private sector, because the mat was pulled out from under it. Morale at the prison has plummeted, particularly amongst management. The widely held view is that even if market testing and the SLA were not a sham at the outset, they were soon a shambles in practice.

This saga is instructive, for it demonstrates one of two things: either a governmental determination to forestall improvement in the public sector prison system or a profound failure by the most senior management to comprehend the implications of the policies that they themselves had developed. The cross-sectoral benefits of privatization cannot be fully identified or exploited with such half-hearted commitment.[3] As for Buckley Hall, it was no great surprise that Group 4 outbid the Prison Service here. The Manchester exercise had caused much organizational discomfiture, and there was little enthusiasm for risking a replay.

Woodford

The Queensland Corrective Services Commission (QCSC) has been characterized as having initially been captured by, indeed readily surrendering to, the private sector. But escape always remains an option. Its decisive handling of market testing at Woodford suggests that this may now be a possibility.

In May 1994 the government announced that a new 400-bed (subsequently increased to 600-bed) prison would be built at Woodford, north of Brisbane. The private sector (narrowed down after expressions of interest to CCA and ACM) and the QCSC were invited to bid. The contract would be to design, construct and manage the prison, but building costs would be met directly by the government on the basis of a fixed-price contract. To bid, therefore, the QCSC would have to put together a consortium including a construction company as a joint venturer. This was done. An independent Tender Evaluation Committee was set up, with elaborate safeguards, including a Chinese wall within the QCSC, to ensure that personnel seconded to the Committee could not influence the QCSC's own bid. The outcome was that the QCSC consortium was the successful bidder. The related management contract was let for five years with an option to renew for a further five years.

Capital costs were obviously a major component of the total bid. The experience of the QCSC mirrored what private operators have always maintained – that prison design and management regime are inextricably interrelated. Building a 'standard' prison first and trying to work out management and programme matters second is not only inefficient but also more expensive. As for staffing levels, these had been influenced by experience of the private sector at Borallon and were lower than for a comparable public prison. Programme delivery, it is claimed, will be just as good.

These claims have yet to be tested. The prison will not become operational until mid-1997 at earliest. However, the tangible fact is that the public sector agency has beaten the private sector at its own game. Of course, if it has done so by lowering its quality, there is no cause for celebration in that. But so far, and subject to there being a better monitoring regime at Woodford than has hitherto been the case at the Queensland private prisons, there is no evidence that that will be the case. Moreover, the present rhetoric is that the bid price will be honoured, including the annual escalations. If that is done, there truly will be an opportunity to see what the public sector is capable of when operating in a competitive environment.

Summary

The point of privatization is system-wide change and improvement. This chapter has sought to show that this is already occurring and to identify the mechanisms which facilitate this. The catalyst is competition. So far it has been a one-way street – the public sector responding to the private. But that is not a structural inevitability. As the public component of the single system improves, whether in response to competition or to any one of a variety of broader socio-political stimuli, it can cause the private sector to improve also. One of the most interesting models for change may be market-tested prisons run by the public sector. In the USA this is a novel concept; in the UK the experiment has been almost throttled in infancy; and in Australia it is about to begin. This development should be kept under review.

The objective above all, by whatever means it may be achieved, is to launch an upward spiral of improved penal practice from the stagnant plateau which has all too often over many decades characterized purely public systems in the USA, the UK and Australia. However, if governments set out to undermine this process, then it will not occur.

Notes

1 Borallon was the first prison in Australia to have on-site presence of medical or paramedical personnel 24 hours a day.
2 It is possibly in tacit recognition of this that the oft-announced market-testing exercise in relation to a tranche of UK prisons (featuring in particular some run-down ones) has not to date taken place.
3 These comments are based on the author's direct observations, discussions and analysis of the relevant documentation (February 1995). Subsequently, in October 1995, the chief inspector of prisons carried out a full inspection. His report,

released in July 1996, has vindicated the position taken in the above text. It was stated that:

> In our view the SLA was not treated in accordance with the spirit of Treasury guidance. It appeared from interviews and correspondence that senior managers in the Prison Service (having been successful in ensuring that the in-house bid achieved the lowering of Manchester's staff's expectations about staffing costs) were no longer interested in the Treasury guidance. Instead, Manchester was treated no differently than any other public sector prison . . . Understandably, managers and staff at Manchester were frustrated at the Prison Board's response to the SLA.
>
> (Tumim 1996: 21)

Later, the Report stated:

> If market testing of the management of existing prisons is to establish credibility within and outside the Prison Service, more effective arrangements must be in place for compliance with Treasury guidelines, and the prison treated as closely as possible to a privately-run establishment.
>
> (Tumim 1996: 14)

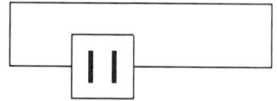

11

The future growth of privatization

There are two possible growth areas for prison privatization: expansion within existing markets and entry into completely new ones. Existing markets are found only in developed, westernized, anglophone nations – the USA, the UK and Australia, with New Zealand committed and Canada dipping its toe in the water. The extent of likely expansion in these countries will depend upon a variety of factors which should by now be familiar. Included in these is public and political confidence that private prisons will be effectively accountable. A model for accountability is thus not merely ethically essential in itself but pragmatically important because it will have a bearing upon future growth.

What of new markets? It was earlier foreshadowed that the fascinating anomaly that private prisons have so far not spread beyond the developed anglophone countries would be explored. Perhaps a deeper understanding of the apparent reluctance of other nations to go down this road will heighten awareness of the dilemmas posed by privatization.

Potential new markets and barriers to privatization

To judge from their rhetoric, the biggest players seem confident of expansion not only within their existing markets but also into new ones. Wackenhut has established 'a central corporate infrastructure capable of sustaining global operations,' whilst CCA asserts that 'there are powerful market forces driving our industry, and its potential has barely been touched'. Indeed, in 1994 CCA agreed with a French corporation, Sedexho SA, that the latter should acquire a 20 per cent share holding in the former. Sedexho is a major provider of 'hotel' and programmatic prison services in France, and a general services supplier to more than 60 countries. Another major player, Group 4, also possesses a multinational character through Securitas, a Swedish corporation with which it is associated.

In discussions with industry leaders, possible target areas which come up are: mainland Europe; Africa, particularly South Africa; South America; the former Soviet empire; and Israel. Other areas which merit at least passing comment are Asia and the South Pacific, particularly Papua New Guinea.

Europe

In 1987 the government of France decided to expand prison accommodation by 13,000 beds. This involved building about 25 new prisons in all parts of the country. Because of the recent rapid increase in prisoner population, speed was essential. The private sector was accordingly invited to participate. Successful bids came from four private companies; they designed and constructed the prisons in two years. At the outset, the expectation had been that the operation of these new prisons should likewise be privatized. But in the face of opposition from various parliamentary, bureaucratic and academic sources (Boulan 1987), privatization of the core operational side was cancelled before it even got under way. Management and custodial functions therefore remained with the Service Publique Penitentiaire. However, the hotel functions, prison industries, vocational training, educational programmes and the like were privatized, the contracts being awarded to the companies which had originally made the successful package bids. Sedexho SA, incidentally, was one of the most prominent contractors.

This arrangement, described as *prisons semi-privées*, remains in force. In 1993 the Belgian Ministry of Justice decided to follow down the same path; tenders were invited to build and supply non-custodial services for a 400-bed maximum-security prison in Andenne. This is expected to be operational by the end of 1996 (Beyens and Snacken 1994).

This Franco-Belgian experience is not paralleled anywhere else in mainland Europe (Ryan 1996). Nevertheless, it has apparently caused the big US players to imagine that the door has now been flung open for privatization. In reality, the type of service delivery which has been privatized is philosophically quite different from that found in the anglophone states. The most teasing moral conundrum of all – whether punishment becomes delegitimized if delegated to private operators – does not have to be confronted, for the custodial functions remain with the state.

In fact, France's momentary flirtation with the notion of full, US-style privatization was no more than that; and its retreat was a reoccupation of the mainstream philosophical ground as to the nature of the state which has underpinned European affairs since at least the time of Napoleon. Writing the 'Introductory Report' for a Council of Europe conference on privatization of crime control, Jung (1990: 10) spelled this point out as follows:

> At least for continental Europe the links between the development of states and the maintenance of public peace are obvious. The emergence

of the modern public police and penal law must be seen in this context. In the continental European tradition, the state is considered to be the proper guarantee of public order and equal standards. On the other hand, the notion prevails, despite some bitter lessons, that the state can be controlled better than private individuals.

It is this philosophy which makes it highly improbable that prison privatization will take hold in mainland Europe in the way that it has in those anglophone states which reflect Anglo-Saxon common-law traditions and values.

At the same conference Rosenthal and Hoogenboom (1990: 20–1) had also expatiated on this point:

> Whereas in the Anglo-Saxon context, privatization may be just one among many alternatives to attain a better delivery of goods and services to the public, it has a very fundamental connotation in the continental setting . . . The abandonment of governmental tasks and responsibilities, in particular, is not taken light-heartedly in the continental context. The relative effectiveness and efficiency of the public versus the private sector may be a matter of serious concern, but it will never be a sufficient criterion. Before it is ready for a test of its effectiveness and efficiency, continental theory (and for that reason practice as well) has to deal with more intrinsic considerations . . . First and foremost, in the continental culture, the state is seen as much more than a 'service institution'.
>
> Even if one runs the risk of embracing a mythical notion of one state, one should be aware that in many countries on the continent people may have internalized the state as an integrative symbol. Abandoning tasks may then be put to a test of a totally different nature. Does it affect the organic identity of the state? Does it weaken . . . the sovereignty of the state? Only when such questions are answered negatively may effectiveness and efficiency come to the fore.

Christie's Norwegian objections to privatization (Christie 1993: 102) can now be better located; he has 'internalized the state as an integrative symbol'. And in this regard he epitomizes the approach of the Nordic states; the imposition of punishment and the concomitant attempt to realize useful penal objectives are matters far too solemn to be devolved. There is a duty and a responsibility for the state to carry the whole of these burdens, directly, on its own back.

For those European nations – like France itself – which are perhaps less concerned with the possibly constructive side of incarceration than with symbolizing the central importance of state control, the same broad philosophical point remains: punishment is a state responsibility and entitlement. Privatization would be the abandonment of a governmental task. This value is indeed entrenched in the German constitution (Ryan 1996).

The prognosis must, therefore, be that prison privatization will not become a feature of continental European penal practice for the foreseeable future. This is likely to be so, however shrewd the commercial alliances which are made and however persuasive the salesmanship. That is not to say that a foot might not at some time somewhere be thrust in the door. But it is far more likely that private sector (and as at present non-government sector) involvement will increase on the hotel, programmatic and services side of prisons, not the custodial.

Africa

Africa would seem to be unpromising territory for private prisons. In the majority of states incarceration and punishment are an essential tool for political survival; it is almost inconceivable that the dictator of the day would risk letting control of prisons slip out of his hands. Nevertheless, some companies seem to think that opportunities could arise there.

This very fact raises profound ethical issues. Whatever their faults, the present private prison nations all subscribe to the notion of due process. A prisoner, once sentenced, can be presumed to have had a fair trial. Miscarriages of justice occur, of course, but they are not endemic to the system. No such presumption, indeed quite the contrary, can be made in most African states. If private prisons are to remain a respectable part of the total prison system in the USA, the UK and Australia, their operators must not allow themselves to become part of the apparatus of unjust oppression elsewhere. Lilly and Knepper (1992) would have been on stronger ground had they focused on such issues rather than on a rather diffuse notion of the perils of the US military-industrial complex.

It is possibly because South Africa does possess those trappings of due process that the private prison industry is much more confident about exploring opportunities there. The supposition seems to be that South Africa's ability to manage an effective prison system lags behind its ability to manage an acceptable judicial system, and that it may be possible to export management know-how and technology wholesale. Certainly, that country's view of the state has been more influenced by its British than its Dutch past, so that there may not be deep philosophical objections. But one would have thought that, politically, it would be hazardous for the black government of a newly freed state to hand over any part of its incarceration responsibilities to predominantly white foreign companies, or even to local subsidiaries of those companies.

Other geo-political regions

Enough has been said for it to be apparent what are the main sorts of barriers against the expansion of private prison markets. In this context, some of the suggested areas for expansion are, frankly, incomprehensible: Israel above all, and also the former Soviet empire where capacity to pay might in any case have a cautionary effect upon the companies.

Perhaps the lowest barriers are currently found in South America or at least the US-dominated part of it. Already Puerto Rico has contracted with CCA for two private prisons. Of course, this is a US protectorate, but perhaps it can equally be seen as an outpost of Spanish-speaking South America. Panama also might seem receptive enough to US culture and susceptible enough to political dominance to be a possible new market. Some companies talk about Venezuela and, rather less plausibly, Brazil in much the same way. Certainly, the European notion of the role of the state has not taken root in these and other South American countries to the same extent as in Europe itself.

In Asia the most likely candidate would seem to be the Philippines, again because of the influence of the USA and the lack of a strong notion of state. Thailand is also thought to have given some consideration to the possibility, though at the time of writing any such moves remain unformulated. However, it is almost inconceivable that other parts of mainland Asia would permit privatization. The prevailing value in criminal justice terms – whether through Marxism, Confucianism, Shintoism, Buddhism or Islam – is that, for the greater good of the greater number, the individual should conform to the state; the corporate welfare is more important than that of the individual. An aspect of that is that the state should retain the ultimate power of incarceration and exercise it directly. That is not inconsistent with very widespread non-government or voluntary sector participation in corrections, other than prisons, in much of Asia.

South Pacific prisoner numbers and distribution are generally not suitable for privatization; such an undertaking would not be economically viable. A possible exception to this is Papua New Guinea. That country has had a desperate law and order crisis throughout the 1990s, and it is expected that with Australian economic aid more prisons will be built. With Australia itself already being committed to a wide degree of privatization, it is by no means fanciful to contemplate that, for reasons of efficiency, familiarity, speed and cost, prison construction and management may go down the road of privatization.

Overview

New markets, then, seem problematical; they will certainly not be easy to penetrate. It is significant that, even though the discussion paper of the Secretariat had flagged privatization strongly as a possible development (United Nations 1995a: 7–10), the Ninth United Nations Congress on the Prevention of Crime and the Treatment of Offenders, held in Cairo in 1995, did not even address the issue (United Nations 1995b). Evidently, for the bulk of the world's nations, privatization was simply not worth discussing.

The reasons for this resistance or indifference boil down to the central premise which sometimes the private companies have not sufficiently recognized even in those areas where privatization is a proven option. It is this: that the use of imprisonment and the management of prisons have profound cultural connotations. If these are unreceptive or positively antipathetic to privatization, it will not take hold. To date and not coincidentally, private prisons have established themselves only in the most sympathetic markets – developed, westernized, anglophone countries possessing traditional Anglo-Saxon notions of the role and place of the state in civic life.

Expansion of existing markets

The continuation of those circumstances that spawned privatization in the first place will underpin future expansion. These circumstances were discussed at various points in Chapters 1 and 2. The principal ones are: continuing increase in prison populations; consequential shortage of accommodation; overcrowding and the risks it creates; governmental reluctance or inability to put up capital funds for the construction of new prisons; a belief that running costs can be reduced or at least provide better value for money; a strong desire in some quarters to break down union power and associated restrictive work practices; and, in more liberal circles, a belief that privatization might be a catalyst for compelling the state to confront the question whether the prison system must irrevocably remain a standing reproach to decency in public affairs and a permanent barrier to optimism in correctional practice.

These factors are not necessarily embedded permanently into penal affairs. For example, the union factor is already being eroded and the question of running costs, always in any case difficult to measure in truly comparable ways, is responding to competition and change. So the question has to be asked: will privatization, by being successful, destroy its own *raison d'être*? Similarly, if the preconditions such as increases in prison population disappear, will the catalyst for privatization likewise disappear? Each of these scenarios seems highly unlikely.

Take, for instance, the increase in prison populations. If, magically, this trend came to a halt tomorrow, there is still an immense amount of slack to take up in terms of current overcrowding. This is so in all the countries under review. More accommodation would be needed to cope even with a steady-state prison population.

Moreover, much of the existing plant is by any criterion substandard, and even admitted to be so by governments. There will be a need for replacement or refurbishment of existing prisons not only in a steady-state but also in a reducing prison population. In Australia, plant replacement has been a prominent factor in privatization: for example, in Queensland to enable the disgraceful Boggo Road prison to be closed and in Victoria to move away from the fetid rabbit warren of the Coburg complex (including the maximum-security Pentridge prison). It will be recalled also that, as at 31 December 1995, 11 out of 92 US private prisons had been renovated by the operator, and that in the UK the home secretary has spoken of the need to involve the private sector in refurbishing 25 prisons.

However, the pressure on governments is such that it is improbable for the foreseeable future that capital outlays on prisons will ever, in terms of priority, precede outlays on hospitals or schools or roads or other infrastructure projects. Unless governments decide deliberately to let existing prison systems gradually deteriorate through non-investment – a hazardous policy at the best of times – up-front capital outlays will continue to be required for the replacement or refurbishment of plant. From these two points – capital scarcity and capital needs – it logically follows that governments will continue to try to shift some of the burden on to the private sector, amortizing outlays into annual payments calculated over long-term, interlinked management contracts – 25 years in the UK and 40 years in Victoria, for example. These periods, incidentally, each seem too long from the point of view of ensuring effective and ongoing review of management performance. However, the point for present purposes is that DCFM contracts will increasingly become the norm; and management-only contracts will become rare.

That is the prognosis, then – steady expansion within existing markets, more rapid as prison populations continue to increase but not drying up completely if they plateau or even begin to decline. How far will this process go? This will vary from place to place; but in states with moderate or large prison populations (as opposed, say, to the tiny Nova Scotia population, where contracting out of the total system has been contemplated), it could be that there would be strong cultural and political resistance well before the 50 per cent point is reached. Even in those countries where the state is seen very much as a 'service institution', it might be expected that there would be concern if it was reduced to the point of being the minority provider of this particular service.

This is all speculative. What can be predicted with more certainty is that gross or repetitive or system-wide failures by the private sector will cause the debate to be relocated and perhaps to commence all over again. If the chain of private prisons in the UK were ransacked and torched, as was a chain of public prisons in 1990 leading to the Woolf inquiry, it is likely that any review would examine not only what went wrong, not only what to change for the future, but also whether the private sector should be permitted to continue in this role at all. In that regard, the private sector will always be more vulnerable than the public sector whose malfeasance, however negligent or brutal or incompetent, will never lead to its having its prisons taken away from it.

That observation brings one back to the question of accountability, for a sector or system which has been regulated effectively and which is publicly accountable is by definition far less likely to suffer terminal crises than one which is not.

Summary

There are significant cultural and political reasons which lead one to think that expansion of private prisons into new markets will be slow and fragmented. In existing markets, whilst there are some natural barriers beyond which privatization is unlikely to proceed, steady growth can be anticipated. However, gross failures or system-wide malfeasance could force governments to reopen the whole question of the legitimacy and propriety of privatizing prisons.

12

A model for public accountability of private prisons

A model of public accountability must satisfactorily cover the ten key tenets identified and discussed. These are:

(i) The distinction between the allocation and the administration of punishment must be strictly maintained, with the private sector's role being confined to its administration.

(ii) Penal policy must not be driven by those who stand to make a profit out of it.

(iii) The activities of the private sector and their relations with government must be open and publicly accessible.

(iv) What is expected of the private sector must be clearly specified.

(v) A dual system must not be allowed to evolve in which there is a run-down and demoralized public sector and a vibrant private sector.

(vi) Independent research and evaluation, with untrammelled publication rights, must be built into private sector arrangements.

(vii) Custodial regimes, programmes and personnel must be culturally appropriate.

(viii) There must be control over the probity of private contractors.

(ix) There must be financial accountability.

(x) The state must in the last resort be able to reclaim private prisons.

It has emerged that some systems are strong on some points but weak on others. No system meets every tenet, but no system is in breach of every tenet. Moreover, though some breaches of some tenets by some states are flagrant, mostly they are matters of emphasis – a shade of grey rather than black. Also, most failures are a function of naivety or lack of imagination rather than bad faith, though elements of bureaucratic arrogance and commercial insouciance which are tantamount to bad faith sometimes emerge as barriers to accountability.

All states have recognized that, whatever their public prison accountability mechanisms, there must be an add-on component for private prisons. This component is variously known as the monitor or controller or liaison officer. However, a weakness shared by all states is that the monitoring system has often been less rigorous than it should. This is mainly because of the principle of capture, discussed in Chapter 3 and illustrated at points throughout the book. Some degree of capture is structurally inevitable in relation to all of the systems examined here (except possibly Florida) because they are in breach of a key theoretical proposition of public regulation. That proposition is that whenever the principal operator in a public service industry is empowered to contract and delegate to others some part of its own operational responsibilities, and in so doing it takes on the role of regulatory agency in relation to the activities of those delegates, there is a high risk that some degree of capture or co-optation will occur.

The ultimate justification for private prisons lies in their capacity to contribute to enhancement of the total prison system – cross-fertilization with the public component of what should be seen as a single system. If monitoring is partially ineffective and the tenets of accountability are breached, the basis for productive cross-fertilization is correspondingly eroded.

A model of accountability, then, should be structured to achieve three things: routine compliance by the private sector with the ten key tenets of accountability; avoidance of capture; and encouragement of cross-fertilization. The models which have been adopted by the various states will now be spelled out, their deficiencies identified, and a new model proposed.

The basic model

The basic model is that found in most US states and most of the Australian states. This model places the public sector correctional agency at the centre of privatization decisions: setting the terms, awarding the contracts and monitoring compliance. The monitor is employed by and works to the public correctional agency. Capture occurs frequently. At all stages, external input is minimal. Typically, there is no mechanism for cross-fertilization, which at best may be a fortuitous by-product. This model is represented in Figure 12.1 (page 160).

The UK model

This follows the basic model but in one respect is preferable. This is because the role of the chief inspector of prisons brings some external scrutiny to the prison system generally, including the private sector: see Figure 12.2. This aspect of the accountability system is vigorously independent, with no danger

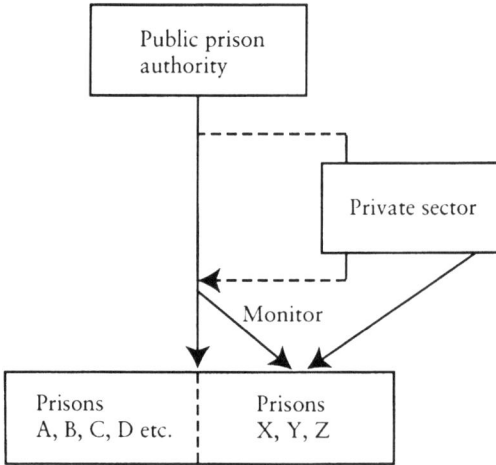

Figure 12.1 The basic model for public accountability.

of capture to date. But a crucial limitation upon its effectiveness is the fact that the chief inspector's reports are recommendatory only; the office is outside the line of command. Moreover, suggested moves to give it more teeth have studiously been ignored by government, most notably in relation to the Woolf inquiry's recommendation that UK prisons – public and private – must be accredited according to criteria applied by the chief inspector of prisons as an aspect of the inspection and reporting function. An accountability system which does not enable the external agency to see that things identified as wrong are put right is deficient.

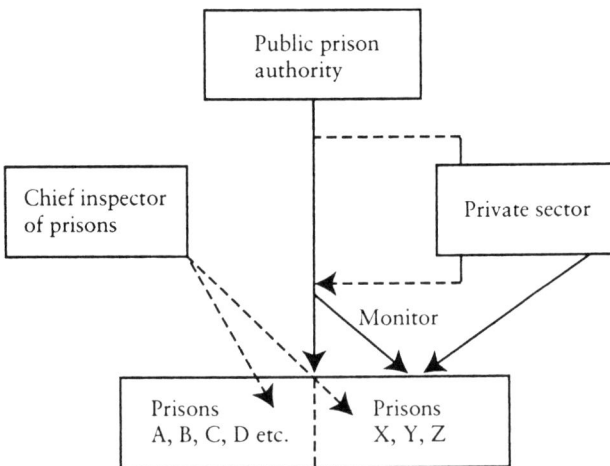

Figure 12.2 The UK model for public accountability.

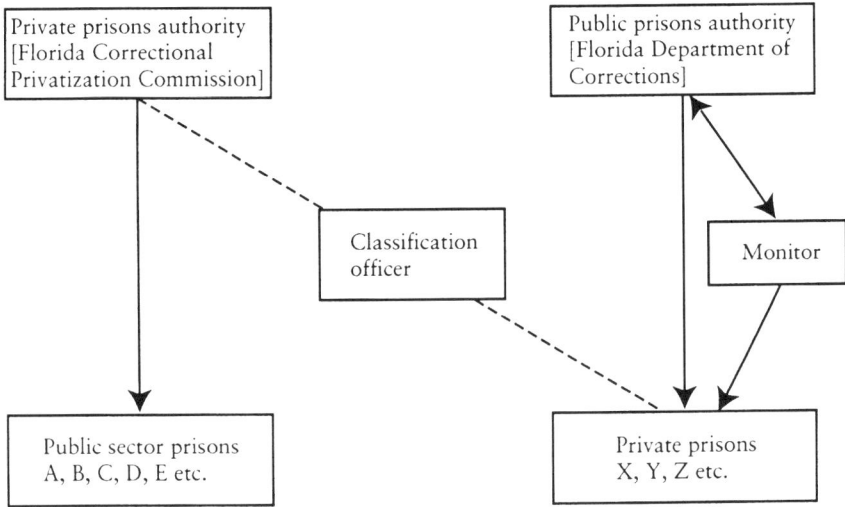

Figure 12.3   The Florida model for public accountability.

The Florida model

The strength of this model, set out in Figure 12.3, is that it is independent of the public system. Because its monitors are not public prison system employees, the danger of capture is minimized. However, the private system is in a sense a little too self-contained. The separateness of the public and private components of the total prison system – with cross-system links only found in the disciplinary role of classification officers – reduces opportunities for cross-fertilization. There is also a danger that the monitors may develop a loyalty to the Privatization Commission which in turn might inhibit their willingness to make public criticisms – a variant of the capture principle.

A new model

An effective model for accountability must be based on the notion that the prison system is a single system, with two components. Just as it would be regarded as absurd to make the public system accountable to the private prison hierarchy, so it is inappropriate to make the private system accountable to the public prison hierarchy. Each should be equally accountable to an independent body, one which is not in the business of managing prisons in a day-to-day sense but which nevertheless possesses powers to impose sanctions upon those, from either sector, who fall short of acceptable performance. This independent body, conversant with the standards and practices of both sides of the single system, would be well placed to lead the process of cross-fertilization – picking out the best and discarding the worst, to the benefit of the system as a whole.

The independent body – let it be called for convenience the Prisons Authority – should not only scrutinize the existing prison system, but also play a central role in shaping that system. It is proposed that, subject to general governmental direction as to prisons policy and the allocation of resources, the Prisons Authority should take over new prison projects from the outset. Its remit would be to determine the siting, security rating, size, programme mix and so on and then to call for tenders. These may be sought from both the private and the public sector – rather as with Woodford prison in Queensland. The contract would be awarded not just on the basis of cost but taking into account probity, reliability, the range of services and programmes offered, and value for money generally.

After a contract (or a service-level agreement, to use the UK terminology applicable to public prisons) has been let, and the agreed option periods taken up, there would then be rebidding in relation to that prison; this would be open to both the public and the private operators. In other words, there may in principle be turnover or 'churning' not only within the private sector but also from the private to the public sector, and vice versa. This naturally would reinforce the general sense of accountability, as well as the idea of cross-fertilization. Obviously, an aspect of decision-making at this time would be the reports of the monitor – a person who would be in direct line of command to the Prisons Authority. The schematic model of this proposed system is set out in Figure 12.4.

If such a model were adopted, suitably adapted to local conditions, other desirable features could hang off it. For example, in the UK and Australia, which lack accreditation systems, the Prisons Authority would be able to take up that responsibility. A related point, perhaps particularly apposite to the USA, where so many prison systems have been under federal court order, is that the Prisons Authority would be ideally placed to ensure that a dual prison system did not develop, with run-down public prisons and comparatively up-market private ones. For all systems, as the need for some kind of prisons ombudsman comes increasingly to be acknowledged, the Prisons Authority would provide a natural reporting point. Generally, cross-sector training needs could be identified at that level, and the research–evaluation–modification loop strengthened. Expertise about contract specifications would be enhanced more quickly and with greater refinement, because every new prison contract would have to be reviewed. Existing public prisons could progressively be brought within this integrated approach, and contracts or service-level agreements worked out. However, as mentioned earlier, it would not be publicly acceptable for the private sector contribution to become predominant. The Prisons Authority could decide as a matter of general policy and system-wide needs from time to time what would be the optimum mix of public and private prisons, and plan against that background.

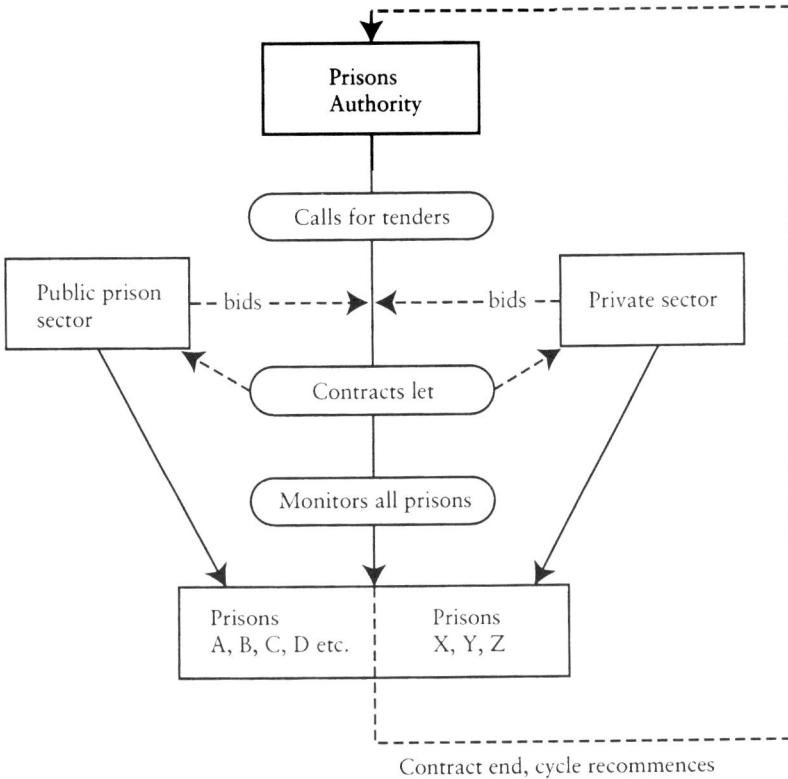

Figure 12.4 A new model for public accountability.

This takes one back to the turnover or 'churn' rate. It is essential that neither part of the system should be able to take the extent of its participation absolutely for granted; at that point accountability starts to erode. A key factor to enable churning in reality to occur rather than existing merely as a theoretical possibility is that the length of the initial contract, whilst sufficient to enable the operator to implement its regime and programmes, should be short enough to ensure the operator does not start to think of itself as indispensable and virtually unaccountable. The 25- and 40-year periods in recent UK and Victoria contracts are far too long, and the fact that there are provisions enabling the state to reclaim management in the event of gross breach of contract does not meet the objection. The Prisons Authority would be well placed to develop workable guidelines as to optimum contract lengths and renewal or rebidding protocols.

Of course, it has already been shown that the majority of future contracts will be DCFM. A constraint upon public sectors everywhere would seem to be the reluctance of government to capitalize them. To do so would defeat one of the very purposes of privatization – to enable governments to shuffle

up-front capital expenditure into the form of long-term recurrent expenditure. The reason why the government of Victoria, for example, has refused to
permit the public sector to bid against the private (thereby missing one of the
tangible benefits of privatization) was the belief that it would have had to
corporatize and capitalize it to enable it to do so. It is evident that, if this view
is correct and if the forecast that future contracts will be predominantly
DCFM is also correct, the suggested model would lack one of its foundations.

However, the market-testing exercise in Queensland with regard to the
Woodford contract belies this fear. It will be recalled that the public authority
successfully put together a consortium, which included a construction
company, to bid for the contract. As it happened, the construction side of the
project was fixed-price with the usual arrangements as to periodic payments,
penalty clauses and the like. In other words, the company did not have to
carry the capital costs on its books beyond the completion of the project.
However, the experience elsewhere – in Victoria, New Zealand, the USA and
with the later UK contracts – shows that carrying such costs is in itself no
disincentive to participation. The agreed formula for contract payments
simply reflects those costs – and from the point of view of the government or
the contracting authority it is of no consequence whether the consortium is
made up entirely of private sector partners or also includes a public sector
partner.

As for running costs – the pure management side of the contract – where
the successful consortium includes the public sector prisons authority, there is
potentially a problem of cost overrun. If there is an unexpected blow-out or
there has been a miscalculation, private corporations must simply absorb the
costs as best they can. But where the management side of the DCFM contract
is being carried by the public authority, how can the Prisons Authority
impose financial sanctions for breach or insist on costly performance of the
contract? The only funds available to the public authority are those allocated
for the purpose of running their part of the prison system generally. There is
no other source from which funds can be diverted. Thus, to impose sanctions
or mandate exact compliance in these circumstances would inevitably have
knock-on effects with regard to purely public prisons – hardly a just outcome
for prisoners.

The Queensland solution to this dilemma is as follows. The public
authority's bid included a specified amount as a governmental contingency
fund to cover possible shortfall or sanctions. In considering the bids and
making a recommendation, the Tender Evaluation Committee took account
of the likelihood of this fund having to be drawn on over the duration of the
contract. If it is not drawn on, it represents in effect a 'dividend' for the
government. And if it is, that alone would not turn an acceptable bid into one
which should never have been accepted in the first place.

This is more than enough detail. The point is not to produce a legislative
outline but to identify a new model and to confront some of the most difficult

problems it poses. If the broad objectives are agreed, the model can be implemented according to local conditions and priorities. One issue of principle remains, however. How can one be sure that the Prisons Authority itself is not captured? What guarantee is there that governments would permit such an authority to operate according to the somewhat optimistic scenario one has proposed? The answer, obviously, is that one cannot be sure, there is no such guarantee. But no model of public administration can ever be completely immune from governmental antagonism or calculated lack of support. However, short of that sort of governmental attitude, this model is more robust than any currently in existence, far better designed to derive the best from privatization and to control the worst. That is all one can seek from a model.

Conclusions

Accountability is often presented as a rather negative idea – a system to ensure that standards are not breached. In the context of prison privatization, that aspect of accountability is crucial. But accountability also has more positive connotations – to make a system work better than it previously has done. The system in question is the prison system as a whole, not just the private sector component. The model of accountability developed in this book rests on the premise that the public component of the prison system is no less in need of effective regulation than the new private sector.

Privatization of prisons has become a fraught topic for penologists. Undoubtedly, some of its supporters have brought to the debate values which have lost sight of equitable penal policies and are focused more on ideological agendas such as economic rationalism or workplace reform. Conversely, some of its opponents dismiss or ignore fundamental questions such as how to improve prison conditions and make the prison experience less destructive.

Donahue (1989: 225–6) has stated:

> [I]t is perverse to reject privatization simply because some enthusiasts favor it for the wrong reasons. Even for those who believe in government – perhaps *especially* for those who believe in government – any opportunity to serve the public interest more efficiently warrants respectful appraisal.

This book has attempted to appraise how private prisons have so far worked in practice and how their performance could be enhanced. The evidence is clear that private prisons could act as a catalyst for improvement across the whole prison system, but only if they are effectively regulated and properly accountable.

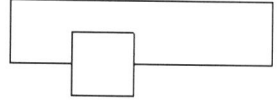

References

Aldrich, H. (1979) *Organizations and Environments*. Englewood Cliffs, NJ: Prentice Hall.

American Correctional Association (1990) *Standards for Adult Correctional Institutions* (3rd edn). Washington, DC: ACA.

Anderson, S. (1981a) 'The Prison Work of the New Zealand Ombudsman'. *Ombudsman Journal*, 1: 24–40.

Anderson, S. (1981b) 'Overseeing Fairness: The Corrections Ombudsman'. In D. Fogel and J. Hudson (eds), *Justice as Fairness: Perspectives on the Justice Model*. U.S.A.: Anderson Publishing Co.

Baldry, E. (1994a) 'USA Prison Privateers: Neo-colonialists in a Southern Land'. In P. Moyle (ed.), *Private Prisons and Police: Recent Australian Trends*. Sydney: Pluto Press, pp. 125–38.

Baldry, E. (1994b) 'Private Prison Entrepreneurs and the NSW Experience'. *Socio-Legal Bulletin*, No. 12: 11–15.

Bernstein, M. (1955) *Regulating Business by Independent Commission*. Princeton, NJ: Princeton University Press.

Beyens, K. and Snacken, S. (1994) 'Privatization of Prisons: An International Overview and the Debate'. Paper presented to the Prisons 2000 Conference, University of Leicester, April.

Biles, D. and McDonald, D. (1992) *Deaths in Custody Australia, 1980–1989*. Canberra: Australian Institute of Criminology.

Birkinshaw, P. (1985) 'An Ombudsman for Prisoners'. In M. Maguire, J. Vagg and R. Morgan (eds), *Accountability and Prisons: Opening up a Closed World*. London: Tavistock Publications, pp. 165–74.

Black, D. (1976) *The Behavior of Law*. New York: Academic Press.

Bottomley, K., James, A., Clare, E. and Liebling A. (1996a) 'Evaluating Private Prisons: The Criminological Challenge'. Paper presented at the Annual Conference of the Australian and New Zealand Society of Criminology, Wellington.

Bottomley, K., James, A., Clare, E. and Liebling, A. (1996b) *Wolds Remand Prison: An Evaluation*, Research Findings No. 32. London: Home Office Research and Statistics Unit.

Boulan, F. (ed.) (1987) *Les Prisons dites 'privées': une solution à la crise penitentiaire?* Aix-en-Provence: Presses Universitaires d'Aix-Marseille.

Bowery, M. (1994) *Junee: One Year Out.* Sydney: New South Wales Department of Corrective Services.

Braithwaite, J. (1985) *To Punish or Persuade: Enforcement of Coal Mine Safety.* Albany: State University of New York Press.

Brakel, S. (1988) 'Prison Management, Private Enterprise Style: The Inmates' Evaluation'. *New England Journal on Civil and Criminal Confinement*, 14: 175–244.

Branham, L. and Krantz, S. (1994) *Sentencing, Corrections and Prisoners' Rights* (4th edn). St Paul, MN: West Publishing Company.

Brown, A. (1994) 'Economic and Qualitative Aspects of Prison Privatization in Queensland'. In P. Moyle (ed.), *Private Prisons and Police: Recent Australian Trends.* Sydney: Pluto Press, pp. 194–218.

Brown, D. (1992) 'The Prison Sell'. *Alternative Law Review*, July: 32–4.

Bureau of Air Safety Investigation (1994) *Investigation Report 9301743: Piper PA31–350 Chieftain, Young, NSW, 11 June 1993.* Canberra: Department of Transport.

Carl Vinson Institute of Government (1993) *Selecting Prison Sites: State Processes, Site Selection Criteria and Local Initiatives.* Atlanta: University of Georgia.

Carson, W. (1982) *The Other Price of Britain's Oil.* Oxford: Martin Robertson.

Carter, K. (1995) 'The Occupational Socialisation of Prison Officers: An Ethnography'. University of Wales Cardiff: Unpublished PhD thesis.

Christie, N. (1993) *Crime Control as Industry: Towards GULAGS, Western Style?* London: Routledge.

Clarke, M. (1990) *Business Crime: Its Nature and Control.* Cambridge: Polity Press.

Criminal Justice Newsletter (1995) 'Three Strikes Causing Problems in California, Studies Indicate'. *Criminal Justice Newsletter*, 26(7): 1–3.

Cross, R. (1971) *Punishment, Prison and the Public: An Assessment of Penal Reform in Twentieth Century England by an Armchair Penologist.* London: Stevens and Sons.

de Witt, C.B. (1986) 'Ohio's New Approach to Jail Financing'. *Construction Bulletin, National Institute of Justice*, November: 1–12, Washington, DC: US Government Printing Office.

DiIulio, J.J. (1988) 'What's Wrong with Private Prisons?'. *The Public Interest*, 92: 66–83.

DiIulio, J.J. (1991) *No Escape.* New York: Basic Books.

Dinitz, S. (1981) 'Are Safe and Humane Prisons Possible?'. *Australian and New Zealand Journal of Criminology*, 14(3): 3–19.

Donahue, J. (1989) *The Privatization Decision: Public Ends, Private Means.* New York: Basic Books.

Downes, L. (1994) *Performance Review of Junee Correctional Centre: June 1994.* Sydney: New South Wales Department of Corrective Services.

Ericson, R., McMahon, M. and Evans D. (1987) 'Punishing for Profit: Reflections on the Revival of Privatization in Corrections'. *Canadian Journal of Criminology*, 29(2): 355–87.

Ethridge, P. and Marquart, J. (1993) 'Private Prisons in Texas: The New Penology for Profit'. *Justice Quarterly*, 10(1): 29–48.

Feeley, M.M. (1991) 'The Privatization of Prisons in Historical Perspective'. *Criminal Justice Research Bulletin*, 6(2): 1–10.

Fitzgerald, M. (1977) *Prisoners in Revolt*. Harmondsworth: Penguin.

Fowles, A. (1989) *Prisoners' Rights in England and the United States*. Aldershot: Avebury.

Freiberg, A. and Ross, S. (1995) 'Change and Stability in Sentencing: A Victorian Study'. *Law in Context*, 13: 107–42.

General Accounting Office (1991) *Private Prisons: Cost Savings and the Bureau of Prisons' Statutory Authority Need to be Resolved*, GAO/GDD 91-21. Washington, DC: General Accounting Office.

General Accounting Office (1996) *Private and Public Prisons: Studies Comparing Operational Costs and/or Quality of Service*, GAO/GDD 96-158. Washington, DC: General Accounting Office.

Genders, E. and Player, E. (1995) *Grendon: A Study of a Therapeutic Prison*. Oxford: Clarendon Press.

George, A. (1989) 'The State Tries an Escape'. *Legal Service Bulletin*, 14(2): 53–7.

Grabosky, P. and Braithwaite, J. (1986) *Of Manners Gentle: Enforcement Strategies of Australia Business Regulatory Agencies*. Melbourne: Oxford University Press.

Gration, P. (1994) 'The Civil Aviation Authority'. *Canberra Survey*, 47(22): 1–6.

Greenwood, P. and Zimring, F. (1985) *One More Chance: The Pursuit of Promising Intervention Strategies for Chronic Juvenile Offenders*. Santa Monica, CA: The Rand Corporation.

Grindrod, H. and Black, G. (1989) *Suicides in Leeds Prison: An Enquiry into the Deaths of Five Teenagers during 1988/89*. London: The Howard League for Penal Reform.

Gunningham, N. (1989) 'Asbestos Mining at Baryulgil: A Case of Corporate Neglect?'. In P. Grabosky and A. Sutton (eds), *Stains on a White Collar*. Sydney: Federation Press.

Hallenstein, H. (1989) *Finding of Inquisition Held at Coroner's Court, Melbourne, into the Deaths of James Richard Logloughnan and Others*. Melbourne: Office of the State Coroner.

Harding, R. (1992) 'Private Prisons in Australia'. *Trends and Issues in Crime and Justice*, 36: 1–8.

Harding, R. (1993) 'Inside Trading', *The Bulletin*, 6 April: 36–7.

Harding, R. (1994a) 'Models of Accountability for the Contract Management of Prisons'. In P. Moyle (ed.), *Private Prisons and Police: Recent Australian Trends*. Sydney: Pluto Press.

Harding, R. (1994b) 'What Can We Learn from Suicides and Self-injury?'. In A. Liebling and T. Ward (eds), *Deaths in Custody: International Perspectives*. London: Whiting and Birch.

Harding, R. (1995) 'Prison Privatization in Australia and New Zealand'. *Overcrowded Times*, 6(5): 1, 15–18.

Hatry, H., Brounstein, P., Levinson, R., Altschuler, D., Chi, K. and Rosenberg, P. (1989) *Comparison of Privately and Publicly Operated Corrections Facilities in Kentucky and Massachusetts*. Washington, DC: The Urban Institute.

Hatry, H., Brounstein, P. and Levinson, R. (1993) 'Comparison of Privately and Publicly Operated Corrections Facilities in Kentucky and Massachusetts'. In G.

Bowman, S. Hakim and P. Seidenstat (eds), *Privatizing Correctional Institutions*. Brunswick, NJ: Transaction Publishers.

Hayes, L. (1994) 'Jail Suicide Prevention in the United States: An Overview of Yesterday, Today and Tomorrow'. In A. Liebling and T. Ward (eds), *Deaths in Custody: International Perspectives*. London: Whiting and Birch.

Home Office (1993) *Local Economic Impact of New Prisons in Urban Areas*. London: Home Office.

Home Office (1996) *Protecting the Public: The Government's Strategy on Crime in England and Wales*, Cm. 3190. London: HMSO.

HM Chief Inspector of Prisons (1987) *Report of an Inquiry into the Disturbances in Prison Service Establishments in England between 29 April/2 May 1986*. London: HMSO.

HM Prison Service (1995) *Greater Manchester Community Prison: A Final Report by Pieda plc*. London: HM Prison Service.

Hopkins, A. (1989) 'Crime without Punishment: The Appin Mine Disaster'. In P. Grabosky and A. Sutton (eds), *Stains on a White Collar*. Sydney: Federation Press.

Jacobs, J. (1977) *Stateville: The Penitentiary in Mass Society*. Chicago: University of Chicago Press.

Johnson, C. (1989) 'Complaints-Grievance Procedures for Prisoners'. *Ombudsman Journal*, 7: 123–37.

Johnston, E. (1991) *Report of the Royal Commission into Aboriginal Deaths in Custody*. Canberra: Australian Government Publication Service.

Jung, H. (1990) 'Introductory Report'. In *Privatisation of Crime Control*, Collected Studies in Criminological Research, 27. Strasbourg: Council of Europe.

Kauffmann, K. (1988) *Prison Officers and their World*. Cambridge, MA: Harvard University Press.

Kennedy, J.J. (1988) *Final Report of the Commission of Review into Corrective Services in Queensland*. Brisbane: Government of Queensland.

Keve, P. (1996) *Measuring Excellence: The History of Corrections Standards and Accreditation*. Washington, DC: American Correctional Association.

Kinkade, P. and Leone, M. (1992) 'The Privatization of Prisons: The Wardens' Views'. *Federal Probation*, 56(4): 58–65.

Kleinwort Benson (1989) *Investigation into Private Sector Involvement in the N.S.W. Corrective Services*. Sydney: Kleinwort Benson.

Kramer, R. (1992) 'The Space Shuttle *Challenger* Explosion: A Case Study of State-Corporate Crime'. In K. Schlegel and D. Weisburd (eds), *White Collar Crime Reconsidered*. Boston: Northeastern University Press.

Learmont, Sir John (1995) *Review of Prison Service Security in England and Wales and the Escape from Parkhurst Prison on Tuesday 3rd January 1995*, Cm. 3020. London: HMSO.

Levinson, R. (1985) 'Okeechobee: An Evaluation of Privatization in Corrections'. *Prison Journal*, 65: 75–82.

Liebling, A. (1994) *Suicides in Prison*. London: Routledge.

Liebling, A. and Ward, T. (eds) (1994) *Deaths in Custody: International Perspectives*. London: Whiting and Birch.

Lilly, J. and Knepper, P. (1992) 'An International Perspective on the Privatization of Corrections'. *The Howard Journal*, 31(3): 174–91.

Livingstone, S. (1994) 'The Changing Face of Prison Discipline'. In E. Player and M. Jenkins (eds), *Prisons after Woolf: Reform through Riot*. London: Routledge.

Livingstone, S. and Owen, T. (1993) *Prison Law: Text and Materials*. Oxford: Clarendon Press.

Logan, B. (1993) *Ministerial Inquiry into Management Practices at Mangaroa Prison*. Wellington: Department of Justice.

Logan, C. (1990) *Private Prisons: Cons and Pros*. New York: Oxford University Press.

Logan, C. (1992) 'Well Kept: Comparing Quality of Confinement in Private and Public Prisons'. *Journal of Criminal Law and Criminology*, 83(3): 577–613.

Logan, C. and McGriff, B. (1989) 'Comparing Costs of Public and Private Prisons: A Case Study'. *NIJ Reports*, 216: 2–8.

Macionis, S. (1992) 'Contract Management in Corrections: The Queensland Experience'. Paper presented to the Conference on Private Sector and Community Involvement in the Criminal Justice System, Wellington, New Zealand, November/December.

Maguire. M. (1985) 'Prisoners' Grievances: the Role of Boards of Visitors'. In M. Maguire, J. Vagg and R. Morgan (eds), *Accountability and Prisons: Opening up a Closed World*. London: Tavistock Publications, pp. 141–56.

Maguire, M. and Vagg, J. (1983) 'Who Are the Prison Watchdogs? The Membership and Appointment of Boards of Visitors'. *Criminal Law Review*, 1983: 238.

Maguire, M., Vagg, J. and Morgan R. (eds) (1985) *Accountability and Prisons: Opening up a Closed World*. London: Tavistock Publications.

Martinson, R. (1974) 'What Works? Questions and Answers about Prison Reform'. *The Public Interest*, 35: 22–54.

Matthews, R. (ed.) (1989) *Privatizing Criminal Justice*. London: Sage Publications.

McConville, S. (1987) 'Aid from Industry? Private Corrections and Prison Overcrowding'. In S.D. Gottfredson and S. McConville (eds), *America's Correctional Crisis*. Westport, CT: Greenwood Press.

McConville, S. (1990) 'The Privatisation of Penal Services'. In *Privatisation of Crime Control*, Collected Studies in Criminological Research, 27. Strasbourg: Council of Europe.

McDonald, D.C. (ed.) (1990) *Private Prisons and the Public Interest*. New Brunswick, NJ: Rutgers University Press.

McDonald, D.C. (1992) 'Private Penal Institutions'. In M. Tonry (ed.), *Crime and Justice: An Annual Review of Research*, vol. 16. Chicago: University of Chicago Press, pp. 361–419.

McDonald, D.C. (1994) 'Public Imprisonment by Private Means: The Re-emergence of Private Prisons and Jails in the United States, the United Kingdom and Australia'. In R. King and M. Maguire (eds), *Prisons in Context*. Oxford: Clarendon Press.

McGivern, J. (1988) *Report of the Enquiry into the Causes of the Riot, Fire and Hostage-Taking at Fremantle Prison on the 4th/5th January 1988*. Perth: Department of Corrective Services.

Morgan, R. (1985) 'Her Majesty's Inspectorate of Prisons'. In M. Maguire, J. Vagg and R. Morgan (eds), *Accountability and Prisons: Opening up a Closed World*. London: Tavistock Publications, pp. 106–23.

Morgan, R. (1994) 'An Awkward Anomaly: Remand Prisoners'. In E. Player and M. Jenkins (eds), *Prisons after Woolf: Reform through Riot*. London: Routledge.

Morgan, R. and Bronstein, A. (1985) 'Prisoners and the Courts: the US Experience'. In M. Maguire, J. Vagg and R. Morgan (eds), *Accountability and Prisons: Opening up a Closed World*. London: Tavistock Publications, pp. 264–80.

Moyle, P. (1992) 'Privatising Prisons: The Underlying Issues'. *Alternative Law Journal*, 17(3): 14–19.

Moyle, P. (1993) 'Privatisation of Prisons in New South Wales and Queensland: A Review of Some Key Developments in Australia'. *The Howard Journal of Criminal Justice*, 32(3): 231–50.

Moyle, P. (1994) 'Private Prison Research in Queensland, Australia: A Case Study of Borallon Correctional Centre, 1991'. *British Journal of Criminology*, 34(1): 34–62.

Nagle, J. (1978) *Report of an Inquiry into the New South Wales Department of Corrective Services*. Sydney: State Government Printer.

National Audit Office (1994) *Report by the Comptroller and Auditor General: Wolds Remand Prison*. London: HMSO.

National Prison Project (1989) *Status Report: The Courts and the Prisons*. Washington, DC: National Prison Project.

Nellis, M. (1991) 'Electronic Monitoring of Offenders in England and Wales: Recent Developments and Future Prospects'. *British Journal of Criminology*, 31(2): 165–88.

New South Wales Public Accounts Committee (1993) *Infrastructure Management and Financing in New South Wales*, Report No. 73. Sydney: Parliament of New South Wales.

O'Hare, N. (1990) 'The Privatization of Imprisonment: A Managerial Perspective'. In D.C. McDonald (ed.), *Private Prisons and the Public Interest*. New Brunswick, NJ: Rutgers University Press.

Paulus, P. (1988) *Prison Crowding: A Psychological Perspective*. New York: Springer-Verlag.

Prison Reform Trust (1995) *HM Prison Doncaster: The Doncatraz File*. London: The Prison Reform Trust.

Prison Reform Trust (1996) 'August incidents in CCA jails'. *Prison Privatization Report International*, issue no. 4, October.

Public Sector Management Commission (1993) *Review of the Queensland Corrective Services Commission*. Brisbane: Public Sector Management Commission of Queensland.

Richardson, G. (1985a) 'The Case for Prisoners' Rights'. In M. Maguire, J. Vagg and R. Morgan (eds), *Accountability and Prisons: Opening up a Closed World*. London: Tavistock Publications, pp. 19–28.

Richardson, G. (1985b) 'Judicial Intervention in Prison Life'. In M. Maguire, J. Vagg and R. Morgan (eds), *Accountability and Prisons: Opening up a Closed World*. London: Tavistock Publications, pp. 46–60.

Richardson, G. (1993) *Law, Process and Custody: Prisoners and Patients*. London: Weidenfeld and Nicolson.

Richardson, G. (1994) 'From Rights to Expectations'. In E. Player and M. Jenkins (eds), *Prisons after Woolf: Reform through Riot*. London: Routledge.

Rosenthal, U. and Hoogenboom, B. (1990) 'Some Fundamental Questions on Privatisation and Commercialisation of Crime Control'. In *Privatisation of Crime Control*, Collected Studies in Criminological Research, 27. Strasbourg: Council of Europe.

Rowan, J. (1994) 'Prevention of Suicides in Custody'. In A. Liebling and T. Ward (eds), *Deaths in Custody: International Perspectives*. London: Whiting and Birch.

Rutherford, A. (1990) 'Prison Privatization in Britain'. In D.C. McDonald (ed.), *Private Prisons and the Public Interest*. New Brunswick, NJ: Rutgers University Press.

Ryan, M. (1996) 'Prison Privatization in Europe'. *Overcrowded Times*, 7(2): 1, 16–18.

Ryan, M. and Ward, T. (1989) *Privatization and the Penal System: The American Experience and the Debate in Britain*. Milton Keynes: Open University Press.

Sechrest, D. and Shichor, D. (1993) 'Corrections Goes Public (and Private) in California'. *Federal Probation*, 57(3): 3–8.

Shaw, S. (1989) 'Penal Sanctions: Private Affluence or Public Squalor?'. In M. Farrell, *Punishment for Profit? Privatisation and Contracting Out in the Criminal Justice System*. London: Institute for the Study and Treatment of Delinquency.

Shaw, S. (1992) 'The Short History of Prison Privatisation'. *Prison Service Journal*, 87: 30–2.

Sherman, L. (1980) 'Three Models of Organizational Corruption in Agencies of Social Control'. *Social Problems*, 27(4): 478–91.

Shichor, D. (1993) 'The Corporate Context of Private Prisons'. *Crime, Law and Social Change*, 20: 113–38.

Shichor, D. (1995) *Punishment for Profit: Private Prisons, Public Concerns*. Newbury Park, CA: Sage Publications.

Sneddon, G. (1995) *Performance Review Report: Junee Correctional Centre, August 1995*. Sydney: New South Wales Department of Corrective Services.

Sparks, R. (1994) 'Can Prisons Be Legitimate? Penal Politics, Privatization, and the Timeliness of an Old Idea'. In R. King and M. Maguire (eds), *Prisons in Context*. Oxford: Clarendon Press, pp. 14–28.

State of Florida: Office of the Auditor General (1993) *Certification of Correctional Facility Actual Per Diem Costs*, Report 12192. Tallahassee: Office of the Auditor General.

Staunton, J. (1996) *Commission of Inquiry into Relations between the Civil Aviation Authority and Seaview Air*. Canberra: Australian Government Publication Service.

Stern, V. (1993) *Bricks of Shame: Britain's Prisons*. London: Penguin Books.

Tennessee Select Oversight Committee on Corrections (1995) *Comparative Evaluation of Privately-managed CCA Prison and State-managed Prototypical Prisons*. Nashville: Tennessee Legislature.

Thomas, C. (1991) 'Prisoners' Rights and Correctional Privatization'. *Business and Professional Ethics Journal*, 10: 3–46.

Thomas, C. (1994) *Private Adult Correctional Facility Census* (7th edn). Gainesville: University of Florida.

Thomas, C. (1995a) *Private Adult Correctional Facility Census* (8th edn). Gainesville: University of Florida.

Thomas, C. (1995b) *Planning for the Future of the Florida Correctional Privatization Commission*. Gainesville: University of Florida.

Thomas, C. (1996) 'Correctional Privatization: The Issues and the Evidence'. Paper presented at the Privatization of Correctional Services Conference, Toronto, Canada, July.

Thomas, C. and Bollinger, D. (1996) *Private Adult Correctional Facility Census* (9th edn). Gainesville: University of Florida.

References 173

Thomas, C. and Logan C. (1993) 'The Development, Present Status, and Future Potential of Correctional Privatization in America'. In G. Bowman, S. Hakim and P. Seidenstat (eds), *Privatizing Correctional Institutions*. New Brunswick, NJ: Transaction Publishers.
Tumim, S. (1993) *H.M. Prison and Remand Centre, Cardiff: Report by H.M. Chief Inspector of Prisons*. London: Home Office.
Tumim, S. (1994a) *Wolds Remand Prison: Report by H.M. Chief Inspector of Prisons*. London: Home Office.
Tumim, S. (1994b) *H.M. Prison, Leeds: Report by H.M. Chief Inspector of Prisons*. London: Home Office.
Tumim, S. (1995) *H.M. Prison Blakenhurst: Report by H.M. Chief Inspector of Prisons*. London: Home Office.
Tumim, S. (1996) *H.M. Prison Manchester: Report of a Full Inspection by H.M. Chief Inspector of Prisons*. London: Home Office.
United Nations (1995a) *Criminal Justice and Police Systems: Management and Improvement of Police and other Law Enforcement Agencies, Prosecution, Courts and Corrections; and the Role of Lawyers*, A/CONF.169/6. Vienna: United Nations.
United Nations (1995b) *Report of the Ninth United Nations Congress on the Prevention of Crime and the Treatment of Offenders*, A/CONF.169/16. Vienna: United Nations.
Vagg, J. (1985) 'Independent Inspection: The Role of Boards of Visitors'. In M. Maguire, J. Vagg and R. Morgan (eds), *Accountability and Prisons: Opening up a Closed World*. London: Tavistock Publications, pp. 124–37.
Vaughan, D. (1990) 'Autonomy, Interdependence and Social Control: NASA and the Space Shuttle Challenger'. *Administrative Science Quarterly*, 35: 225–57.
Vickers, J. and Yarrow, G. (1988) *Privatization: An Economic Analysis*. Cambridge, MA: MIT Press.
Vinson, T. (1982) *Wilful Obstruction: The Frustration of Prison Reform*. Sydney: Methuen.
Vinson, T. and Baldry, E. (1993) 'It's Jackpot for Some in Bottom-line Jails'. *Sydney Morning Herald*, 30 December: 9.
Weiss, R. (1991) 'Attica: 1971–91. A Commemorative Issue'. *Social Justice*, 18(3).
Westley, W. (1966) *Violence and the Police*. Boston: MIT Press.
Wicker, T. (1976) *A Time to Die: The Attica Prison Revolt*. London: Bodley Head.
Williams, T. (1983) 'Custody and Conflict: An Organisational Study of Prison Officers' Roles and Attitudes'. *Australian and New Zealand Journal of Criminology*, 16: 44–55.
Woodcock, J. (1994) *Report of the Enquiry into the Escape of Six Prisoners from the Special Security Unit at Whitemoor Prison on Friday 9th September 1994*, Cm. 2741. London: HMSO.
Woolf, H.K. and Tumim, S. (1991) *Prison Disturbances, April 1990: Report of an Inquiry by the Rt. Hon. Lord Justice Woolf (Parts 1 and 2) and His Honour Judge Stephen Tumim (Part 2)*, Cm. 1456. London: HMSO.
Zdenkowski, G. and Brown, D. (1982) *The Prison Struggle: Changing Australia's Prison System*. Melbourne: Penguin.

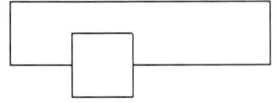

Index